Soviet
Foreign Aid

Soviet
Foreign Aid

MARSHALL I. GOLDMAN

FREDERICK A. PRAEGER, *Publishers*
New York · Washington · London

FREDERICK A. PRAEGER, PUBLISHERS
111 Fourth Avenue, New York, N.Y. 10003, U.S.A.
77–79 Charlotte Street, London W.i, England

Published in the United States of America in 1967
by Frederick A. Praeger, Inc., Publishers

Second printing, 1967

Library of Congress Catalog Card Number: 66-21779

This book is Number 181 in the series of
Praeger Publications in Russian History and World Communism

Printed in the United States of America

To
MERLE

Contents

Preface

To undertake a complete study of Soviet economic relations with the less developed countries of the world is almost as quixotic as it would appear. Hindered on the one hand by the sense of Soviet secrecy and on the other by the remoteness and inaccessibility of most of the works on the subject, the student has not always found it easy or possible to obtain the desired information. Nevertheless, in recent years more data have been made available. A careful study of the existing literature, a firsthand inspection of numerous aid projects, and relatively candid discussions with government and foreign-aid officials around the world—this combination enabled me to etch out what I hope is a fairly complete and unbiased picture. Unfortunately, the picture has numerous gaps. However, until there is easy access to the government archives in the U.S.S.R. and all the Afro-Asian countries (although six countries have already opened their files to me), these gaps will probably remain unfilled.

In the pages that follow, I have made a sincere effort to attribute praise and criticism where they are deserved. I have done this despite the realization that many of the observations made here will be taken out of context and slanted to prove a particular point of view. In fact, this has already happened. Some of the preliminary findings of my research first appeared in an article I wrote entitled "A Balance Sheet of Soviet Foreign Aid," which appeared in the January, 1965, issue of *Foreign Affairs* and parts of which are reprinted here with the kind permission of the Council on Foreign Relations, Inc., New York. Depending on whom you read, you emerge with two entirely different interpretations of that analysis.

In an interview in the Soviet newspaper *Krasnáia Zvezda (Red Star)* of June 15, 1965, P. Grigorev, a member of the Government Committee of the Council of Ministers of the U.S.S.R. for Foreign Economic Relations (GKES), praised Soviet foreign aid and cited my views to substantiate his position:

By invitation from the governments of the emerging countries, the Soviet Union does everything possible to help establish basic industry in these countries. Without such industry it is impossible for these countries to be economically independent and attain a high level of economic development. It is noteworthy to read the conclusions of the American economist Marshall Goldman in his article "The Results of Soviet Help to Foreign Governments," [*sic*] which appeared in the journal *Foreign Affairs*. He acknowledges that the success of the Russians in "rendering help to foreign governments has come from concentrating on certain key projects which are often industrial in nature. These major-impact projects not only excite the imagination but often have productive and visible results."

Exactly the opposite conclusions have been drawn by those who seek to discredit Soviet foreign aid. The descriptions of a number of incidents contained in my article were drawn upon by Victor Lasky in his book *The Ugly Russian*. I do not concur with Lasky's treatment of these incidents since, in my judgment, it unduly emphasizes the shortcomings of the Soviet record in foreign aid. Lasky selected material only from the last part of the article, where Russian aid was criticized, while Grigorev quoted only from the first part, where the Russians were complimented. Balance is difficult to attain.

Probably it is to be expected that similar misinterpretations will follow the appearance of this study. Nonetheless, this is no reason to abandon the quest. If both those who want to praise and those who want to criticize Soviet efforts can continue to extract what they want in this book, then perhaps I have found the middle ground.

Whatever the desirability of seeking a balance and making such a study, the effort would have been impossible without the help of several institutions and many individuals. First, the Brookings Institution provided me with a Research Professorship that allowed me to inspect and discuss Russian aid projects in Africa, Eastern Europe, and Asia. In addition, Wellesley College gave me a Junior Leave from teaching, which made it possible for me to find the time to travel, read, and write. The leave, combined with the Brookings grant, meant that I could see Soviet and American aid projects myself and discuss their results with Russian, American, and local officials. In every country I visited, except Burma (and that was because I could stay only twenty-four hours in Rangoon), I was graciously received by Soviet officials, who discussed American and Russian aid programs with varying degrees of candor. In some cases, the Soviet ambassador himself received me and in some cases the local economic counselor, but in almost all cases the reception was surprisingly warm and friendly. The interviews ranged in duration from one of forty-five minutes to one of five hours that was spread over three days. American aid people and foreign-service officers were equally helpful and often spent extra hours outside the office arranging for me to see projects and talk with technicians. Local government officials and businessmen also spent time with me and provided me with data heretofore unavailable outside their offices. Finally, Wellesley College alumnae living in remote areas around the world welcomed me as a friend and made it possible for me to obtain something of the local flavor of each country which is generally denied the average tourist.

Of course, there are the old stand-bys who also deserve my thanks. The Russian Research Center at Harvard University and its Executive Director, Abram Bergson, and Executive Secretary, Helen Parsons, have provided me with working facilities for several years now. Without the help of the Center's library and the librarians Ina Bonnell, Ruth Seidman, Susan Shill, and Taras Butoff, it would have been impossible to find the necessary material. The Center's typists, especially Rose di Benedetto, have put up with impossible deadlines and illegible manuscripts for so long that they no longer know what normal working conditions are. Finally, my wife and children deserve my thanks. It was not easy for them while I was gone. My wife, in addition, invariably ends up spending as much time editing and correcting my work as she does writing her own. That she manages both and the children as well is forever a source of wonder. To her I am deeply indebted.

Introduction

Soviet economic activity in Eastern Europe dates back to 1945, and in the Afro-Asian world to 1954. By the mid-1960's, some projects had been completed, and some loans had even been repaid. Enough time has elapsed, therefore, to make possible an examination of the Soviet record. This would seem to be an especially appropriate project now that some of the past recipients of Soviet aid have become less reluctant to discuss the merits of the help they have been receiving. Previous studies, such as Nicolas Spulber's excellent analysis *The Economics of Communist Eastern Europe* and Joseph Berliner's pathfinding monograph *Soviet Economic Aid,* were written either before the Russians began to react to the Polish and Hungarian uprisings or while the Soviet aid program was still in its infancy.[1] Consequently, the problems were less complicated, and there was little to be criticized since little had actually been visibly accomplished. Moreover, no one has heretofore attempted to examine and compare Russian relations with *all* the less developed countries—that is, not only with the neutralist nations, but with the countries of Eastern Europe and Communist Asia.

At first glance, it might appear that there is nothing to be gained by lumping Soviet economic relations with both Communist and neutralist countries together. To provide the proper perspective, however, a study of Soviet relations with the developing countries should begin with an examination of how the U.S.S.R. has treated the less developed countries within its own orbit. This was the Soviet Union's first major experience in economic relations with weaker countries, and certain patterns that were first established in Eastern Europe and China continue to be of significance in the Soviet aid program today. After a brief look at Soviet policy in the various Communist countries, we will devote the remainder of the study to an examination of Soviet economic practice in the emerging nations. The Russian record is considerably better there than in Eastern Europe, but by no means is it perfect.

For the most part, criticisms of Soviet aid and trade have been overshadowed by praise. For an American, this is especially intriguing.

Why is it that the Soviet Union seems to have obtained such a high return for its rubles? Consider that the United States since 1948 has spent over $100 billion in foreign aid throughout the world (including Marshall Plan aid to Western Europe) and that the Russians since 1945 have committed themselves to only about $14 billion (including about $10 billion to their satellites) and actually have spent no more than three-quarters of that; how is it that the Russians have achieved such disproportionate success? [2] Bring up the subject of Soviet aid, and immediately someone will say, "Oh, the Aswan Dam in Egypt," or "the Bhilai Steel Mill in India." Who knows the name of even one American project? How many Americans know about such equally spectacular American accomplishments as the Sharavathi Dam in India and the Eregli Steel Mill in Turkey? (Maybe the secret of Russian success is that they manage to find projects with names that are easier to pronounce.)

The major Soviet triumphs at Aswan and Bhilai, along with several other projects, have helped to create the general impression that the Soviets are more adept at handling foreign aid than we in the United States. A close look at American and Russian aid projects reveals, however, that just as we have had our successes which no one seems to have heard about, the Russians have had their failures which have gone unnoticed. In particular, their shortcomings in the satellite countries are rarely mentioned. Nonetheless, the Russians can boast with legitimate pride about the effectiveness of a large portion of their aid to the developing countries. In seeking to find why the Russians have been successful, we may learn a little about how to improve our own aid-giving operations.

In addition to searching for the secret of Soviet success, there is something else we should seek to explain. What accounts for the sporadic way in which Soviet aid agreements are made? After a late start, the Russians began to commit themselves to foreign-aid projects at an astonishing pace. Soviet promises of aid mounted rapidly until, at their peak in 1960, they were announcing new projects at a rate of $1 billion a year. In terms of gross national product, this was about the same proportion as the United States was providing at the time. Subsequently, however, in late 1961, promises of Soviet aid fell off sharply and remained at an insignificant level until late 1963. Then Russian aid promises again began to flow, until late in 1964, when once more the Russians retreated and the volume of new commitments was sharply reduced. What is the explanation for this on-again off-again policy? The answer will provide us with additional insight into the problems confronting the Soviet aid program.

In this analysis of Soviet foreign aid, it seemed best to arrange the material on a country-by-country or continent-by-continent basis wherever possible. This allows the reader to focus his attention on the sequence of events as they occur in each country or area. However, to ensure that each chapter is something more than the enumeration of various Soviet aid projects, an attempt has been made to focus each chapter on a particular issue which has been of special importance in that country. Thus the chapter on India gives considerable attention to Soviet commercial-trade policy, as well as to the Soviet oil offensive. The section on Nepal contains a discussion of the Sino-Soviet dispute as it affects the developing countries, and the section on Yemen includes a consideration of racism. Similarly, Guinea is used as a case study of unsuccessful Soviet economic aid, and Indonesia is cited to illustrate the difficulties inherent in any aid program. Finally, the concluding chapter attempts to draw some implications for American aid policy.

Soviet
Foreign Aid

1. Satellite Aid to the Soviet Union: Reparations, Prices, and Joint Stock Companies

The Soviet Union's economic policy toward its less powerful allies sometimes has been as imperialistic as anything devised by the most avaricious firms in the West toward the developing countries. By means of war reparations, joint stock companies, and discriminatory pricing, the Russians have contrived schemes that would make even such masters of intrigue as Union Minière du Haut-Katanga, United Fruit, and Standard Oil blush with embarrassment. The extent of Soviet exploitation is especially shocking if one considers the Russian stance as the chief defender of weak and defenseless nations. Criticism of the economic imperialism of Western firms has been well publicized, but somehow the record of Soviet foreign economic relations has been obscured.[1] The next two chapters will attempt to right this imbalance.

Although Soviet economic exploitation of other nations actually began in the 1920's (as we shall point out in our discussion of Mongolia and China), it became significant only in the aftermath of World War II. Soviet intentions first became evident from the manner in which the Russians pressed their claims for reparations, especially in the Communist-controlled areas. Because it was one of the victors, had suffered immense losses in the war, and had won extensive political concessions from the Western Allies, Russia was given a free hand in the economic life of both Eastern Europe and Manchuria. Like the other Allies, the Russians were entitled to some compensation from the Germans and the other members of the Axis. Unlike the other Allies, however, Russia counted on collecting the full measure of what it was entitled to. While the other Allies—especially the United States, which suffered relatively little in the war—were often as intent on reconstruction as they had previously been on destruction, Russia claimed everything it could put its hands on. This was immediately manifested in the widespread confiscation of billions of dollars' worth of goods and machines. That which was not readily portable was lifted out by the foundation in both Europe and Asia. Unfortunately, the pervasiveness

3

of the Russian drive for war booty affected some of the less powerful members of the Allied nations, like Poland, as well as the former enemies.

Reparations

GERMANY. Naturally, Germany bore the heaviest reparation burdens. Compensation took the form of commodities and fixed assets. Just as Germany had helped itself to the choicest goods in the countries it had occupied, so the Russians claimed whatever they wanted in Germany. Moreover, at Potsdam and at other conferences, the Soviets were awarded the foreign holdings of German investors and corporations located in Eastern Europe. The Russians insisted on this provision even though some of this property had formerly belonged to owners in Allied countries and had only recently been confiscated by the Germans. The Russians, who have always regarded German industrial technology with awe and envy, felt this to be an important compensation for the damage inflicted on the U.S.S.R. during the war. Not only did the reparation agreement provide a steady flow of goods in the years to come, but it also made available whole factories either for direct shipment to the U.S.S.R. or for control and operation in Eastern Europe.

It is difficult to place a precise value on the material actually obtained by the U.S.S.R. in the form of reparations. First, it is hard to evaluate used capital under the best conditions. Second, the intrigue, the destruction, and the chaotic market conditions and inflation that characterized the postwar era could hardly be described as the "best conditions." What is the value of an operating drill press when almost all the other drill presses in the country have been destroyed? Finally, many of the data are unavailable and those figures which are published may not be complete or accurate.

Originally German reparations to the U.S.S.R. were set at about $10 billion (in terms of prewar prices) by the conferences at Yalta and Potsdam.[2] By late 1951, the Soviets acknowledged that they had received $3,658 million worth of reparations valued at prewar prices. They had also taken over ninety-nine East German enterprises which made such things as machine tools, chemicals, and metallurgical equipment.[3] Much of the machinery in these factories was shipped to the U.S.S.R. for use in Soviet factories. At the same time, East Germany, as was true of West Germany, was required to bear the maintenance costs of the occupation troops on its soil.

As passions quieted in the postwar era, the Russians realized that the original reparation burden was too much for East Germany to bear. It became apparent that continued insistence on the original terms of the reparations agreement would turn an asset into a liability. Thus in May, 1950, the Russians agreed to cancel one-half of the unpaid reparation debt due after late 1951. This left $3,171 million to be paid over a 15-year period in addition to the already collected $3,658 million. The famous but short-lived German rebellion of June 17, 1953, and the battle of men versus Soviet tanks accelerated the efforts to reduce the burden. Soon after quiet had been restored, it was announced that East Germany would be freed of all reparations as of January 1, 1954. Similarly, it was decided at this time to return free of charge the 99 German factories which had been confiscated by the U.S.S.R. This included 66 former German firms which had already been returned in 1952 but for which an as yet unpaid redemption fee had been levied by the Soviet Union. Finally, Soviet troop maintenance costs for approximately 20 Soviet divisions were reduced so they totaled no more than 5 per cent of the East German national budget. Reportedly, this still amounted to more than $700 million, but it nonetheless was an improvement over the officially cited costs of $900 million collected in 1949. This reduced burden continued until the unrest of 1957, when it was again halved. It took until 1959 for the Russians to agree to free the Germans from this one last obligation.[4] Estimates of what all of this directly cost East Germany range from $4 billion at 1938 prices for the reparations to as much as $25 billion if plant confiscation and troop maintenance costs are included and the reparations are valued at postwar prices.[5]

OTHER EUROPEAN SATELLITES. Because Germany treated the Russians so ruthlessly during the war, it is not too hard to understand the initial Soviet insistence on such demanding terms, even after East Germany's conversion into a People's Socialist Democracy. The Soviet attitude toward the other Communist satellites in Eastern Europe, some of whom were Russia's wartime allies, is less easy to comprehend.[6] Hungary, a former member of the Axis Pact, was required to pay the U.S.S.R. $200 million in goods at 1938 prices. Rumania, another Axis power, was fined $300 million, one-half of which was to be paid in the form of oil deliveries.

While bearing the cost of their own sins, Hungary and Rumania, along with Bulgaria, were precluded from seeking redress for damages inflicted by the Germans. This came about because, despite Soviet promises, local property seized or acquired by the Germans during the war was not always returned to the people or governments of Eastern Europe. Instead, it was generally kept by the Russians. This included not only property long held by German corporations, but also assets originally controlled by Western organizations such as the Société Générale de Belgique and subsequently confiscated by the Nazis for German banks, especially the Dresdner and Deutsche banks. Only Czechoslovakia, Poland, and Yugoslavia managed to recover what the Germans had previously taken. The other countries in Eastern Europe found that virtually all former German or Western factories located within their borders were now claimed by the Russians regardless of how the Germans had gained control. Similarly, the former Axis partners were forced to sign waivers agreeing to renounce any claims they might have had in Germany from September, 1939, to May 8, 1945. They were forced to do this even though several of the countries were neutral or on the Allied side during at least a portion of this time. Thus Hungary, Bulgaria, and Rumania were unable to make any claims on Germany, although the reverse did not hold. As a result, Rumania was actually forced to pay its debts to Germany which of course meant they paid them to the U.S.S.R.

Ultimately the penalties for Hungary, Bulgaria, and Rumania were lightened somewhat. Thus after having paid Russia $56 million at 1938 prices, Hungary's unpaid reparations balance was reduced by one-half to $66 million plus $45 million for so-called Hungarian debts to Germany. Rumania too found its burden reduced. It was difficult enough to meet its reparations obligations to the U.S.S.R. and its own requirements for postwar reconstruction. On top of this it had to maintain Soviet troops and restore Russian property taken by Rumanian troops during the war. In a short time, the Rumanian economy appeared to be on the verge of bankruptcy and anarchy. Also, the Rumanian drought in 1945 proved a severe blow. The Russians quickly realized that instead of collecting they would have to lend. In late 1945 and early 1946, they were forced to lend Rumania about a half a million tons of grain. At the same time, they agreed to reduce the reparation debt by half. It was necessary to halve the debt once again on June 7, 1948. By this time, Spulber estimates, the Rumanians had delivered to the Soviet Union goods worth $153 million in 1938 prices. According to his calculations, the annual burden of reparations at times amounted to one-half of the Rumanian national budget.[7]

Poland, being an ally, was officially excused from paying reparations. Nonetheless, due to some heavy-handed dealings, Poland was made to bear a reparation-like burden until at least 1956. This came about in the following manner: as compensation for the damage inflicted by the Germans, the Soviet Union declared its willingness on August 16, 1945, to provide Poland with all the German property held in Poland as well as 15 per cent of the value of reparations due to be received by the Russians from West Germany.[8] As a quid for this somewhat less than lavish quo (one would think Poland would be entitled to German property within its borders as a matter of right), the Poles agreed to provide coal to the U.S.S.R. at a "favorable price." This price was maintained until November, 1953, when it was increased from about $1.25 a ton to about $15.50, which more closely reflected the world rate.[9] Thus, while the rest of the world hungered for coal, Poland provided close to 50 million tons to the Soviet Union at gift prices. Originally, the Poles had contracted to supply 8 million tons of coal in 1946, 13 million annually in the years from 1947 to 1950, and 12 million a year thereafter. But in March, 1947, the Soviet Union agreed to accept reduced deliveries of 6.5 million a year. As we shall see, during the Polish uprising of October, 1956, the Soviets acknowledged that there had been a lack of fraternal helpfulness in this arrangement. (The Poles' attitude was reflected in one of their famous jokes. Question: The sun and Polish coal are sources of heat. How do they differ? Answer: The sun disappears in the West; Polish coal disappears in the East.) As compensation for grabbing (an ideologist might say exploiting) Poland's coal resources, the Soviets announced they would cancel Poland's outstanding debt to the Soviet Union, which they said totaled approximately $626 million.[10] This, the Russians acknowledged, more or less equaled the gains they had made on the purchase of Polish coal at bargain prices. Nevertheless, by that time, coal was no longer in short supply, and whatever chance the Poles had to buy Western machinery for their coal on more favorable terms had passed. Thus, whatever the ultimate compensation, the effect from 1947 to 1953, and to some extent to 1956, was as if Poland was paying reparations to the U.S.S.R. with the one internationally accepted currency it had, coal.

The whole question of the fairness of bloc prices has been the subject of heated controversy. It seems worth while at this point to consider the matter in more detail. While the inequity of Polish coal was an extreme situation, there were other commodities provided the Soviet Union at prices that occasionally did not even cover costs. Thus, the Russians obtained Rumanian oil at 1938 prices for a number of years after the conclusion of the war, despite the increase in world prices and domestic costs.[11]

The general feeling for some time has been that similar one-sided pricing prevailed, although to a lesser degree, between the U.S.S.R. and all the countries of the bloc. This was nourished by reports of refugee groups and periodic complaints by the affected satellites. As one-time Russian subordinates like Yugoslavia, Albania, China, and North Korea started to splinter from the Soviet branch of leadership, they be-

gan to justify their actions by citing the shabby treatment they had received from the Russians. Inevitably, this included a charge of price
discrimination.[12] This substantiated testimony offered at the purge
trials conducted in the aftermath of Tito's defection in 1948. The Bulgarian Vice Premier was accused of selfishly defending Bulgaria's interests without regard to fraternal relations. To mention only a few of
the charges, he was criticized for arguing over every bargaining point,
over the exchange rate of the ruble, and over prices. Similar accusations
were made at the Slansky trials in Czechoslovakia.[13] While the indict-
ment against such defendants was that they were trying to take advantage of the U.S.S.R., their actions are generally interpreted in the
Titoist sense that they were just trying to protect their own interests.

When the Russians began to release official foreign trade statistics
covering the years 1955 and thereafter, Western economists sought to
show that the terms of trade for the satellites with the U.S.S.R. were
unfavorable. Horst Mendershausen found there was a tendency for the
U.S.S.R. to charge the satellite countries more than it charged Western
Europe for similar Soviet exports and to pay the bloc less than it paid
to Western Europe for imports.[14] Disputing the political significance
of these findings, Franklyn Holzman argued that if one viewed the
terms of trade from the vantage point of the satellite countries, the
argument could equally well be made that the bloc countries discriminated against the U.S.S.R.[15] He pointed out that because of the
artificial nature of the Eastern bloc trading group, the satellites were
forced to buy their products within the bloc and therefore were unable
to avail themselves of the best bargains in the West. In addition, in
order to crack capitalist markets, Communist firms were generally
compelled to reduce their prices. Similarly, for political and other reasons, in order to purchase goods from Western companies, it was often
necessary for Communist trading agencies to pay premium prices.
Holzman called the net result of such practices an "autarky," or
"customs-union" effect, which would inevitably result whenever nations try to isolate themselves voluntarily or involuntarily from the
opportunities of the world markets.

In the midst of the debate between Mendershausen and Holzman, a
Russian economist, F. Abramov, wrote an article in *Vneshniaia
Torgovlia* arguing that neither Mendershausen nor Holzman was correct.[16] Abramov accused Mendershausen of making improper use of
the data, arguing that it was misleading to assume that a single price
for the commodity "steel" could be calculated. Various grades of steel
are naturally sold at varying prices, and failure to account for this, or
to include a large enough sample, distorts the results. Abramov at-

tacked Holzman for suggesting that there is such a thing as a "customs union" or anything other than a "voluntary, mutually beneficial" arrangement between fraternal socialist states.

For the period of time examined, there does not seem to be a simple answer to the dispute. Nonetheless, a few observations can be made. Unfortunately, the argument between Mendershausen and Holzman centers on the years after 1955. Because complete Soviet data are unavailable for any earlier period, it is impossible to make even an imperfect analysis of the period prior to 1955. Yet it was in the period from 1945 to 1956, especially 1945–53, that the most aggravated excesses supposedly occurred. Those were the years in which Polish coal and Rumanian oil were sold to the Russians at completely unrealistic prices. According to Frederic Pryor of Yale University, there was also extreme discrimination against Bulgaria at this time, although the terms of trade improved markedly after 1954.[17] Approximately the same claim is made about trade relations between the U.S.S.R. and East Germany.[18] Nor does the debate take account of what could have been obtained in exchange in Western Europe at a time when coal and oil were relatively so important. Similarly, the argument does not reflect the unrealized benefits to Eastern Europe that would have come if it had been allowed to participate in the Marshall Plan. Until ordered to withdraw, Czechoslovakia was prepared to join in the Plan along with the West European countries. Whatever theoretical merits there are in the arguments, then, the fact remains that the era of greatest discrimination is not covered in the analysis. Furthermore, as Holzman himself indicated, there is little reason to believe that the East European countries formed their "customs union" or sought "autarky" voluntarily. So even if there is a theoretical explanation, because of the "customs union" or "autarky" effect, it seems unlikely that the East European countries would have turned eastward voluntarily for their trade to the extent that they did.

Apparently this kind of intimidation did not end in the early 1950's. On December 3, 1965, Dr. Erich Apel, Chief of the Planning Commission of East Germany, committed suicide in protest over the unfair terms of a trade agreement imposed on East Germany by the U.S.S.R. Reportedly he was particularly distressed by the demand that the Germans sell 300 or more freighters and other ships at 30 per cent less than prices prevailing on the world market. Not surprisingly, a few days later, the Russians announced the sale of $105-million worth of ships to Greece at world prices, of which $75 million was to be paid for in convertible currency. This was almost the same pattern the Russians had followed in the late 1940's and early 1950's.

ASIAN SATELLITES. It was not only in Eastern Europe that the Soviets managed to press their claims for reparations and economic concessions. Even though their overt military activity in Manchuria lasted for less than one week, the Russians were awarded extensive compensation rights there.[19] Their claims even extended onto the territory of one of the wartime allies, the Republic of China. According to the Yalta Agreement of February 11, 1945, the commercial port at Darien was to be internationalized. The lease to the naval base at Port Arthur was to be restored to the U.S.S.R., and the Russians were given a half interest in the Chinese Eastern Railway and the South Manchurian Railway. The name was changed to the Chinese Changchun Railway and control was to be shared with the Nationalist Chinese.

In September, 1945, only a month after the Russians declared their little war on Japan, their troops began to loot Manchuria. Marshal Malinovsky, then in command of Soviet forces in the area, declared that unless the Chinese under Chiang Kai-shek agreed to the formation of joint stock companies with the Russians, the Russians would declare most of the industrial equipment in Manchuria war booty and take what they wanted. This action infuriated local Chinese and Manchurian Communists. They fiercely resented the sacking of their country, whether by Japanese or by Soviets, and they eventually expressed their anti-Soviet feelings openly.[20] Edwin Pauley, in his survey for the United States Government, estimated that Soviet confiscations caused damage totaling nearly $900 million, although restoration and repair would have cost close to $2 billion.[21] The Russians replied that their removals totaled only $97 million. Whatever the actual figure, the Russians apparently took everything they could. After the expulsion of Chiang Kai-shek from the mainland in 1949, the Russians began a partial restoration of equipment and property. This alone resulted in the surrender of 320 major pieces of property, including 44 factories, 33 warehouses, 188 dormitories, and 11 movie houses.[22]

Joint Stock Companies

The tale of the Soviet joint stock companies (JSC) sounds as if it were taken from a diatribe of the most violent anti-Soviet propaganda. To paraphrase, truth is often stronger than fiction. Unlike the reparation demands, for which there was often a moral justification, or discriminatory pricing, for which there may have been at least some theoretical justification, the formation of the JSC was in the best tradition of a colonial power. Few if any American or European companies have been so "imperialistic," and when they have been, the outcry has been always loud and anguished. Ironically, for almost four decades in some cases, there has been nothing but painful silence about the Soviet JSC. Although Yugoslavia protested against the JSC in its attack on the Soviet attempt to dominate Yugoslavia, other countries, such as Rumania and China, have only recently broken the silence of their muted suffering.

NATIONALIST CHINA AND MONGOLIA. The history of the Soviet JSC dates from the revolution. At first, the Soviets voluntarily disavowed all economic claims on other countries in the form of debts and property rights. It was not too long, however, before they reconsidered and decided to hold onto at least some of their Czarist inheritance in the Far East. In 1924, they resumed joint responsibility for the operation of the Chinese Eastern Railway with China. Russian interest in this area continued until 1935, when the Soviets decided it might be politically and economically expedient to sell their share to Manchukuo, Japan's puppet state. Apparently the Russians were not bothered by the thought of accepting payment for an investment on foreign territory.

The other area of Soviet economic penetration prior to World War II was in Mongolia. The Russians had also made inroads here under the Czar, but their activity seems insignificant in comparison to what the Soviets eventually managed to do. After freeing Mongolia of its Czarist debt, the Soviets attempted to re-establish their economic position in the country. Shortly after the end of the Civil War in the Soviet Union, the Soviets again established branches of Russian companies in the Mongolian market.[23] Among the first were Sherst, which was to handle wool procurement and export, Kozhsindikat, which did the same for leather, and Sibgostorg and Dalgostorg, both of which were trading companies. The Soviet consumers' cooperative organization, Tsentrosoiuz, was also allowed to open up branches. The acknowledged purpose of these organizations was to force out foreign competition, primarily Chinese and Anglo-American firms. Not surprisingly, the authorized Soviet companies had some measure of success. The number of Chinese firms in Mongolia fell from 470 in 1924 to 270 in 1926, and the number of Anglo-American firms from 12 in 1924 to 9 in 1926.

In a short time, the Soviet firms were merged into joint stock companies with existing Mongolian enterprises. These JSC were owned jointly by Soviet and Mongolian interests, but for the most part they were managed or effectively controlled by the Soviets. There were many reorganizations, but the Russians were usually able to retain their power. Thus in 1932, the JSC Monsovbuner was formed to handle foreign and domestic trade for all of Mongolia. It even absorbed some of the activities of Montsenkoop, the Mongolian Central Cooperative Society. In turn, even though the functions were unchanged, Monsovbuner was superseded by Gostorg on September 14, 1934, which was replaced by Gossnabtorg in 1938. In November, 1939, Monkoopsoiuz assumed a monopoly in domestic trade. Foreign trade was then transferred to Optorg. All of these organizations plus Pishchetrest, a newly organized firm, were either aided or partially directed by Soviet interests. In the field of transportation, Sovtorgflot was formed to handle maritime traffic. With the Mongolian Ministry of Transportation, the two were formed into Mongoltrans in 1925. In November, 1929, Mongoltrans absorbed the Mongolian highway transportation company. Soviet interests in this company were turned back to Mongolia in 1935. However, Soviet interest in Mongolian transport continued, and on February 27, 1946, the Russians announced that they had presented Mongolia with the Altan-Bulek to Ulan Bator and the Chorbalean to Under-Khan highways and were charging Mongolia only one-half of the cost of the roads. As we shall see, this was to become the way in which the Russians dissolve a JSC: they not only claim half of the earnings while the JSC is in operation, but they try to obtain compensation for 50 per cent of the assets once it is dissolved.

Prior to World War II, the Russians had penetrated into almost every sector of the Mongolian economy. In addition to the areas already mentioned, the Russians were also part owners or major influences in the Mongolbank (Mongolian State Bank) set up on June 2, 1924, the Trade and Industrial Bank set up in 1939, and the Mongolian Radio and Communication Company organized in March, 1931. Thus the Soviets were involved in finance, communications, transportation, and trade. There were not many other heights left to command.

After the war, there was a renewed flurry of activity. In February, 1949, Mongolneft was authorized to drill and refine oil. The next month, Sovmongolmetall was created to conduct geological surveys and undertake mining activities. Later that year, on June 6, 1949, a JSC, the Ulan Bator Railway Company, was set up and also authorized to build a railway from Ulan Bator to Nashuki.

The Russians' withdrawal from the Mongolian JSC began in 1953, apparently at the same time that they moved out of their East European companies. The process of withdrawal, however, was considerably more prolonged in Mongolia. This was partially due to the much greater degree of Soviet involvement in the economy. It also reflects the absence of the protest about the Russian presence that existed in Eastern Europe. Interestingly, the major concessions by the Soviets to the Mongolians were made much later than elsewhere and seem to coincide with the outbreak of Soviet tensions with Communist China, at which time China criticized the Soviet Union's imperialistic role in Mongolia.[24]

Without having to compensate the U.S.S.R., Mongolia was given the Soviet share of the Selenga Steamship Line, sixteen meteorological stations, all long-distance telephone lines, and airports at Ulan Bator and Sain-Shande, together with five Ilyushin airplanes. These transfers were made in 1953 and 1954. The Russians claimed that this amounted to a gift of $25 million. A second round of Soviet withdrawals began in 1956. In advance of the major activity that was to follow at the end of the year in Europe, on April 8, 1956, the Mongols obtained sole title to the Ulan Bator Railway. The Russians claimed this was worth about $6 million and they transferred it free of charge. In May, 1957, the Russians also made the Mongols a gift of the oil trust, Mongolneft. At the same time, when the Russians withdrew from the metallurgical jsc, Sovmongolmetall, the Mongols agreed to compensate the U.S.S.R. for its 50 per cent share. The Russians claim that the value of their gifts to the Mongols from 1947 to 1959 totaled between $75 and $110 million.[25] However, as just mentioned, the Mongols were also required to pay for one-half the value of many of the jsc turned over to them by the Soviets. For this purpose, the Russians extended a thirty-year loan. Repayment was to begin in 1962.[26]

EUROPE. Although the Soviets made extensive use of jsc in Asia, the most valuable companies were formed in Eastern Europe. Because of their widespread use and because at least some of the East Europeans have spoken openly about these organizations, most of our knowledge about the operating characteristics of Soviet jsc comes from East Europe.[27]

The attention of the outside world was first drawn to the jsc by the complaints of the Yugoslavs during their quarrel with the Russians that began in 1948. In a unique document, the *White Book on the Aggressive Activities by the Governments of the U.S.S.R., Poland, Czechoslovakia, Hungary, Rumania, Bulgaria, and Albania Toward Yugoslavia,* the role of the jsc and the host country's attitude toward such an organization is spelled out in detail.[28]

Unlike Bulgaria, Hungary, East Germany, Rumania, and Austria, where jsc were also created after World War II, Yugoslavia had not been a member of the Axis. But, in accords of June 8, 1946, and February 4, 1947, the Yugoslavs voluntarily entered into an arrangement to create two jsc. The jsc were to promote the economic development of the country and were to serve as gateways through which the Russians would channel capital goods and technical assistance. In return for this expected help, the Yugoslavs consented to split the profits of such companies on a 50-50 basis. As was the case in virtually all the other JSC we will study, the Yugoslavs also agreed that such companies would have certain property and legal rights within the host country not enjoyed by purely domestically owned firms. Moreover, they were normally freed from taxation, custom duties, and most foreign-exchange restrictions. Just as in the days of the Open Door Policy in China, such privileges amounted to extra-territoriality, which inevitably gave such firms an all but insurmountable competitive advantage. Finally, the Yugoslavs agreed that half the members of the Board of Managing Directors in each firm would be Russian.

Whatever hopes Yugoslavia had about the JSC were quickly shattered. In the breast-beating that followed the split between Yugoslavia and the Soviet Union, the Yugoslav government declared in an official report that

> It should be emphasized, and this was confirmed by the experience of running these companies, that mixed companies are not and cannot be a form of economic cooperation guaranteeing equal relations between their partners. The formal parity (paid-up capital on a 50-50 basis, parity distribution of profits, etc.) was only a screen to conceal direct exploitation and appropriation of profits by the utilization of Yugoslavia's natural resources and of the value created by the labor of the Yugoslav working people.[29]

The Yugoslavs subsequently rejected Soviet attempts to set up additional JSC in areas such as oil and banking.

The Yugoslav experience with the two JSC that were formed provided them with plenty of reason for distrust. JUSTA, the Soviet-Yugoslav Civil Air Transport JSC, succeeded in taking away most of the traffic from the national Yugoslav State Air Transport Company. The Soviet Director General operated on the assumption that JUSTA not only had the right to utilize domestic airports for its operations, but that it had exclusive control over the entire air transport service in the country. This included all means of communication and radio navigation. Eventually JUSTA became so powerful that it felt it unnecessary to notify the Yugoslav government of the arrival and departure of foreign aircraft.

In the case of the Soviet-Yugoslav Danubian Shipping JSC, or JUSPAD, the unfair competition with Yugoslav firms assumed equally blatant forms. The best river craft of Yugoslavia were turned over to JUSPAD as Yugoslavia's share of the investment pool. The Russian technicians were given a free hand in the selection of ships from the Yugoslav fleet. Although the Russians later complained that what they found was of poor quality, no one disputed the Yugoslav contention that it was the best Yugoslavia had to offer. Not only did the Russians take the best equipment, but JUSPAD often charged Yugoslavia three times the amount it charged the Soviet Union for the haulage of freight. The Russian explanation that the difference was due to the economies of scale involved in the longer haul to the U.S.S.R. is not entirely convincing. The Yugoslavs also complained that, wherever possible, JUSPAD chose not to utilize the tugboat service of the national Yugoslav State River Shipping Company. Instead, they chose to hire and pay the wholly Soviet-owned Soviet-Danubian State Shipping Company. All of this naturally hurt the Yugoslav balance of payments. Thus the Yugoslavs complained that instead of facilitating economic development, the jsc hampered it.

As an indication of how little the Russians thought of Yugoslav rights, the Yugoslavs point to the Russian attempt to form an international shipping cartel along the Danube. This was to be done not only at the expense of the Yugoslavs and JUSPAD, but to the detriment of Meszhart, the Soviet-Hungarian shipping company; DDSG, the Soviet-Austrian shipping company; and Sovromtransport, the Soviet-Rumanian shipping company. The leader of this cartel was to be the Soviet-Danubian State Shipping Company. Because the director generals of all these companies were Soviet citizens, it was relatively easy for them to meet and draw up a pact without the knowledge of their Yugoslav, Hungarian, Austrian, and Rumanian counterparts on the various managing boards. When the Yugoslavs found out about this conspiracy, on March 27, 1948, they refused to participate. Their immediate fear was that this plan would give the U.S.S.R. complete domination over all transport on the Danube. This fear was doubtless shared by other countries. Yet, at the time, there was no public complaint. Nevertheless, it should be noted that this Soviet move coincided with the first manifestation of overt tension between the U.S.S.R. and Yugoslavia. That same month marked the first hostile exchange of notes and the Russian announcement of their withdrawal of Soviet military and civilian advisers from Yugoslavia. It is likely that economic exploitation was a factor in the ultimate split and that the Yugoslavs had considerable support for their position in other countries in the Eastern bloc.

In the process of dissolving both Yugoslav joint stock companies, further evidence of Russian rapacity came to light. First, it turned out that the Russians had failed to put in the full amount of their promised share of the capital stock. (The Yugoslavs also held back their full share.) Second, the Soviets insisted that the Yugoslavs pack up and ship, at Yugoslav expense, all the equipment supplied by the U.S.S.R. that was still in the possession of JUSPAD and JUSTA. They also demanded that the Yugoslavs return all cash that had been sent in by the Russians as their share of the capital. The Russians also tried to make the Yugoslavs bear the full cost of liquidating the companies and paying the debts. The Yugoslavs claim that this amounted to about $2 million. The Yugoslavs refused to accede to Soviet demands that they compensate the Russians for the machinery that had already depreciated in the course of operations and that they bear a major portion of the liabilities toward third parties.

Probably there were other injustices. Yugoslavia has hinted that the Soviet Union had its Rumanian jsc cut off the flow of oil to JUSTA in April, 1948, as a means of exerting pressure. The Russians followed this up with a formal complaint that the Yugoslavs were trying to hamper JUSTA's operation. Lest the reader generate too much sympathy for Yugoslavia, it should be noted that Yugoslavia has not been completely innocent in such operations. It is ironic to find that Yugoslavia set up similar jsc in Albania. Indeed, Yugoslav penetration in Albania was much more complete than the Soviet efforts in Yugoslavia, extending into such fields as railroad operation, oil drilling, mining, electrical generation, banking, and import-export. Albanian complaints about Yugoslavia sound much like the Yugoslav complaints about the Russians. Thus they have charged that the Yugoslavs failed to make any actual investment in Albania and instead "exploited the riches of our country at the same time unjustly trying to dictate to it." [30] This goes a long way toward explaining the suspicion with which members of the East European satellites viewed economic ties not only with the U.S.S.R. but with each other.[31]

We have fewer details about the operation of the jsc in countries other than Yugoslavia, but what we know suggests that the pattern is much the same. If anything, Soviet exploitation is greater, since the Russians felt less need to invest and bring in equipment from their own country. The Russians saw no need to build up the economies of former Axis nations, even if in the meantime they had become People's Democracies. For the most part, actual investment by the U.S.S.R. in such companies was quite small. By claiming the bulk of German assets in Eastern Europe as war booty, the Russians found themselves in control of important sectors of the various economies without having to bring in their own equipment. In some cases, the plants had previously been wholly or partially German-owned because of ownership of stock by German investors or banks. For the most part, the

Russians simply replaced the German capitalists who had preceded them—although in some cases the Germans had themselves only recently assumed control during the war from the Allies.

Initially, the Russians took a good portion of former German property as reparations. But because of the chaotic conditions that prevailed throughout Eastern Europe at the time, much of the material never reached its ultimate destination. The Russians therefore decided to use the equipment where it was. This meant either running the plant as a wholly Russian-owned subsidiary, selling the plant to the country where it was located, or operating the enterprise jointly with the host country.

In Bulgaria, there were five jsc plus some wholly Soviet-owned power stations, a credit institution, and some real estate. The first jsc, Gorubso, the Soviet-Bulgarian Mining Company, was formed in 1946.[32] Created originally by the French and subsequently confiscated first by the Germans and then by the Russians, Gorubso accounted for 90 per cent of the nonferrous mining activity in Bulgaria. The other jsc were Sovbolstroi (construction), Korbso (ship-building), Tabso (civil aviation), and a uranium-ore company. All the jsc except Tabso, which continues in operation apparently at Bulgarian request, were sold to Bulgaria in 1954–56. This was a direct response to the Berlin uprisings and the revolts in Poland and Hungary in 1956. The Soviets gave 20 per cent of "their" equity in these jsc to Bulgaria free of charge, while the remainder was to be paid back by Bulgaria over an eight-year period.

As a more advanced country in which there had been considerable German economic involvement, Hungary found itself exposed to significantly more Russian penetration than did Bulgaria.[33] Immediately after the war, the Soviets took over complete control of all former German assets. Thus, at one stroke, the Russians owned 201 firms, including 17 financial institutions, 82 mining and manufacturing firms, 2 electric power stations, and 2 steamship companies. The Russians kept at least 69 of these enterprises until the fall of 1952, when they were sold "at favorable terms" to the government of Hungary. Included were a large wool factory and the Budapest Electrical and Cable Company, formerly owned by the German firm Siemens. In early 1946, the Russians decided to take the remaining firms which had been confiscated from the Germans and convert them into jsc. As was the usual practice, the Soviet share of investment in such firms was to consist of the assets of the confiscated companies. Six of the jsc were of special importance: Meszhart (navigation on the Danube); Maszovlet (civil aviation); Maszovol (producing, drilling, and distributing oil);

Molaj (processing and marketing oil products); Maszobal (mining of bauxite); Danube Valley Alum Earth Company (constructing plants for the bauxite industry). It is also claimed that there was a jsc created to operate Hungarian uranium-ore mines.

The importance of the jsc was increased in 1949 when the Hungarians nationalized all business activity in the country except the Russian-owned firms and the jsc. In the process, some of the jsc were consolidated and expanded. They were also aided by the receipt of approximately $30 million obtained through the sale of other German assets in Hungary.

On November 6, 1954, the Soviets decided to sell their interest in the jsc to Hungary. After the revolution of 1956, the Soviets concluded that they had better close out their interests completely. They canceled the remaining debt owed them for the jsc, the wholly Soviet-owned firms, and reparations. Reportedly this totaled more than 1 billion forints.[34]

Soviet involvement in Rumania was even greater than it was in Hungary. From the more than 400 enterprises the Russians took over from the Germans, 16 jsc were formed.[35] The first companies were established as early as July, 1945, when Sovromneft, an oil company, was created. There followed in rapid succession Sovromtransport (river transport), Tars (civil aviation), Sovrombank (banking), and Sovromlec (lumber). In 1948–49, eight new jsc were formed: Sovromkhim (chemicals), Sovromtraktor (tractor manfacturing), Sovromgaz (natural gas), Sovromugol (coal), Sovrommetall (metallurgy), Sovromconstructio (construction), Sovromasigurari (insurance), and Sovromfilm (movies). In 1952, Sovromfilm was dissolved, but three new jsc were created: Sovromutilaj (oil equipment), Sovromnaval (ship-building), and Sovromcvart (uranium-ore mining).*

Apart from aircraft and the right to use selected airfields in the U.S.S.R., the Russians contributed little of their part of the bargain except their claim to captured German assets. To the Rumanians, this was an especially delicate issue. In the case of Sovromtransport, for example, the Soviet contribution consisted of ships originally owned by Rumanians that had been confiscated by the Germans and reconfiscated by the Red Army. Furthermore, the method for calculating the Rumanians' share of the capital stock discriminated heavily against them. As was often the practice in the other East European countries, goods shipped to the U.S.S.R. as payment for the reparation debt were

---

* See Appendix 3 for the text of the Soviet-Rumanian Agreement on Sovromneft.

valued at a 1938 price level. Given the postwar inflation, this meant that actual deliveries had to be much larger than it first appeared. Finally, some Rumanians questioned the right of the Russians to any German war booty, on the grounds that the Rumanians themselves had ousted the Antonescu fascist government in August, 1944, and thus should not have been treated as an enemy. They also charged that Moscow had even encouraged the Communists in Rumania to seek an alliance with Hitler after the signing of the Nazi-Soviet Pact in 1939.[36]

As they did elsewhere in Europe, the Russians began to dissolve their Rumanian jsc after the 1953 riots in East Germany. In September, 1954, the Soviets sold out their interests to Rumania in all but Sovromneft (oil) and Sovromcvart (uranium). Sovromneft was eventually liquidated in December, 1955, and Sovromcvart a year later, in November, 1956. More important, in late 1956, after the Hungarian uprising, the Russians freed their partners from the debt owed for the Russian share of the jsc. For the Rumanians, this amounted to $710 million and meant a significant easing of their balance of payments burden.

Information about Soviet jsc in other East European countries is much less complete. For a time such companies did exist in Austria and in Albania. Soviet interests in the latter were presented as a gift to Albania in 1957, thus freeing the Albanians from a debt of about $87 million. There was a jsc in Czechoslovakia which, like those in Rumania and Hungary, operated the uranium mines. The Russians also had a joint uranium company in East Germany. Called WIS-MUT, it was in operation as late as 1958, well after most such ventures had been dissolved.

In addition to the Soviet jsc, there were other jsc formed between East European countries themselves without Soviet participation. Following the example of Yugoslavia and Albania, Rumania and Hungary in June, 1952, formed Romagkhim to develop the gas and chemical industry. Rumania also joined in a similar operation with East Germany in September, 1952, and Poland and China formed a shipping jsc in 1950.[37]

COMMUNIST CHINA. Oddly enough, the system of jsc established with Nationalist China continued after the Communist victory. The new partners in the jsc had been neither hostile to nor dependent on Soviet help prior to their accession to power. If anything, Mao and his followers defeated Chiang Kai-shek in spite of Stalin. Nonetheless, the concessions obtained from Chiang Kai-shek by the Russians were not canceled. Instead the number and influence of the jsc were increased.

As mentioned earlier, the Soviets reasserted their Czarist rights of control in Port Arthur and the Chinese Changchun Railway at the end of World War II. In the case of Port Arthur, Soviet domination was facilitated by the fact that the Director and three of the five members of the Managing Board were Russians. With the expulsion of the Nationalist government from the mainland, the JSC that operated the Chinese Changchun Railway was simply reorganized, with Chinese Communists taking the place of Nationalists. The Russians agreed to return complete control of the railway to the Chinese in 1952 without charge. Nevertheless, the Russians managed to persuade the Communists to permit the creation of four additional JSC.[38] On March 27, 1950, Sovkitmetall and Sovkitneft were formed. The former was authorized to prospect for uranium and nonferrous and rare metals in Singkiang, and the second was to drill for oil there. Ironically, the Russians had tried to open such firms in Singkiang in 1949, but the Nationalists, who were then in control, resisted. It was only when the Communists took power that the Russians could move in. The third new JSC was Skoga, the civil airline, which was formed on March 27, 1951. This airline was given the key franchise on the routes Peking–Sheyang–Chita; Peking–Ulan Bator–Irkutsk–Moscow; Peking–Sian–Urumchi–Alma-Ata; and Urumchi–Kashgar. As opposed to the usual pattern of complete Russian domination, the manager of Skoga every other two years was to be Chinese. The metal and oil companies were to remain in existence for thirty years, while the airline company was to continue for ten. In 1951, a fourth JSC was formed, Sovkitsudostroi, the Sino-Soviet Shipbuilding Company in Darien. Again, except for some airplanes, the Russians brought in very little equipment. Even though profits were to be shared equally, the capital assets of the companies were formed either from equipment captured from the Japanese or from material contributed by the Chinese, both Nationalist and Communist.

In October, 1954, Khrushchev visited Peking and agreed to return the four JSC to China by the following January, with the provision that the Chinese would continue to make deliveries of uranium to the U.S.S.R. from what once was Sovkitmetall. The Russians withdrew from Port Arthur a few months later, "after having stayed on a bit longer at China's request."[39] The Soviets were to be reimbursed for their share in the JSC through Chinese exports to the U.S.S.R. In contrast to subsequent policy in Eastern Europe after the Hungarian uprising, this obligation was apparently never revoked by the Russians.

Undoubtedly in China, as in Eastern Europe, the Soviet JSC were very much resented. Despite official praise at the time, it seems clear that these organizations were viewed as an imperialistic device. We have already presented the Yugoslav evaluations of the jsc. Now that the Chinese have become similarly disenchanted with the U.S.S.R., they have been equally critical. The Chinese have much to complain about. In addition to being virtually the only satellite that had to pay back the Russians in full for the Soviet share in the jsc, the Chinese claimed that the Russians had tried to hold back Chinese industrialization. Referring to the jsc, and to Soviet economic policy toward the satellites in general, the Chinese scolded the Russians:

> You bully those fraternal countries whose economies are less advanced and oppose their policy of industrialization and try to force them to remain agricultural countries forever and serve as your sources of raw material and as outlets for your goods.[40]

The Russians replied by reminding the Chinese that such policies were started by Stalin, and by mocking Chinese support of him. The Russians claimed that the Chinese had approved when the

> Central Committee of the Communist Party of the Soviet Union corrected Stalin's errors and restored the Leninist principle of equality in its relations with fraternal parties and countries. We liquidated the economic joint stock companies in China and in other countries and took a number of other measures. It is not superfluous to note that the Central Committee of the Chinese Communist Party at one time fully approved and set a high value on these steps taken by our Party.[41]

To sum up, the jsc served as a bold instrument of economic penetration. By imposing them on countries that had been friendly as well as hostile, the Russians managed not only to obtain a steady source of income in the countries affected, but also to secure priority shipments of goods to the U.S.S.R. from their partially owned companies at a time of severe international shortages. Similarly, they assured themselves of supplies of uranium ore and nonferrous metals, which have always been in short supply in the U.S.S.R. Through their jsc, they managed to control the airlines of virtually all the countries in Eastern Europe, as well as Mongolia and China. They attempted to do the same in river transportation on the Danube.

That the Russians themselves were aware of the imperialistic effect of the jsc is indicated in the letter to the Chinese cited above. They conceded that in order to correct Stalin's errors and restore the Leninist principle of equality among socialist countries, it was necessary not only to withdraw Soviet troops but to dissolve the jsc. Yet when they did come to this decision, the Russians made sure that the principle of equality did not cost them too much: they tried to convert their share holdings into imports by requiring that their partners pay for the Soviet share of the JSC. Only the events in Hungary lifted this burden from the countries in Eastern Europe (although it apparently did not help the Chinese).

In conclusion, by means of a tough policy on reparations, terms of trade, and the JSC, the Russians managed to take what they could from the satellite economies for themselves. Unfortunately, this still did not compensate for the devastation suffered by the Russian economy during World War II. But by the same standards, it is inaccurate to claim, as the Russians do, that "in a short period of time, the Soviet Union reestablished its economy after the war without the help of foreign credits." [42] The satellites may not have extended "foreign credits" in the traditional sense, but until 1956, at least, they did provide more than they received.

2. Soviet Aid to the Satellites

We turn now from a study of Soviet taking to a study of Soviet giving. Not surprisingly, we will see that there is a close correlation between foreign and domestic political events and the generosity of Soviet economic policy. Official Soviet sympathy and understanding, not to mention financial responsiveness, are directly related to political and economic difficulties within, as well as to pressures from outside, the bloc. The unanticipated threat of anarchy and revolution in the Communist bloc in the early 1950's not only forced the Soviet Union to cancel reparations, dissolve joint stock companies, and adjust prices, but also induced the Russians to offer large-scale credits. Actually, the Russians had been periodically helping their satellites for some time, but on balance the Russians were recipients rather than suppliers. Now, because of political and economic developments, they became net donors.

Before embarking on an analysis of Soviet aid to the satellites, it is necessary to re-emphasize the shortcomings in the data. The task of tabulating the size and time of promised Soviet loans to the satellites is especially frustrating. A compilation that it is hoped is as complete and reliable as can be prepared is presented in Table II-1. But there is some question whether Soviet authorities themselves actually know the precise amount of aid that has been promised and delivered. There are several reasons for this:

1. A major difficulty is that the Russians do not have a hard and fast definition of foreign aid. Normally, Russian foreign aid consists of goods and equipment supplied on a credit basis with repayment to be in the form of cash or bartered goods over at least a five-year period. In some cases, however, exports are supplied by the U.S.S.R. for what it expects will be immediate repayment, but the recipient is unable to fulfill its part of the agreement. Because Soviet exports thus unexpectedly exceed Soviet imports, the resulting deficit may be converted into a foreign-aid credit, even though such a step was not originally contemplated and there was no announcement beforehand.

Table II-1

A PARTIAL LISTING OF SOVIET LOANS, DEBT AND REPARATION CANCELLATION, JOINT STOCK COMPANY CANCELLATION, AND GRAIN LOANS
(in Millions of Dollars[a])

	1945-46	1947	1948	1949	1950	1951	1952	1953	1954	1955
Albania										
Loans										
Debt cancellation										
Release of JSC										
Reparation reduction										
Bulgaria										
Loans		5				d				
Debt cancellation			5							
Release of JSC										
Reparation reduction			10-11							
China										
Loans					300				130	
Cuba										
Loans										
Czechoslovakia										
Loans			32							
Grain loans		600,000								
East Germany										
Loans								121-28		
Debt cancellation										
Release of JSC									200	
Reparation reduction					3,171			3,171		
Hungary										
Loans										
Debt cancellation	6	155								
Release of JSC										
Reparation reduction	b							b		
Korea										
Loans				53				250		
Debt cancellation										
Mongolia										
Loans							225			
Poland										
Loans		28-30	450		100					
Debt cancellation										
Grain loans	140,000	500,000								
Rumania										
Loans		10							50	
Debt cancellation			c							
Release of JSC										
Grain loans	300,000									
Vietnam										
Loans										100
Yugoslavia										
Loans			200							
Debt cancellation										90

Sources: See pages 247-48.

[a] Grain loans in tons.
[b] Reduced, but amount not confirmed.
[c] Reduced by one-half.
[d] Quantity unconfirmed.

1956	1957	1958	1959	1960	1961	1962	1963	1964	1965	1966	U.S. Government Estimate 1945-62
	48 18 87	84		40							246
92	50	33		163 40	202			333-605			569
					360						790
				100		403				89	
	14										62
	85	28				225-310					1,353
			270								
35	344 37 250										381
75				225							690
	61			262				500	d		658
200-300 626 1,400,000											914
68	24										189
700-1,100 400,000				d							
7.5	12	40		194						800	369
194											

2. Many of the loans are provided in kind. This creates a problem in valuation, especially on those loans which were extended in the early postwar period when the prices used were sometimes prewar and sometimes postwar.

3. The category "socialist countries" keeps changing. Thus it is hard to say how much has gone to the satellite bloc and how much to the neutralists. Cuba, at one time classified by Russia as a developing country, is now included in the satellite grouping. Yugoslavia is even more of a problem. Initially it was included as a "socialist country"; in the late 1940's and early 1950's it was excluded. Albania is variously included or excluded; loans to China always seem to be included.

4. Aid promises do not always equal aid deliveries. Usually the promises exceed the deliveries, but sometimes deliveries may be higher. Yugoslavia is one country where the deliveries are way below aid promises. The Russians made large pledges to Yugoslavia and then canceled them all in 1948, only to renew them again in 1955. China and Cuba are cases where deliveries exceeded, at least for a time, the aid promises.

5. Another difficulty arises from the inclusion of the value of canceled reparation debt in the total of Soviet economic aid.

6. The liquidation of the joint stock companies is apparently handled in the same way. As already noted, when the Soviets withdrew from the joint stock companies, their partners were compelled to buy out the Russian share. Since large sums of money were involved, the Russians agreed that the payments could be extended over a period of several years. To make the obligation formal, the debt was converted into a long-term loan. In any event these obligations were often included in the total loan figures, although no new funds or goods were provided the recipient countries.

7. Finally, there is an apparent lack of uniformity in handling loans that were either canceled or extended. Sometimes they are counted twice and sometimes they are not counted at all.

The combination of such factors naturally makes any precise statement about the size of Soviet loans extremely difficult. This is reflected in Soviet descriptions of their own aid program. Frequently Soviet studies will disagree about the quantity of aid provided the various countries. Some even differ as to the size and timing of the aid provided in a given year.[1] Inevitably this leads to some overstatement of the actual new credit provided. For the reader, as well as for the writer who likes precision in the materials he utilizes, this predicament is unsettling. Unfortunately this makes it advisable to use a range of estimates.

The Russians claim to have published annual statistics about the size of foreign aid "drawdowns" (actual aid deliveries) since 1955. In a personal interview in June, 1964, in Moscow, officials of the Ministry of Trade indicated that the Soviet Union provides specific information about the size of aid deliveries. D. F. Fokin, Chief of the Economic Planning Administration of the Ministry of Foreign Trade, reaffirmed that information about aid drawdowns is contained in the statistical handbook *Vneshniaia Torgovlia SSSR* (hereafter referred to as *VT SSSR*). According to Fokin, Item 16, "Equipment and Material for Complete Plants," represents the ruble value of technical services as well as the material goods supplied by the Soviet Union to aid-receiving countries, both Communist and neutral.* If this is correct, total Soviet drawdowns from 1955 to 1965 to the satellites as shown in Table II-2 amounted to $3,462 million. Fokin also pointed out that the figures published in *VT SSSR* are not a measure of the balance of trade, since they also include the cost of technical services.

While it is fairly certain that most foreign-aid shipments, other than materials presented in gift form, are reflected in Item 16, there is at least one unanswered question that makes it necessary to use this figure with caution. Item 16 may also include the value of equipment and material for complete plants that are purchased for cash or on short-term credit which would not normally be considered as a foreign-aid credit. This is a crucial unknown, and until more definite information is obtained this figure can only serve as a guide. Consequently, where it appears reasonable, Item 16 will be cited as an indication of the size of aid drawdowns. In other cases, Item 16 will be utilized with reservations.

Soviet foreign aid to the satellites can be divided into the immediate postwar loans, the loans offered as consolation for the rejection of the Marshall Plan, the loans and concessions that followed the death of Stalin and the subsequent Berlin uprising, and the massive aid program introduced after the Polish and Hungarian uprisings of 1956. The case of China will be dealt with separately (see pp. 38–51).

Postwar Loans

In the chaos and hunger that followed in the wake of World War II, it was frequently necessary to provide relief in one form or another, often to prevent starvation. But the Russians were hardly in a position to be particularly generous. They themselves were receiving food and

---

* Item 16 is reproduced in the Appendix pp. 204–5.

Table II-2

ANNUAL FOREIGN AID DELIVERIES (DRAWDOWNS) TO BLOC AND
FORMER BLOC COUNTRIES, 1955-65
(In Thousands of Dollars)

	Albania	Bulgaria	China	Cuba	Czechoslovakia	East Germany	Hungary	North Korea	Mongolia	Poland	Rumania	North Vietnam	Yugoslavia
1955	1,373	13,861	141,359		3,283		4,502	1,736	2,715	88,801	17,769		
1956	2,472	12,763	216,733		1,936	1,150	2,122	4,321	5,295	37,838	7,293		
1957	2,472	8,394	208,815		2,776	1,242	1,224	6,613	6,681	31,010	3,735	167	
1958	1,796	16,753	165,995		4,274		1,331	2,807	5,831	17,476	9,797	75	
1959	5,189	20,560	399,361		971	3,353	19,515	2,272	9,967	14,479	23,392	128	
1960	12,808	35,140	373,469		864	7,105	13,894	897	13,094	12,535	26,112	3,243	
1961	3,286	47,799	78,830	1,850	2,525	8,160	12,794	1,234	11,789	14,301	22,295	11,634	
1962		63,929	8,836	11,137	7,970	9,846	14,947	9,795	28,393	23,955	18,263	21,747	4,256
1963		78,728	14,555	57,904	10,453	11,432	17,851	13,734	29,860	30,060	35,503	24,355	3,419
1964		93,524	12,416	35,430	15,609	14,649	18,356	18,691	33,762	9,078	27,545	18,587	8,553
1965		128,323	3,899	16,319	4,628	19,411	14,912	13,150	36,247	19,106	26,408	32,383	7,062
Total	29,396	519,764	1,624,268	122,640	57,616	76,348	121,448	75,250	183,634	298,639	218,212	112,319	22,890

Sources: See page 248.

credit shipments from UNRRA as well as from the United States under Lend Lease. Consequently, Soviet grants and credits were not very large. Yet, for reasons best known to Stalin, food loans were sometimes extended by the U.S.S.R. despite the existence of food shortages and near-starvation conditions at home.[2] In other cases, Soviet food loans turned out to be grain originally grown by the recipient, subsequently delivered to the Russians as reparations, and returned again by the Russians. In other cases, Russian aid took the form of a postponement or cancellation of contracted or obligated deliveries from the satellite nations.[3] Thus in the case of the Rumanians, the Russians agreed to scale down the reparation payments and provide a wheat-and-corn loan in 1945. They were forced to do much the same thing in 1946, when they provided a grain loan of 300,000 tons. About the same time, Poland was supplied with a grain loan of 140,000 tons and Hungary's reparation burden was lightened. Simultaneously, a fine of $6 million which had been imposed by the U.S.S.R. on Hungary for failure to meet delivery commitments was suspended.

The year 1947 was a bad one throughout all of Europe; it was particularly difficult in Eastern Europe. This was not only because of climatic and economic conditions, but also because of growing tension between the East and West. As a result of a variety of pressures, there was a considerable increase in Soviet economic aid that carried over into 1948. Almost the whole East European bloc received some help in this period. Poland seems to have benefited the most. On March 5, 1947, the Russians extended their first financial aid to a satellite country. Heretofore Soviet loans had been in the form of commodities, not cash. Now the Poles were given about $28 million–$30 million in gold and convertible foreign exchange. They were also provided with 500,000 tons of grain.[4] Equally if not more important, in March, 1947, the Russians agreed to reduce the quantity of low-priced coal they purchased from Poland. The most spectacular loan, however, was announced in January, 1948, and was a direct result of Poland's agreement not to participate in the Marshall Plan.

Reaction to the Marshall Plan

Following Secretary of State George C. Marshall's Commencement Address at Harvard in June, 1947, several of the Eastern bloc countries evidenced interest in cooperating with the West European countries and the United States in the economic reconstruction of Europe. After the Paris Conference in July, 1947, it appeared that both Poland and Czechoslovakia would request help. Neither one seemed to heed the Soviet warning that participation in the Marshall Plan would enslave them to the United States and force them to accept unwanted consumer goods from America's glutted warehouses. Only Soviet help, the Russians claimed, would ensure the provision of capital goods and sound economic recovery.[5] To quell any lingering doubts the Poles may have had about Soviet intentions, the Russians officially announced in January, 1948, a $450-million loan to cover machinery imports and the construction of a new steel mill at Nova Huta.

The political events of 1948 were of equal if not more importance for their effect on Russian generosity. Although the full significance of the move was not appreciated for some time to come, in late March, 1948, the Soviets announced the withdrawal of their military advisers from Yugoslavia. The civilian advisers left soon after and the Cominform resolution condemning Yugoslavia was adopted in June of the same year. In response to these political developments, and perhaps to head off any further defections, the Russians extended about $10 million in loans to Rumania and agreed that Rumania could cancel half of its debt to the U.S.S.R. Much the same type of aid was provided Bulgaria, which obtained a $5-million loan and was permitted to reduce reparation payments and postpone the payment of certain other debts. The Russians even found it necessary to extend economic credit to Czechoslovakia, the showcase of the Eastern bloc. Although the date and terms of the loan are ambiguous, the Russians apparently agreed to provide 600,000 tons of grain and 1,150 million crowns in November, 1947.[6] The following year this was followed by an industrial loan for $32 million.[7] In a way, the Yugoslav defection made it easier for the Russians to undertake these new loans. Now the U.S.S.R. was freed from fulfilling its promise to deliver the full $200 million in aid it had committed to Yugoslavia in the period 1945–48.

The temper of the times called for something more than loans, however. Even though Stalin's rule was absolute, he felt it necessary to provide an institutional counterbalance to the growing cohesion of the West European nations which had been stimulated by the Marshall Plan. He also hoped to halt the spread of dissension among the East European nations which had been provoked by Yugoslavia's disaffection. With this in mind, the Council for Mutual Economic Assistance (COMECON, or CMEA) was created in January, 1949. Its purpose was to facilitate economic relations between members of the bloc by promoting economic integration and mutual growth and the expansion of trade. It preceded by some years the creation of the European Common Market. In fact, at the time of its formation, CMEA was heralded as something that could be created only in a socialist society, where states would willingly yield their sovereignty. Actually, CMEA continued the domination of the U.S.S.R. spelled out in the preceding chapter. It was later charged that Soviet embassies even had the power to decide the selection of the goods to be entered in foreign trade and the composition of the Ministries of Foreign Trade within the various satellites until 1956.[8] It was to be some time before CMEA would provide any concrete advantages for the smaller nations. At first, it seems to have antagonized its members and caused them to distrust it and each other, as we shall see.

During the next few years, Stalin reasserted his control over Eastern Europe. Except for a $100 million loan to Poland on June 29, 1950, the release of some captured German factories, and a loan to Bulgaria of unspecified size in 1951, it appears there were no other loans provided Eastern Europe until after Stalin's death in 1953. That is virtually a five-year period with only minor new loan commitments. Despite a generous loan of $300 million for China in February, 1950, the Soviet Union directed its economic efforts inward and apparently capitalized on its advantageous position relative to its East European satellites.

The Death of Stalin

The policy of draining the East European satellites was radically altered after the death of Stalin. The disappearance of Stalin's iron hand was the signal for the release of long built-up frustration. This was manifested in the 1953 street riots in Germany, and later, by the two revolutions of 1956: the peaceful one in Poland and the violent one in Hungary. It was during this period that the Russians not only dramatically expanded their loan program, but, as mentioned earlier, also found it expedient to close out their interests in the joint stock companies.

The uncertainty that followed the death of Stalin affected all the Communist countries, not only Russia. The first overt demonstrations took place in East Berlin amid growing rumors of strikes and restlessness. Tensions reached a breaking point on June 17, 1953, in the famous confrontation of men and rocks with Russian tanks and shells. Although the outcome of that particular battle was never in doubt, there was no particular reason to anticipate the economic actions that were to follow. In the face of pressure, the Russians made economic concessions.

Yielding to the German unrest, the Russians granted a loan of $121 million–$128 million in August, 1953, of which $34 million was in convertible currency.[9] More important, the burdensome terms of the war settlement were lightened. Under the original conditions, rehabilitation of the East German economy was virtually impossible. This was

made all the more evident by the growing contrast with life in West
Berlin and West Germany. Consequently, the Russians agreed that
reparations totaling 10 billion German marks (about $3.2 billion)
would be annulled. The Russians also canceled a redemption fee for
sixty-six confiscated firms returned to Germany in 1952 and worth an
estimated 430 million marks ($200 million). Furthermore, the East
Germans were freed from paying occupation costs in foreign currency
and those costs were lowered from about 12 per cent of the country's
budget to 5 per cent. Even though the Germans were not entirely
freed from the financial load of maintaining Soviet troops until 1959,
the reductions made in 1953–54 were of considerable help.

In the immediate confusion and tension following Stalin's death, the
only other East European country to receive a loan was Rumania,
where what were described as "economic difficulties" necessitated a
credit of $50 million.[10] Loans were also extended to the Asian Com-
munist countries (see pages 37–38). In addition to providing for the
new governments of North Korea and North Vietnam, these loans,
especially to China, also reflected some of the uncertainty and instability which followed Stalin's death. Otherwise the Russians seemed content with the status quo, at least until 1956. When Yugoslavia decided
to welcome Khrushchev's peace overtures in 1955, the Russians agreed
to forgive some of the credits originally issued to Yugoslavia prior
to 1948. But since there seemed to be little chance that any money
would ever be collected from the Yugoslavs, this appeared to be more of
a political gesture by the Soviets than an economic sacrifice.[11]

The Hungarian Revolution

In 1956, the Russians extended several loans in Eastern Europe, apparently for the first time since 1952. The first loan was part of a series
to Yugoslavia that came early in the year. In recognition of the new
thaw in political relationships, Tito was given a loan of $110 million on
January 12, 1956. This was followed within a month by two new loans,
bringing the total to $194 million.[12] At about the same time, a poor
harvest in Bulgaria necessitated a request for aid which the Russians
met with two loans of $75 million and $17 million. This was to provide
both food and equipment.

The main outflow of economic aid, however, took place at the end of
the year. It marked an entirely new dimension in Soviet economic policy toward Eastern Europe and once again was necessitated by outside
pressure, the uprisings in Poland and Hungary. The combination of
these protests triggered an outpouring of economic aid without prece-
dent in Soviet history. Almost every country in Eastern Europe received some major concession or loan.

The events of 1956 were set off by Khrushchev's secret speech attacking Stalin, presented in February to the Twentieth Party Congress of the Soviet Communist Party in Moscow; its impact thundered throughout Eastern Europe. The official acknowledgment of Stalin's villainy added to the uncertainty and instability already evidenced in Germany in 1953. The readmission of Tito to the comradeship of the East European countries and his elevation to the position of favored son with loans and embraces did nothing to reduce the ferment. Heretofore, mere suspicion of sympathy for Tito was sufficient cause for punishment. Eternal truths and gods were being shattered on all sides.

The first clear sign of trouble after Khrushchev's speech occurred in Poznan, Poland, on June 28, 1956, where a workers' protest spread into a general uprising that resulted in forty-four deaths and the wounding of hundreds. This set off a period of hurried maneuvering which ultimately led to the election of Wladyslaw Gomulka as head of the Communist Party on October 21, a move taken in defiance of Soviet preferences.

The next outbreak was the more serious and widespread rebellion in Hungary. A few days after the events in Poland, the entire government of Hungary announced its rejection of Soviet domination and refused to submit any longer to Soviet dictates. After initial hesitation, Soviet troops acted firmly. Further resistance was suppressed by November 4. While this put an end to physical violence, it left political and economic confusion in its wake. But instead of resisting and applying retaliatory force throughout the bloc, the Soviets, as before, succumbed to the pressure from the satellites. In an attempt to compensate for the past, the Russians released a huge outpouring of economic loans, grants, and concessions.

Even before the climactic days in October, the Russians had found it expedient to come to the aid of Poland with a loan of $25 million in convertible currency. To ameliorate the effects of a bad harvest and prevent any more Poznans, the Russians in September, 1956, provided Poland (as it had Bulgaria) with the means to replenish its depleted grain stocks on the world market. Evidently this came nowhere near assuaging Polish demands. After Gomulka's accession to power, a series of new loans and concessions was announced. As a first step, the Russians agreed to stretch out the payment date of some of the earlier loans and allow the repayment of the 1947 gold loan with goods instead of gold or convertible currency. One estimate put the cost of these concessions at about $200 million. But this also failed to answer Polish needs and demands. Accordingly it was decided on November 1, 1956, to cancel all Polish debts to the U.S.S.R. Officially, it was agreed that this would compensate for the low prices paid by the Russians for Polish coal.

Considering the opportunities missed because Poland could not obtain Western equipment for its industry, it is questionable whether the $626-million worth of canceled debt did in fact provide adequate compensation. In any event, it was a dramatic move which indicated the seriousness of the situation. Yet it was still not enough to pacify and satisfy the Poles. Eighteen days later, a grain loan of 1.4 million tons was promised by the Russians. In addition, a new loan of $175-million worth of equipment was announced. This reportedly brought the total of new Soviet aid to Poland in the period 1956–57 to $300 million. With the abrogation of all outstanding debts in 1956, the effect of the new loan was ultimately to make the U.S.S.R. a net lender to Poland for the first time.[13]

Shortly after the Russians announced their loans, other members of the bloc also extended aid to Poland. In 1957, East Germany promised to provide $100 million in coal-mining equipment. This was followed by another loan of $64 million in January, 1961, for financing the Polish section of the Druzba oil pipe line from the U.S.S.R. through Eastern Europe. Similarly the Czechs presented Poland with a loan of $25 million for sulphur-mining equipment and in May, 1958, they provided another $62.5 million for coal-mining improvement. In early 1961 they also gave the Poles a loan for $125 million to finance the sale of copper-mining equipment.

Much the same pattern of events prevailed in Hungary. There, too, the Russians found that there was a limit to how much they could extract. They attempted to replenish the nearly exhausted Hungarian treasure chest. Moreover, joint participation by fellow satellites reached an even larger scale than it did in Poland. The credit spree began in October, 1956, when the Russians announced a loan of 100 million old rubles, or $25 million, to Hungary. Of this amount, $10 million was made in convertible currency so that purchases could be made outside the bloc. This was followed later in the year by another loan of approximately $10 million. These initial loans were supplemented with at least two other major Soviet loans in 1957. In March, loans totaling $219 million were made, including about $50 million in convertible currency.[14] In December, another loan of $75 million was made.[15]

Again as in Poland, the Russians made other concessions in addition to the extension of a new loan. They agreed to postpone about $37 million due on loans extended earlier. More important, they not only liquidated their interests in the Hungarian joint stock companies, but agreed to free the Hungarians from having to pay for the Soviet share. It is estimated this amounted to about $250 million. There is a question as to why Hungary should have had to pay for this in the first place, but the ultimate decision was a welcome one. As mentioned in the last chapter, the Russians subsequently canceled the debt for all the joint stock companies except those in China and a few in Mongolia.

Because of the violent nature of the crisis in Hungary, more of the satellites came forward with loans. Total loans from within the bloc (other than from the U.S.S.R.) came to at least $100 million. Apparently every Communist country except Mongolia, North Korea, and North Vietnam came forth with some offering. Even the Poles, despite their own needs, made a loan of $25 million.[16] The Czechs made two loans, of $19 million and $25 million; the Rumanians offered $15 million; East Germany provided $25 million, with an extra $3 million in 1957; Bulgaria supplied $3 million; and even Albania managed to come up with $50,000. There is some disagreement as to whether China provided $25 million or a higher figure, but it and Yugoslavia, which offered $2 million, were both involved.[17] In fact, this was one of the last acts about which all members of the Communist bloc could agree before the schism between the U.S.S.R. and China.

Even though the other members of the bloc promised to give aid to Hungary, this did not prevent countries like Rumania, Bulgaria, and East Germany from seeking help for themselves as well. We have just seen how Poland was somehow able to find the funds for a loan to Hungary while simultaneously it was being provided with close to $300 million in new loans from the U.S.S.R. and being forgiven over $600 million in old loans. Almost every bloc country in Eastern Europe received Soviet help from 1956 to 1958.

The Russians walked through Europe as if they had an open check book and were trying to make up for the greed of ten years in one. Even Czechoslovakia was given a gold loan for $13.5 million. Many recipients had never before received any significant help from the U.S.S.R. For example, Albania was presented with two loans in 1957, one for $8 million in April, 1957, and another for $40 million in November, 1957. The following year it was promised an additional $9 million for oil equipment and $75 million for general industrial equipment. It was also freed from paying for the Soviet half of the Albanian joint stock companies, which the Russians claimed amounted to about $90 million. At the same time, Albania was released from having to repay $18 million in old debts. In 1960, an additional $40 million was promised Albania, but the following year, when Khrushchev denounced Albania for reactionary views, the 1960 loan as well as the 1957–58 loans were suspended.[18] Like the Yugoslavs in 1948, the Albanians had gone too far, and the aid strings were cut.

The East Germans had no such difficulties. In January, 1957, a loan for $85 million in convertible currency was announced. This was followed in February, 1958, by a credit for $27.8 million for the chemical industry. Equally important was the belated decision to free the Germans from the cost of maintaining Soviet soldiers on German territory. As previously indicated, this went into effect on January 1, 1959. A few years later, the Russians provided East Germany with a commodity grant of $310 million on March 5, 1962.

The story is much the same in Bulgaria. After the early loans in 1956, the Bulgarians received two additional loans. The first one, in 1957, was for $50 million for a coal-enriching plant and a zinc refinery; the second, in 1958, for $33 million to be used to build an oil refinery. These were followed in 1960 by a new loan of $163 million for a metallurgical plant. At the same time, the Russians agreed to the postponement until 1966 of a debt for $40 million which was originally to have been repaid in 1961. According to one Soviet authority, this brought Soviet loans to Bulgaria from 1948 to 1962 to a total of $1 billion.[19] Another series of loans was promised in 1964. Beginning with $330 million, a second loan of $183 million and perhaps a third of $72 million were offered apparently in an effort to prevent Bulgaria from following the path of Rumania, which by the mid-1960's had started to make independent noises.[20] Actual aid deliveries exceeded $500 million by 1966.

After the Hungarian revolt, Rumania was overwhelmed with kindness by the Russians. Following a series of hurried negotiations in November and December, 1956, most of Rumania's past debts were written off and some new credits were extended. For example, the Russians agreed to drop their demands that the Rumanians buy up the former Soviet interest in the Rumanian joint stock companies. This was estimated to have saved Rumania between $700 million and $1,100 million. The Rumanians were also allowed four more years to pay off some of their older debts. As a new credit, the Russians provided grain loans of 400,000 tons of wheat and 60,000 tons of feed. More important, additional loans of $68 million in food and industrial equipment were promised. Shortly thereafter, this was increased to $92 million. In one last gesture before Rumania started to veer off on its own course, the Russians provided another short-term grain loan in 1960 after a poor harvest in Rumania.

In sum, the unrest in Eastern Europe necessitated a new economic policy by the U.S.S.R. Not only were past claims and pressures renounced, but new loans and gifts were generously spread about. There can be no doubt that after 1956 the Russians gave more than they took from Eastern Europe. If heretofore the European satellites had served as a private reservoir to quench the Soviet thirst for resources and technology, the flow was decisively reversed as Russian aid to East Europe rose from little more than zero in 1954 and 1955 to approximately $620 million in direct loans in 1956 and $500 million in 1957. In addition, roughly $2 billion in 1956 and $500 million in 1957 were provided in the form of loan cancellations or other benefits.[21]

Aid to the Smaller Asian Satellites

Except for China, Soviet aid to the Communist countries in Asia has been less spectacular than in Eastern Europe. After having been abused for many years, Mongolia eventually received considerable help. While it is hard to pinpoint in just what year Soviet aid was promised or delivered, especially before 1955, the Russians assert that they provided $225 million in economic loans to Mongolia in the ten years from 1947 to 1957. In 1957, a new loan to Mongolia for $61 million was extended. In addition, a loan was created to finance the acquisition by Mongolia of the Soviet interest in the Mongolian joint stock companies. This was a step behind the complete disavowal of the debt that had been made in Eastern Europe. The abrogation of this debt did not follow in Mongolia until 1960-61. As China and the U.S.S.R. began to compete more openly for Mongolia's favor, the Russians stepped up their loan program. They promised about $500 million to Mongolia for 1961-65, and they have promised to provide the exceptionally large sum of $733 million for 1965-70.

Soviet economic aid to Korea actually predates aid to China. Because a Communist government took control in North Korea before it did in China, the Russians found it necessary to supply Korea with $53 million to finance imports from the U.S.S.R. as early as March, 1949. After the Korean War, in 1953, the Russians gave the country a gift of $250 million and a loan of $75 million in 1956 in addition to a write-off of previously contracted debt. The Russians also canceled a $190-million loan in 1960 and postponed one for $35 million. In July of the following year, a new loan was issued so that by July, 1964, the Russians assert, they had loaned Korea $550 million.[22]

North Vietnam received a loan for $100 million in 1955 for twenty-five projects. A series of other loans followed, including a $7.5-million credit in December, 1956, to finance an adverse balance of trade; $12 million in 1957; $40 million in late 1958; $87 million in June, 1960, for food-processing and production; and $107 million in December, 1960, for 206 different projects. Thus from 1955 to 1961 the Russians claim they supplied North Vietnam with loans of about $350 million, of which $105 million was a gift.[23] This may have been supplemented with other credits. In addition, during Kosygin's visit to Vietnam in early 1965, the Soviet Union agreed to reduce the terms of the loans it had provided to Vietnam in 1960–62. Similarly, in late 1965, the Russians agreed to finance Vietnamese trade deficits for 1964, and in late 1966, the Russians reportedly provided another $800 million.

Even before the intensification of the war in 1964, North Vietnam was a recipient of loans from other Communist countries. As of 1961, this aid was reported to total about $750 million, which would mean that Communist countries other than the Soviet Union had provided about $400 million. Of this, China gave about $300 million.[24] Among others who have come to Vietnam's aid were Bulgaria, which offered $3.5 million; Hungary, $2.5 million; Germany, $15 million; Poland, $7.5 million; Czechoslovakia, $26 million; and Rumania, $37 million. Unverified reports in the Western press indicate that total Communist aid by 1965 exceeded $1 billion.[25] It is reasonable to assume that other Communist countries have supplemented their original loans. Apparently they pledged an additional $200 million in late 1966 alone.

The Chinese Dragon

The relations between the U.S.S.R. and China are important enough to warrant a special section. The precise dimension of Soviet economic aid to China is even more difficult to ascertain than is Soviet aid to other countries. The formal long-term credits appear to have been liberally, albeit unwillingly, supplemented with additional short-term credits. Thus, the full impact of Soviet economic aid to China is best evaluated by studying the formal aid agreements in relation to the Sino-Soviet balance of trade and certain major components within that balance.

From the 1949 victory of the Chinese Communists until 1961, only two formal economic credit agreements between the Soviet Union and China were widely publicized.[26] The first, on February 14, 1950, at an interest rate of 1 percent, committed the Russians to deliver $300 million in goods from 1950 to 1954. This came at a time when the Russians were not being particularly generous in Eastern Europe and meant deliveries at a rate of $60 million a year. Repayment in Chinese exports was to begin in 1954 and to continue for ten years. This was supplemented on October 12, 1954, by a loan of $130 million, for a total of $430 million. However, although there were no other formally announced commitments until 1961, there are several factors which indicate that Soviet aid to China considerably exceeded the sum of $430 million. An examination of the foreign-trade relationship between China and the Soviet Union shows that the scale of economic aid is expanded considerably. In the early 1950's, the Soviet Union had a persistent export surplus with China. The extent by which Soviet exports exceeded imports from China is shown in Table II-3. From 1949 to 1955, the Russians shipped China about $1 billion more than they received in return.

Table II-3

SINO-SOVIET TRADE RELATIONS
(in Millions of Dollars)

Year	Soviet Exports	Soviet Imports	Excess of Exports	Excess of Imports
1949	210	140	70	
1950	388	191	197	
1951	478	331	147	
1952	554	414	140	
1953	698	475	223	
1954	759	578	181	
1955	748	643	105	
Total	3,835	2,772	1,063	
1956	733	764		31
1957	544	738		194
1958	634	881		247
1959	954	1,100		146
1960	816	847		31
1961	367	551		184
1962	233	516		283
1963	187	413		226
1964	135	314		179
1965	191	225		34
Total	4,794	6,349		1,555

Sources: See page 249

The significance of this trade gap cannot be evaluated precisely. When one country exports more than it imports from another country, it does not always mean that the net exporter is making up the difference with some form of foreign aid or credit. If this were so, it would appear that several of the Latin American countries were providing economic aid to the United States rather than vice versa. Such a trade gap may simply indicate the countries involved are two members of a three-country multilateral trade arrangement; the full picture is distorted by the lack of trade data from the third country. However, the type of exports, the internal conditions of the Soviet Union and China, the bilateral nature of their economic relationships, and the timing of the aid agreements suggest that trade and aid were closely connected in Russian-Chinese economic dealings and that the trade deficit was largely financed through the expedient of short-term credit.

Even though Sino-Soviet trade throughout this period was primarily bilateral in nature, it cannot be automatically assumed that the *entire* trade gap was made possible through economic credits. Conceivably Soviet military aid during the Korean War of 1950–53 could have been included in the total of Soviet exports, although Soviet practice is to exclude all military materials from its trade statistics. The export trade gap from 1949 to 1955 may have been financed not by a Soviet loan, but by a different kind of capital transaction. It is possible that the Russians may have exchanged machinery or other assets brought in from the Soviet Union in exchange for ownership rights or equity in the joint stock companies. If so, this would mean that such assets were financed by capital stock rather than by capital bonds or loans. However, as already pointed out, except for aircraft and some machinery, Soviet contributions in such companies usually consisted of captured Japanese assets and reparations, with little or nothing brought in from the Soviet Union. Therefore it seems highly unlikely that the export gap was due either to military shipments or to equity contributions by the Russians in Sino-Soviet joint stock companies.

In light of these considerations, two points seem especially important. First, the original 1950 loan called for credit extensions of $60 million a year until 1954. Table II-3 indicates, however, that the annual trade deficit was at least double this amount. In three of the five years, it was more than triple this sum. In fact, the full amount of the loan was used up in 1951—in 1950, if 1949 trade deficits are included. Second, repayments (where Chinese exports exceed Chinese imports from Russia) on the loan were to begin in late 1954. Some token repayments may have been made, but Chinese imports continued to exceed exports and a new but similar loan of $130 million was announced by the Russians. Net repayment was not made and the balance of trade was not reversed until 1956.

When the balance of trade did shift in 1956, there is some question about just how happy the Chinese were about having to export more than they could import—a situation which apparently persisted into 1966. Since the Chinese probably would have preferred an import surplus to facilitate their drive toward industrialization, there is good reason to believe that the switch was made at Soviet insistence. By late 1955, accumulated trade deficits totaled $1,063 million, and military loans may have increased the indebtedness by 50 to 100 per cent. Undoubtedly the Russians were worried about extending so much credit to one country with no sign that it would be paid back. There is also evidence that political relations between the two countries had cooled somewhat as early as October, 1954, when the Chinese demanded the return of the joint stock companies and made territorial claims on the Soviet Union.[27] Apparently the Russians insisted that the Chinese increase their export efforts as a condition for the continued flow of Russian commercial goods and economic aid. These Chinese exports were almost certainly used to repay past economic and military loans.

For a time it seemed as if there were no new promises of Soviet economic aid after 1955–56. However, the Russians have belatedly provided the dates of four other economic accords. This makes a total of six aid agreements that were signed between 1950 and 1959. Together they called for the construction of 336 complete plants, all of which were presumably financed with foreign-aid credits.[28] In addition to the agreements of February 14, 1950, and October 12, 1954, which I have already cited, there were other agreements on May 15, 1953; April 7, 1956; August 8, 1958; and February 7, 1959. These signings passed virtually unnoticed at the time. It is unclear whether these accords involved the promise of new funds or were just the formalization of already created short-term imbalances in trade. But whatever the terms of the contracts, there is considerable evidence to indicate that Soviet aid drawdowns, or at least Soviet technical help, continued even into 1965, despite the shift in the balance of trade and the deterioration of relations. If the meaning of Item 16, Equipment and Material for Complete Plants, in the foreign-trade statistics is being properly interpreted, it appears that Soviet aid may not even have reached its peak until 1959–60. In the years from 1955 to 1965, aid drawdowns or, at the least, the construction of industrial or productive enterprises in China by the Russians totaled more than $1,600 million. If information about aid drawdowns for the years 1949 to 1954 were available and were added in with those of 1955 to 1965, total Soviet economic aid undoubtedly would exceed $2 billion. But how is it possible to say that Soviet foreign aid exceeded $1,600 million from 1955 to 1965 when the total trade deficit never amounted to more than $1,063 million and when that deficit occurred solely in the period from 1949 to 1955?

One partial explanation of why the trade deficit is less than the size of the reported loans or the amount of drawdowns is that the Chinese apparently started to repay some of their economic and military aid in the early 1950's while simultaneously receiving economic aid from the Russians. However, it must be acknowledged that the increased export of Item 16, especially in 1959 and 1960, could have been financed not only by Soviet aid but by the Chinese on a commercial basis by sending a record volume of exports to the U.S.S.R. Nonetheless it is possible to accept the assertion of Soviet officials that Item 16 represents economic aid drawdowns and that Soviet aid to China from 1955 to 1965 exceeded $1,600 million. It would then follow that Soviet aid for both goods and invisibles, or services, during the whole period from 1949 to 1965 amounted to more than $2 billion. The Russians verify that Soviet aid to China continued into and beyond 1960. Their aid program was not terminated despite the outbreak of verbal and physical hostilities and the departure of most Russian technicians from China in July, 1960. In his February 14, 1964, speech to the Central Committee Plenum of the Communist Party of the Soviet Union, Mikhail Suslov declared that in 1960, after the Chinese "turned down a considerable part of the planned deliveries of Soviet equipment, the volume of economic cooperation between the Soviet Union and the Chinese People's Republic in 1962 including trade and technical cooperation fell to 39 per cent of the 1959 level and deliveries of complete equipment and materials dropped by forty times. In 1963, the volume of economic cooperation and trade continued to decline." Yet the Russians did not halt all economic activity as they did in Albania: "Despite the openly hostile actions on the part of the Chinese Communist Party leaders, our country, conscientiously carrying out the obligations undertaken in the past, is continuing *even now* to help China in the construction of eighty industrial enterprises." [29] Even if the Chinese were not being financed by long-term loans from the U.S.S.R. in the 1960's, the Russians were still providing important industrial and technical help despite the tense political climate.

What then was the magnitude of Soviet aid to China? Clearly it was higher than the officially announced $430 million. At a minimum, Soviet loans amounted to $1,063 million, the sum of the trade imbalance at its peak in early 1956. The Chinese themselves agreed that their indebtedness to the Soviet Union exceeded $1 billion. In 1957, they reported receipt of 5,294 million yuans' (approximately $1.3 billion) worth of Soviet loans.[30] For a long time, official Soviet sources quoted only the formally announced loans. Ultimately, when they wanted to show how generous they had been, they came around to accepting the higher Chinese yuan estimate.[31] In the chest-thumping that has accompanied the feuding between China and the Soviet Union, the Russians claim that they have provided even more on credit. The total figure is generally quoted as 1,816 million rubles, or about $2 billion for the period 1950–60.[32] The Russians also say that they provided military loans of about $500 million to the Chinese for the Korean War.[33] It is unclear whether this figure is in addition to the $2 billion or included in it, and whether there was also a special loan to finance the Chinese purchase of the Sino-Soviet joint stock companies. Military aid and the loans for the joint stock companies would not affect the export imbalance, but they might explain why the loan figure was so much higher. However, even if the military aid credit and the debt for the joint stock companies are subtracted from the total of Soviet loans, it still seems fair to say that the Russians had rendered the Chinese at least $1 billion of new economic loans from 1950 to 1956, and possibly $1.5 to $2 billion or more over the fourteen-year period ending in 1965. Whether the Russians provided this much aid with a smile is beside the point. What is important is that industrial and technical assistance was made available at a crucial time in both China's and Russia's economic development.

While the extension of at least $1-billion worth of economic loans over the initial seven-year period does not appear excessive, it was definitely a strain on the Russian economy in the early 1950's. The actual burden was probably greater, for the Russians also exported almost $3-billion worth of goods as of 1956 in addition to that which was provided on credit. While this was paid for with imports from China, a large portion of the *quid pro quo* imports would hardly be considered comparable to the type of exports shipped by the Russians in exchange. In any case, it was not so much the quantity of the aid and trade as the quality. As with the American Lend Lease to the Soviet Union during World War II, the monetary value may have been small in terms of the recipient's gross national product, but the items involved were essential commodities and equipment that otherwise would have been unavailable. Thus over 50 per cent of the Chinese steel produced in 1960 was melted in Russian-built furnaces and almost 50 per cent of the coal extracted was from Soviet-equipped mines. As of 1960–61, Soviet-made equipment produced 30 per cent of China's electrical power and nitrate fertilizer, 25 per cent of its aluminum, 35 per cent of its pig iron,

40 per cent of its copper, 70 per cent of its tin, 80 to 85 per cent of its trucks and tractors, and 100 per cent of its synthetic rubber. By 1962, almost 200 of the promised 336 major enterprises had been put in operation for the Chinese by the Russians.

Even if much of this amounted to no more than the replacement of what originally had been looted by the Russians from Manchuria, there is no doubt that the Soviet Union re-outfitted some of China's largest and most basic enterprises. Furthermore, throughout this period, the Russians trained more than 20,000 Chinese technicians and scientists in Soviet institutes and factories, sent more than 10,000 Soviet technicians to work in China, and provided millions of dollars' worth of blueprints and patents.

An appraisal of Soviet economic support for China in the first half of the 1950's indicates therefore that the Russians were quite liberal with their aid. Although Soviet exports and aid as measured by Item 16 seem to have diminished in 1957 and 1958, they must still be regarded as remarkably generous considering that the Russians were forced to promise so much help to Eastern Europe at this time. Whatever the actual amount of aid included in over-all Soviet exports, clearly the Russians could no longer increase their efforts in Eastern Europe and permit the Chinese to run such large deficits in their trade balance. Furthermore, it was at the same time that the Russians decided to embark on their aid program to developing countries. The burden of the aid program to Eastern Europe and the newly conceived program of aid to the so-called "neutralist" countries, especially India, certainly made continued aid to China an extremely heavy commitment for the Soviet Union. The fact that the Russians continued their aid deliveries and apparently even increased them in 1959 and 1960 seems to indicate that the Russians did not turn their backs on China as the Chinese have claimed.

It is still necessary to explain why China was not assigned absolute priority over the developing countries; there appear to be no economic reasons for this. Suffice it to say that this was a political matter, which in retrospect clearly indicates a degree of distrust and a cause for irritation as early as 1955-56. This seems to mark the beginning of a crucial period in Sino-Soviet economic relations. In 1955 the first Geneva meeting between Khrushchev and Eisenhower took place. This upset the Chinese, who objected to a meeting with the United States and who resented their exclusion. It was also about this time that the Russians began to divert some of their economic favors from China to Eastern Europe and the developing countries. In response the Chinese decided to launch their own counteroffensive. It was in 1956 that the Chinese instituted their own program of foreign-aid loans. This eventually turned the "brotherly cooperation" that had existed between the U.S.S.R. and China into something more like a fratricidal competition for political favor in the neutralist world and ultimately in parts of the satellite world.

One explanation given for the switch in the balance of trade was that the Chinese decided that they could afford to pay for everything they were getting from the Russians. Although it would seem that extra economic help would always be welcome, the Chinese may have been carried away by their own optimism in the Great Leap Forward in 1959. However, even if one accepts this charitable point of view, it must have been distressing for the Chinese to see that at the same time they were in the process of repaying their socialist ally, their ally was apparently engaged in redirecting its aid to the Afghans, Indians, Indonesians, and Egyptians. By 1958, each of these non-Communist countries had received promises of more than $100 million of Soviet aid. As of 1961, the Indians alone had been promised more than $800 million. Moreover, even if industrial aid to China in 1959 and 1960 reached an all-time high, almost all of the aid to the neutralist countries was of a kind that could also have been used in China. While the combined volume of Afghan, Indian, Indonesian, and Egyptian imports from the Soviet Union never amounted to more than comparable Chinese imports, the Chinese by their repayments may have provided the Russians with some of the wherewithal to finance these new credits to the neutralist countries. Yet it is necessary to reiterate that the Russians claim they are directly responsible for the construction of at least 200 major industrial projects in China, and that as of 1964 they were *still* continuing to provide technical help for 80 more.[34]

Paradoxically, the change in the Russian attitude may also account for the introduction of an active aid program by the Chinese themselves. In a series of acts suggesting independence, defiance, and, perhaps, masochism, the Chinese in mid-1956 (the year of net repayment) switched from soliciting aid to dispensing it. Beginning with a loan of $23 million to Cambodia in June, 1956, and followed in the same year with loans to Nepal, Indonesia, and the U.A.R., Chinese promises of aid to neutralist countries soon reached impressive sums. The approximate estimate of Chinese aid shown in Table II-4 indicates that by 1966 the Chinese had provided $873-1,220 million in loans to Communist countries and $859-938 million to neutralist nations. As had been the practice with China's earlier loans to North Korea and North Vietnam, its loan terms were almost always more favorable than those of the Russians. Many countries, including Korea, Vietnam,

Table II-4

COMMUNIST CHINA'S FOREIGN AID PROGRAM
(in Millions of Dollars)

Country	Amount	Agreement Date
Afghanistan	28	March, 1965
Albania	14	Prior to 1961
	123	1961
Algeria	5-10	1957-62
		August, 1962
	50	October, 1963
Burma	4	January, 1958
	84	January, 1961
Cambodia	23	June, 1956
	26.5	December, 1960
	5-10	November, 1964
Ceylon	16	September, 1957
	10.5	September, 1958
	10.5	October, 1960[a]
	4.2	February, 1964
Gongo (Brazzaville)	5	1964
	20	1965
Cuba	60	November, 1960
Ghana	20	December, 1961
	22.4	February, 1964
Guinea	25	September, 1960
	7	1963
Hungary	57	1958-59
Indonesia	16.2	November, 1956
	11.2	1958
	30.2	1961
	50	1965
Kenya	17.8	May, 1964
	10	1965

Sources: See pages 249-50.

[a]Unconfirmed loan.
[b]Amount of loan unconfirmed.

Country	Amount	Agreement Date
Laos	(b)	December, 1962
Mali	20	February, 1961
Mongolia	40 25 50	August, 1956 December, 1958 May, 1960
Nepal	13 21 10 28	October, 1956 March, 1960 October, 1961 (a)
North Korea	4 200 234	1950-52 November, 1953 (a)
North Vietnam	200 100	July, 1954 February, 1959
Pakistan	60 30	July, 1964 January, 1965
Somali	3 18 3	August, 1963 August, 1963 January, 1965
Syria	16.3-20	February, 1963
Tanzania	28.8 14	June, 1963 June, 1965
U.A.R.	4.7 80	August, 1956 January, 1965
Uganda	15	1965
Yemen	16.3 28	January, 1958 May, 1964
Zambia	.5	February, 1964

Mongolia, Nepal, Ceylon, Yemen, Indonesia, Ghana, Guinea, and Cuba, ultimately ended up with loans from both the Soviet Union and China. (See Chapters 7 and 8 for a discussion of the competition between the Chinese and Russians over foreign aid.) [35]

By 1960, the tension had come to a head. In July of that year, the Soviet technicians took their famous walk. According to the Chinese, within a month 1,390 Soviet experts left their uncompleted work, tore up 343 contracts, and scrapped 257 projects of scientific and technological cooperation.[36] This and the work slowdown that preceded the actual departures brought on the collapse of China's Great Leap Forward—or so the Chinese claim. Undoubtedly the Soviet withdrawal did hurt. There were reports that some machinery abandoned by the Soviets in 1960 had not been touched as late as 1966.

The Soviets have replied that their delivery and installation of complete plant and equipment, and perhaps actual drawdowns by the Chinese of foreign aid in 1960, was second only to that provided in 1959. The record level of Soviet exports to China in 1959 and 1960 is not easy to explain. It may have been that the Russians wanted to compensate for their refusal to build China an atomic bomb and for the diversion of other foreign-aid resources to the developing countries. Maybe it was simply that the Chinese increased their shipments to Russia and the Russians agreed to respond. In any case, there is no doubt that the expanded level of Soviet activity in China, together with the demands of Eastern Europe and the opportunities in the neutralist bloc, imposed a strain on the Soviet Union.

Whatever the extra burden, the Russians assert that against their better judgment they were prepared to help the Chinese, and in fact, as we have noted, they did continue to render aid even after the bulk of their technicians withdrew. After the uprisings in Eastern Europe following Stalin's death, the Russians began to realize that their aid efforts were not always warmly regarded, and that the presence of their technicians in satellite countries might serve to create tension.[37] As early as 1956, and again in 1958, the Soviet Union suggested to China that Soviet advisers and specialists be withdrawn. In both instances the Chinese disagreed and the Russians consented to stay on. However, the Soviets claim that the Chinese became openly hostile to Soviet technicians and technology. In 1958, the Chinese adopted the slogan: "Struggle against blind faith in established technological standards and regulations and in foreign experience." This the Russians correctly took to be directed at them. Their views were confirmed, they asserted, when the Chinese began to ignore Soviet advice and abandoned disciplined procedures, going so far as to throw away work instructions and to close up technological departments. This not only hampered working conditions, but jeopardized Russian lives. Conditions at the Hsin-feng-Chiang and Hsin-an-Chiang dam construction projects became so hazardous that Chinese lives were lost.[38] Under such circumstances, Soviet technicians eventually asked to be released from their work. (While there certainly was just cause for the Russian withdrawal, it should be noted that at least equally poor working conditions at the Aswan Dam in Egypt did not lead to a similar Soviet withdrawal. Despite the fact that over 200 Egyptians and several Russians lost their lives at Aswan, the political conditions in the U.A.R. were apparently more propitious than in China in the late 1950's, and the Russians stayed to the end.)

In reply to other Chinese criticism, the Russians point out that the economic sectors that lagged the most during the Great Leap Forward were the ones where Soviet advice had the least impact. On May 1, 1960, there were only one Soviet specialist in the Chinese Ministry of Agriculture, two in the Ministry of Food, and four in light industry. Although they do not indicate how many advisers there were a few years earlier, the point is well taken that the Soviet withdrawal alone did not bring about China's economic difficulties in 1959 and 1960.

There is no doubt, however, that the Russians could have done more to improve their relations with the Chinese. A major agreement was signed in April, 1961, before the Twenty-second Communist Party Congress. In response to the economic crisis in China, the Russians finally came through with what appeared to be their first formal credit since 1954, an interest-free loan of 500,000 tons of raw sugar (worth $45 million). The Chinese were given until 1964–67 to repay this aid. The Chinese, however, were in need of other more important foods than Cuban sugar, of which they already had their share. The Russians later claimed that the loan offer also included 1 million tons of grain, worth approximately $50 million.[39] However, it is not entirely clear that the Chinese ever agreed to accept, or received, the grain. Soviet exports to China in 1961 and 1962 do show that, as opposed to 1960 and 1963, about 650,000 tons ($36-million worth) of grain and flour were delivered to China. This may indicate that a partial loan was made, at least until the Russians had to face their own agricultural problems.

At this time of need (1961), the Russians also agreed to a new five-year loan of $320 million. Unfortunately for the Chinese, it turned out that this was meant to cover cumulative short-term indebtedness, not new shipments. Despite a consistent excess of exports to the Soviet Union since 1956, the Chinese had been unable to liquidate their obligations to the Russians. The Russians thereupon agreed to fund this indebtedness in a new loan, to be repaid in five installments: $9 million in 1962, $55 million in 1963, and $128 million in both 1964 and 1965.

Regardless of the exact terms of the agreement, the Chinese made a substantial repayment to the Soviets in 1961. Although economically this was one of the worst years in the experience of Communist China, the Chinese managed a $184-million export surplus to the Russians, while Soviet exports to China fell to their lowest point since 1950. Soviet exports to China continued to fall; in 1963, 1964, and 1965, they were below what they were even in 1949, which did not represent a full year of trading activity. (See Table II-3.) Simultaneously, the Chinese have continued to pay back the Russians with an export surplus that in 1962 exceeded any previous sum and in 1963 still totaled $226 million. In both years this was far above the agreed-upon repayment schedule. In effect, therefore, by 1965 the Chinese had already more than repaid the Russians for the export credit (which, as mentioned earlier, also includes the cost of technical services) extended to them by almost $500 million. Yet Marshal Chen Yi, the Vice Premier of China, indicated that the complete Soviet debt would not be repaid until 1966 or 1967. As indicated earlier, China's debt to the U.S.S.R. is much larger than the trade deficit alone. The debt undoubtedly includes interest charges, military aid, and probably the purchase of the Soviet share in the joint stock companies.

The need to repay the military debts has been especially distasteful to the Chinese. Chinese commentators have reminded the Russians that they fought the Korean War on behalf of the Russians in order to prevent a head-on clash between the Soviet Union and the United States.[40] The Chinese also charged that they were sometimes forced to take (and ultimately pay for) equipment from the Russians that they did not need, while they could not always obtain equipment they needed.[41] Moreover, some Chinese leaders, such as General Lung Yun, pointed out during the Hundred Flowers Campaign that in contrast to the Soviet Union, the United States had canceled the loans it had supplied its allies (including the Soviet Union) in World War I and World War II.[42] As we have seen, the Russians have retorted that the military loans were only about $500 million of the total sum lent to China. Apparently this response has not entirely satisfied the Chinese. They have been further irritated by the discovery that they cannot obtain spare parts or improved refinements for the military equipment they have already received and paid for. Thus the Chinese were reported to have turned to Indonesia for spare parts for their MIG-15 and -19 jet fighters. It is further reported that both Indonesia and India have the more advanced model MIG-21 which has been denied the

Chinese. (Che Guevara, during his trip to Africa in early 1965, also complained that the Russians were profiting from the sale of arms to Communist groups. He added that the Chinese were just as bad since they, too, were trying to make a profit on the sale of armaments.)

The drop in Soviet aid, the continued burden of debt-repayment, and their own domestic production problems forced the Chinese to turn to the West for the purchase of equipment and grain in 1961. As of June, 1965, China had purchased approximately $340 million worth of grain from Canada, $200 million from Australia, $150 million from Argentina, $45 million from France, about $30 million from Mexico, and reportedly another $40 million from Africa. In October, 1965, a new five-year contract for the purchase of Canadian wheat was announced that may have involved a purchase of up to $900 million. This was followed in November by a $29-million purchase in Australia and an $80-million contract with Argentina. Australia received another $100-million order in 1966. This meant that a billion and a half dollars or more of scarce Western currency has been committed for the purchase of food, and that by 1965 $800 million of it had already been spent. Furthermore, a portion of their grain purchase was diverted to East Germany, Cuba, Albania, and the U.A.R. This was in addition to a new series of foreign loans which amounted in 1963 to about $125 million, in 1964 to about $140 million, and to about $250 million in 1965. (See Table II-4.)

Council of Mutual Economic Assistance

Just as the Soviets discovered that economic aid did not assure continued friendship with China, they also found increasing discontent among the other satellites that had been the recipients of Soviet loans. Clearly Soviet economic help had not sufficed to win the unquestioning allegiance of the East European allies. The restlessness was further sparked by the ever-growing success and prosperity of the countries of the Common Market and the obvious lag and shortcomings of the members of the Council of Mutual Economic Assistance.

The irony of the situation deserves comment. When CMEA was first formed in January, 1949, there was considerable concern in the West that the Communist bloc would function as a well-coordinated and monolithic unit. This would permit division of labor, economies of scale, comparative advantage, and all the other preconditions that normally are deemed necessary for rapid economic growth. At the time, of course, Western Europe was still rent by the memories and the destruction of war. A successful Common Market was considered a serious possibility only by visionaries, for it was widely believed that the fiercely nationalistic countries in Western Europe would never surrender enough of their sovereignty to make a Common Market work. In contrast, it seemed safe to assume that Stalin's heavy hand would eliminate whatever hesitation there might be among the satellites. Therefore it was with skepticism if not disbelief that the Communists watched the eradication of nationalism and economic barriers in Western Europe (at least until General de Gaulle) and the flourishing of chauvinism and economic hostility in their own lands.

As the Common Market continued to grow in strength, it was decided that something had to be done to make CMEA a more effective and competitive economic organization. This became all the more urgent after the new schism within the bloc had been created by Albania's open attacks on the U.S.S.R. As a partial compensation for Albania's ultimate exclusion from CMEA, Mongolia was brought into what had heretofore been a European organization in 1962. This decision reflected the Soviet desire to incorporate Mongolia into the Soviet bloc and to offer it extra protection from the increasingly hostile Chinese.

In the early 1960's, a series of measures was introduced to evoke more active participation by the satellites. After years of talk and frustration, some agreement was reached about the division of labor and the assignment of different production tasks to the various countries. For example, it was agreed that Czechoslovakia would specialize in seamed and seamless pipe, East Germany in steel for bearings, Poland in thin rolled steel, and Hungary in fine bore tubing. This was to be implemented under the supervision of Intermetall, a steel trust set up within CMEA. At least fourteen similar trusts or permanent commissions were set up to supervise and allocate production in such areas as chemicals and machine-tool production. (See the table of organization in the facing diagram.) In 1964, Druzba (Friendship), the long-delayed 2,800-mile oil pipeline from the U.S.S.R. to Eastern Europe, was opened. This involved the joint cooperation of East Germany, Poland, Hungary, Czechoslovakia, and the Soviet Union. Plans were also announced for a power grid uniting Hungary, Rumania, Germany, Czechoslovakia, Poland, and the Soviet Union. These same countries planned to operate a joint pool of 93,000 railroad cars.

The satellites were encouraged to aid one another and formulate joint projects wherever possible. We have already seen how loans were extended to Hungary and the Asian satellites. (A somewhat more comprehensive although still not complete listing of intersatellite loans is presented in Table II-5.) Many of these loans were extended for

THE COUNCIL OF MUTUAL ECONOMIC ASSISTANCE

Sessions of the Council

|

Permanent Executive Committee of the Council

Secretariat | Bureau for Joint
Problems in Planning

Permanent Commissions (and their location)

Coal (Warsaw)
Oil and Gas (Bucharest)
Electricity (Moscow)
Ferrous Metal (Moscow)
Nonferrous Metal (Budapest)
Chemicals (Berlin)
Machine Tool (Prague)
Construction (Berlin)
Light and Food Industries (Prague)
Agriculture (Sophia)
Transport (Warsaw)
Atomic Energy (Moscow)
Foreign Trade (Moscow)
Economic Questions (Moscow)
Air Transport

specific projects. Thus Germany gave Poland a loan of pipe and other goods to complete its share of the Druzba pipeline. Czechoslovakia helped Germany build a plant for the production of potassium fertilizer. Czechoslovakia also provided a loan of $213 million to Poland to develop its sulphur, coal, and copper mines, as well as its nitrogen deposits and electric power. Czechoslovakia is also helping Rumania build two thermal electric plants. Bulgaria and Rumania are cooperating on the construction of a hydroelectric plant on the Danube. Similarly, East Germany provided Poland and Bulgaria with indirect loans, and Czechoslovakia, Poland, and Germany joined together with the intention of building a 200,000-ton cellulose plant at Braila in Rumania. Czechoslovakia and East Germany also combined to finance an electrical project based on Polish brown coal. Hungary and Poland formed the joint stock company of Haldex to reprocess waste from Polish coal mines.

Some of these projects have taken on the appearance of the old joint

Table II-5

INTER-SATELLITE LOANS, AS OF 1965
(in Millions of Dollars)

Donors	Albania	Bulgaria	Cuba	Hungary	North Korea	Mongolia	Poland	Rumania	North Vietnam	U.S.S.R.
						Recipients				
Albania				.05						
Bulgaria	11		6	3	12				3.5	
China	137		60	25	204-466	115-200			300	
Czechoslovakia	25	40	40	43.7	28	22	213	45.5	26	
East Germany	15		10	15-28	118-135		100-164	28	15	
Hungary		9	15		6				2.5	
Poland			27	25	88			2.3	7.5	78
Rumania	7.5		15	15	22				37	
Yugoslavia				2						

<u>Sources</u>: See page 250.

stock companies, with the profits and productions being shared equally. Other projects were to be repaid with product deliveries from the new projects. There was even a return to projects in which the U.S.S.R. was a partner. Hungary and the U.S.S.R. are working on the joint production of potassium salts and aluminum.[43] In some cases, the projects are located in the U.S.S.R. and are financed by countries in Eastern Europe. This seems to be the same old burden with a new twist. For example, in April, 1963, Germany, Bulgaria, Czechoslovakia, Poland, and Hungary agreed to finance the construction of and equip a phosphorus mine in Soviet Estonia at Kingissepsky. In the same year, the Poles agreed to provide a loan to the U.S.S.R. for $78 million in order to develop a potash plant at Soligorsky in Belorussia. The Czechs are aiding Soviet aluminum and steel plants. Even though such joint stock companies often mean that the Soviets are again *taking* foreign aid *from* the satellites, the terms seem to be a little less one-sided. Nonetheless, it seems fair to assume either that the Russians have failed to learn very much from their past experience with joint stock companies or that they are in serious need of economic credits.

The Russians did learn, at least for a time, that foreign-trade prices should be made less discriminatory. After a temporary relaxation in pricing policy following the disturbances in Poland and Hungary in 1956, a harder price policy was once more imposed in 1958. But the price structure was made more liberal again for the satellites in the mid-1960's. Soviet foreign trade officials implied in June, 1964, that it was hoped such price revisions would make bloc trade more advantageous for the satellites and thereby promote increased trade within the bloc. However, in an about-face in 1966, a series of articles appeared, in journals like *Voprosy Ekonomiki,* in which the Russians began to complain about the low prices the East Europeans were paying for Russian raw materials. The Russians also began to hint that East Europeans should provide investment funds if the Russians were to develop any more raw-material bases for East European use.

With the aim of interrelating the economies of the bloc still more, CMEA announced on October 22, 1963, the establishment of its own international bank, the International Bank for Economic Cooperation (IBEC). Though it was to facilitate trade with the West, its main task was to promote multilateral trade among its members. Presumably this would lead to an increase in foreign trade. Reflecting the inflexibility of the system, virtually all trade transactions between members of the bloc had heretofore been of a bilateral nature. Only about 1 per cent of trade within CMEA is multilateral.[44]

IBEC was opened in Moscow on January 1, 1964, under the direction of K. I. Nazakin. The bank coordinates the activities of the foreign-trade banks in the various Communist countries. Transactions and clearing arrangements are conducted in terms of "transferable rubles" (*perovodnye*), which, however, are not freely convertible into Western currencies. To provide the necessary capital of $333 million, each member was required to contribute a share determined by the relative importance of its export activity. Thus the largest share, $129 million, was to be contributed by the U.S.S.R., followed by Germany with $61 million, Czechoslovakia with $50 million, Poland with $30 million, Hungary with $23 million, Bulgaria with $19 million, Rumania with $18 million, and Mongolia with $3 million.[45] Each country was required to contribute 20 per cent of its assessment in the form of "transferable rubles," gold, or freely convertible currency in the first year of the bank's operation and the remainder at the call of the bank.

It soon became apparent, however, that IBEC was not doing much to promote multilateral trade. The Poles were the most outspoken in their criticism of the Bank's shortcomings, but other members voiced similar complaints.[46] The main difficulty, as the Poles saw it, was that no one really wanted "transferable rubles." If the "transferable rubles" could be exchanged after a time for gold or convertible Western currency, it would be all right, but under the original system the "transferable rubles" had no meaning or desirability. They have no value because almost all goods in the Soviet bloc are allocated according to plan. Those goods which are not already designated for some purpose will first be offered for sale in the West for convertible currency. Therefore even though an East European buyer may have "transferable rubles," he does not normally have the authorization to buy what he wants since rubles are not the all-determining consideration. In fact, an article in the Polish newspaper *Glos Pracy* suggested that, under the existing conditions, if a country had a surplus of "transferable rubles" it was a good indication that the only goods available in the whole bloc were items that the prospective buyer either had no need of or did not want because of their poor quality. Thus, while IBEC has brought about some improvement by facilitating clearing and short-term credits, more basic reforms seem to be necessary.

Even more discouraging for the economic integration of Eastern Europe are the growing independence and separatist tendencies shown by such heretofore docile countries as Rumania. To the general astonishment of Western onlookers, Rumania suddenly protested the trend toward specialization within the bloc. Apparently it resented the decision of CMEA to limit the growth of the Rumanian steel industry. In the agreement for the specialization of steel production spelled out in 1962, the Rumanians were told that instead of expanding their own steel production they should rely on the U.S.S.R. and Czechoslovakia for their steel needs. It was argued that the other two countries were better suited for the production of steel.[47] The Rumanians refused to revise their plans to expand their own production. Unlike many of their fellow satellites, they were able to resist any threatened boycott of their steel needs by turning to the West. Since they had an international commodity that "talked"—oil—they were able to do as they pleased. The Rumanians also have refused to participate in Intermetall, the Commission on Ball Bearings, and the railway freight-car pool. Even more astonishing, a cellulose project that was initially to be a joint project with East Germany, Poland, and Czechoslovakia has been opened by the Rumanians to companies from Italy, the United States, and Switzerland. The Rumanians have also awarded orders to GHH-Sterkrade AG of West Germany for the construction of an LD or new oxygen-type converter at the Galati steel mill. At one time, the Soviet Union was to have been the sole supplier of equipment.

Although the other East European countries do not have the means to be so independent, it is clear that they have also been bothered by the implications of the growing integration in CMEA. The Soviets promised that, as opposed to the Western economic organizations where the richer countries have more votes, in CMEA all members would have the same rights. But the smaller countries continued to be distrustful. For example, representatives of the Tatra Works in Czechoslovakia demanded that they be permitted to check the trade agreements to be sure that all CMEA countries were treated equally.[48] The memories of the past examples of "joint economic projects" with the Russians were still fresh. Some of them were reluctant to give up already existing enterprises even when they were inefficient, since there was no guarantee that the future would bring anything better. Moreover, in Soviet-type economies, because of shortcomings in the distribution and transportation systems, a cardinal principle of operation is that a firm should be as self-sufficient as possible. No one wants to rely on anyone else for supplies or raw materials. If this applies to firms within a country, it would be expected to apply even more to firms in different nations. But as before, most of the proposed integration schemes continued to place the U.S.S.R. in the center of all activity.

Industry in Eastern Europe continues to be established on a very fragile basis. Given the fractionalized nature of Eastern Europe and the character of the political boundaries created in the post–Austro-Hungarian era, most of the Communist countries do not have the necessary raw materials to be self-sufficient. Of necessity they have to turn to outside suppliers. Invariably the U.S.S.R. has been selected as a source for one or many of the essential raw materials. Moreover, certain plants, such as the Polish steel mill of Nowa Huta, are located so that alternative sources of supply are uneconomical. On the other side of the coin, since the domestic markets of the East European countries are so limited, a large portion of their industrial production must be exported. The major purchaser is usually the U.S.S.R. Thus even if a country is well endowed with industrial raw materials, and therefore not dependent on the U.S.S.R. as a supplier, it may nonetheless be dependent on the U.S.S.R. as a purchaser. Since the U.S.S.R. is so much larger and so much less dependent on foreign trade, it can place the satellites in this uncomfortable situation with minimal discomfort for itself. When provided the opportunity, the Russians have not hesitated to subordinate weaker economies to their economic system. Only when a country has an unchallenged international currency (like Rumania with its oil) can it expect to break free from such a vise without major economic consequences.

Resistance to Soviet economic policies in Eastern Europe was real enough without heckling from the side. Thus when the Chinese and North Koreans decided to encourage the type of disaffection shown by Rumania, it must have been particularly embarrassing to the Russians. In protesting the way the Russians had treated them, the Chinese warned that the Russians "have no sincere desire to help. They sometimes provide the machinery while holding back the key units and parts. Sometimes they give equipment and hold back technical knowledge trying to make Asian and African countries economically dependent on them. They have even gone so far as to cancel aid, withdraw experts and tear up contracts as a means of applying pressure." [49] The Chinese further warned that there were hidden traps and attached strings to Soviet economic aid even for advanced socialist countries: "You bully fraternal countries which are industrially more developed and insist that they stop manufacturing their traditional products and become accessory factories serving your industries. Moreover, you have introduced the jungle law of the capitalist world into relations between socialist countries. You openly follow the example of the Common Market which was organized by monopoly capitalist groups." [50] Such charges hurt, and there was enough truth in them to intensify the distrust in Eastern Europe.

Finally, although no one publicly voiced such a question, some satellites must have wondered at the Soviet double standard. Why had pressure been put on Rumania to cancel her steel project? As we are about to see, one of the traditional refrains in Soviet aid to developing countries is that any country that wants a steel mill should be aided in financing and building one. "Such efforts are always frustrated," say the Soviets, "because the capitalists fear competition and an end to subservience." Therefore, as some satellites must have asked, why is it that what is good for a neutralist country is not just as good for a Communist country? With that question in mind, we turn now to a study of Soviet aid to the developing countries.

3. The United Arab Republic:
Drama, Repayment, and the Bureaucratic Routine

As long as Stalin was alive, the U.S.S.R. virtually ignored the non-Communist underdeveloped countries. It was too busy with its own reconstruction and relations with its satellites. The Soviet attitude toward the developing countries was generally dogmatic and unrealistic. For example, Gandhi was viewed as a bourgeois nationalist, and India was referred to as a British colony. Economic relations were equally primitive. What economic contact did exist was due to the fact that the Soviet Union was dependent on many of the developing countries for raw materials that were not available in the U.S.S.R. or its satellites. This was especially true of rubber, certain minerals like copper and tin, and foods like cocoa and sugar.

This attitude changed after Stalin's death and the end of the Korean War. The Soviets switched from the hard to the soft sell. Wherever possible, an attempt was made to normalize relations. Perhaps remembering Lenin's injunction that the road to London and Paris lies through Asia and Africa, the Russians decided to do what they could to win the friendship, if not the allegiance, of the developing areas. Ideally, the Russians hoped to Communize these regions; even a disruption of markets and the cessation of the flow of raw materials to the West would be a gain. The Soviet Union also hoped to build up a market for its goods and to improve its adverse balance-of-trade position with these countries. In 1950, the Russians exported $32-million worth of goods to these areas while importing $93-million worth; in 1955, the comparable figures were $142 million in exports and $160 million in imports.[1] Correcting this balance and finding a long-run outlet for Soviet industry had little or nothing to do with spreading Communism: it was primarily a business maneuver. The only way the Communist bloc could overcome the traditional preference for Western-made goods was to extend economic credits which would finance purchases that otherwise would not be made.

It is important to stress that the Russians also believe foreign aid should be given for humanitarian purposes. Although most ordinary

60

Russians realize that much of their aid could be devoted equally well to consumer needs at home, a surprisingly large number of them have a sincere desire to help the poorer countries of the world. The Communist countries recognize and understand the aspirations of those people who want to industrialize their countries. The Russians have generally been willing to help the emerging nations, especially those countries whose ties have heretofore been with the West. Here competition joins with altruism. In any case, like the second-rate politician who surprises everyone by becoming a highly respected judge, the Russians have won praise for their efforts with neutralist countries.

Russia's postwar aid program to the developing countries began in Afghanistan. But its two most ambitious and successful aid programs have been in the United Arab Republic and in India. It is these that have captured the world's imagination and aroused the most interest. We will therefore postpone the examination of Russian efforts in Afghanistan to discuss Russian accomplishments at the Aswan Dam in Egypt and the Bhilai steel mill in India. Because the scope of Soviet activities in both the U.A.R. and India has been so extensive, a description of the Soviet experience in these countries presents an over-all view of Soviet methods.

The Aswan Dam

Soviet aid to Egypt has been especially dramatic. To a large extent, the success of Soviet foreign aid to Egypt is associated with the negotiations and work on one massive project—the Aswan Dam. However, close analysis reveals the difficulties that even a spectacular aid project such as this one can generate.

In Egypt more than anywhere else, the Soviets have managed to link themselves with the long-time aspirations of the aid-receiving country. The Russians are helping to subdue the Nile, and as Herodotus wrote many centuries ago, "Egypt is born of the Nile." Long before the days of the Pharaohs, the life and economic well-being of the country was dependent on the behavior of the Nile. For centuries Egyptians had dreamed of harnessing this poorly utilized natural resource and channeling it into more constructive directions and uses. Napoleon asserted that if he were to rule Egypt, "not one drop of water of the Nile would reach the sea."

As early as 3000 B.C. there were attempts to tame the river by building levees for flood control. But it was like King Canute ordering the sea to stop. The Nile flowed on. In fat years, it fertilized the soil; in lean years, it either washed away or left untouched the thirsty land and hungry people. Some irrigation dams and canals were built in the nineteenth century in the Nile delta and near Aswan. For the most part, however, these projects trifled with, but did not utilize, the power and promise of the river. In modern times, the Egyptians realized that in addition to irrigation potential, the river had industrial possibilities. Lacking energy resources in the form of coal or oil, Egypt was wasting the immense hydroelectric opportunities which flowed through its center in a contemptuous stream. In 1902, under British supervision, a dam was built at the cataracts of Aswan. While this provided some power and some irrigation, it was clearly only a beginning.

Lest the reader be misled, this chapter is not intended to be a panegyric to the Nile. However, to understand the impact of Soviet work on the Aswan Dam it is necessary to appreciate the potential of the Nile and the frustration its unrealized promise has caused many Egyptians. Towering over the nearby banks of the Nile in unproductive and barren glory are the great pyramids, testifying to the construction and engineering skills of early Egypt. But except for the tourist dollars they earn, they can make no contribution to the modern world; if anything, the pyramids have mocked modern Egyptians who resent their country's poverty. Imagine the gratitude and excitement engendered by a project which not only promised to restrain and domesticate the Nile forever, but which would involve construction seventeen times the cubic size of the pyramids. The Aswan Dam project more than anything else aroused the Egyptians and awakened the world to the emergence of the U.S.S.R. as a power in international economic affairs.

The immediate events leading up to the construction of the dam are almost as dramatic as the historic saga of the Nile and Egypt itself. Involved were international power struggles, surging nationalism, explosive military confrontations, and idealistic and stubborn personalities. The first specific plans for the Aswan Dam were drawn up by two engineers, one Egyptian and one Italian, in 1947. But nothing further was done until the revolution of 1952. Excited by the political and economic potentialities of such a scheme, the Egyptian government under Mohammed Naguib, and, later, Gamal Abdel Nasser, decided to sponsor it. Beginning in the fall of 1952, various West German, English, French, and American engineering and banking firms presented Cairo with alternative proposals and plans. Just when it appeared that the United States would be the builder and financer of the dam, the project suddenly became the center of an international dispute.

For some time the Egyptians had been attempting to buy weapons from the United States in order to arm themselves against Israel. Out of fear of a Middle Eastern arms race and dismay over Egypt's growing anti-Western attitude, the United States was reluctant to sell munitions to Egypt. The Egyptians threatened to turn to the Communists for military aid and to the consternation of the West they did. Apparently the first offer of Communist arms was made in May, 1955, by Ambassador Daniel Solod, the Soviet envoy to Egypt.[2] International suspicions were not aroused, however, until the July visit to Cairo of Dmitri Shepilov, then the editor of *Pravda* and later the Soviet Minister of Foreign Affairs. On September 27, 1955, the Egyptians announced that they had entered into an agreement with Czechoslovakia for weapons in exchange for advance commitments of cotton and rice.

Never before had an Arab country demonstrated such defiance of the West and the United States, or opened the door to Communist penetration. Naturally this complicated future negotiations over the dam and raised numerous questions. Did this mean the Communists would take over the army? Did this mean that Cairo had foolishly mortgaged its future income? If so, would it be able to pay for the dam? How would a loan to a maverick like Nasser be interpreted by the other developing countries which had remained loyal to the West and which opposed such a loan? On the other hand, would a refusal by the Americans to finance the dam drive the Egyptians even further into the Soviet camp? Finally, if a bluff were attempted, could the Russians really afford to lend the amount needed for such an imposing project?

In October, 1955, the Russians first indicated they might finance the dam.[3] At the same time, the Americans decided to proceed seriously with the negotiations. They were especially concerned about Egypt's ability to earn foreign currency above and beyond what was needed to pay for Communist arms and the dispute over water rights and compensation for flooded lands with Egypt's neighbors to the south. Secretary of State Dulles' advisers argued that if the Egyptians could handle these issues satisfactorily, the United States should finance the dam. The State Department was supported in this position by the International Cooperation Administration (the foreign-aid dispensing organization) and Eric Johnston, a respected American adviser. On December 16, 1955, Dulles announced that the United States, Great Britain, and the International Bank for Reconstruction and Development had submitted an offer to finance the dam.

Under this proposal, the dam would be financed in two stages. The foreign-exchange needs for the coffer dams, the first stage, would be given outright to the United Arab Republic as a gift: $56 million was to come from the United States and $14 million from England. The funds for the second stage would be presented as a loan: $130 million from the United States, $80 million from Great Britain, and $200 million from the World Bank. The Egyptians would have forty years to repay the loan at a rate of 5 per cent. The remaining $760 million of the nearly $1.3 billion project would come from Egypt itself.

No sooner had the Dulles offer been made than the Russians resumed their international gamesmanship. On December 17, Ambassador Solod announced that the Soviet Union hoped that it would be able to participate in the financing of the dam "unless contrary stipulations in Egypt's accord with the Western powers excludes us specifically."[4] Instinctively, the Americans announced that under no circumstances would the Russians be allowed to participate. This produced the inevitable retort by the Egyptians that such conditions were a slur on the "dignity of Egypt."

Thereafter the bargaining moved slowly. The Egyptians did not take up the Western offer immediately. American Congressmen and committees resented President Nasser's unkind feelings toward both the United States and Israel. The Russians continued to suggest that they might be willing to provide the necessary financing. They also announced their willingness to build an atomic reactor for the Egyptians. On May 15, 1956, Nasser reported that he had bartered away even more Egyptian cotton for steel from Communist China. Finally, in a concluding slap at Dulles and the United States, Egypt declared it would formally recognize the government of Communist China; it was the first Arab country to do so.

Despite growing antagonism for the project in the United States and an increasingly hard line toward neutralist countries by Dulles, the U.S. federal budget released on July 4, 1956, contained an appropriation for the Aswan Dam. However, there was still no word of acceptance from Cairo, only unpleasant rumors. Soviet Minister of Foreign Affairs Shepilov again visited Cairo and was reported to have offered Nasser some kind of deal. Then Dulles publicly expressed doubts about the wisdom of the loan. At the same time, he announced the replacement of the American envoy to Cairo, Ambassador Byroade, who had been a firm supporter of an American loan for the dam. This finally prodded Nasser into action. He hurriedly dispatched Ambassador Ahmed Hussein to the United States for the purpose of accepting the loan, almost seven months after it had been proposed. Apparently at the time of the interview between Dulles and Hussein, on July 19, 1956, Dulles had still not made up his mind about canceling the American offer. He intimated that the United States was finding it harder and harder to serve as sponsor for the project because Egypt had not yet reached an agreement with the Sudan over the water rights and indemnification.

At this point the Egyptian Ambassador became concerned. In an effort to forestall any rejection he said, "Please don't say you are going to withdraw the offer, because we have the Russian offer to finance the dam right here in my pocket." To Dulles this appeared to be blackmail and he immediately replied: "Well, as you have the money already, you don't need any from us. My offer is withdrawn." [5]

The response of Nasser was equally emotional. Replying to Dulles, he declared at a public rally shortly thereafter: "May you choke to death on your fury." Within a week of the withdrawal of the U.S. offer, Nasser nationalized the Suez Canal at the expense of its French and English owners. The immediate justification was that the $100-million annual income of the canal would be used to finance the construction of the dam itself. At this point, Israel, Britain, and France invaded Egypt.

The doors to future negotiation with the United States were closed and the canal seized. Now the question was: would the Russians accept the challenge or had they been bluffing? For a time there was some uncertainty because of the size and cost of the undertaking. The Russians did provide an industrial loan of $175 million in January, 1958, which covered several projects unrelated to the dam. Finally, after two years, the Russians formally committed themselves. Khrushchev's announcement came at the time of a visit to Moscow in October, 1958, by Field Marshal Abdel Amer, the Vice President of Egypt. The Russians agreed to provide a loan of $100 million for the first stage of the dam. The official agreement was signed on December 27, 1958. (See Appendix 4 for the full text.) Thus began the second act of the drama, the construction of the dam itself.

The Russians moved immediately to take up their work. In March, 1959, the first Russians arrived at the site to prepare their plans. The first step was to revise the previously prepared proposals for the construction of the first stage of the dam. The original Western plans called for a series of diversion tunnels of about seven miles in length to be built through the granite on the right bank of the river. Once opened, these tunnels would permit the closing of the original river bed so that the dam itself could be formed. The erection of the dam, the construction of the hydroelectric station, and the erection of the transmission grid would constitute the second stage of construction. The hydroelectric power plant, which also required a water canal, would be placed on the river bank opposite the diversion canal. This is how most Western dams are constructed. To simplify the procedure and reduce the amount of rock excavation and tunneling, the Russians proposed instead that only one bank of the river be used for tunnels.

Thus the power plant would be combined with the diversion canal on the right bank. Moreover, the Russians made the sound suggestion that the tunneling, which promised to be so expensive and difficult, be held to as small an area as possible. Thus instead of tunnels, an open canal was to be constructed along six of the seven miles of granite river bank. This not only reduced the water pressure in the area, but also enabled the Russians to cut the cost estimates of dam construction by at least $35 million and reduce the construction time by as much as a year.[6]

From this point on, the full resources of the Soviet Union were put at the disposal of the dam builders. As one illustration, the research staff of the Hydroelectric Planning Institute of Tushina was assigned to work on the problems of the dam. This involved fifty scientists, who, among other things, constructed a scale model of the Nile as it existed at Aswan in order to anticipate hydraulic problems.[7]

As might be anticipated with the construction of a dam 360 feet high and two miles wide, and a lake about 300 miles long, there were plenty of problems. It turned out that despite the virtually impenetrable granite on the banks of the river, the bed of the river is composed of sedimentary materials down to a depth of about 200 yards. This made seepage a serious threat and thus necessitated a grout curtain filled with impermeable materials. There were also problems of safety: what would happen if the dam broke or was bombed? Finally, there was a question of feasibility: would the reservoir water evaporate or seep away into what once was nothing but desert?

Until some of these questions could be answered, there was no sense in doing too much. Furthermore, no one had agreed to pick up the bill for the revised second stage (erection of the main body of the dam and completion of the hydroelectric works) and the third stage (placement of the electric grid) of construction, both of which promised to be more expensive in terms of foreign currency than the first stage. The Russians appeared reluctant to finance the remaining work. The West Germans, however, evidenced some serious interest. After considerable delay, the Egyptians agreed to accept the West German offer.[8] The day before the Germans were due to fly into Cairo, the Russians decided they could not let the West Germans put a German frosting on a Russian cake. They insisted that they be allowed to finance and build the second and third stages. The Germans were left holding an empty frosting dish.

The complete arrangement for financing the dam was signed on August 27, 1960, and is as follows:[9]

	Total Cost	Soviet Portion	Soviet Percentage
	(in millions of dollars)		
First stage	614	100	16.2
Second and third stage	551	225	40.8
Total	1,165	325	27.8

This was deemed sufficient to build a dam that would have a capacity of 2,700,000 kilowatt-hours of power and an irrigation potential of 2 million acres. When completed, in 1970, the dam would increase Egypt's arable land by one-third. (See pp. 217–21 for the text of the agreement.)

Repayment for the first stage was to take twelve years and was to begin one year after completion of the first stage of the dam, provided this was not later than January 1, 1964. Thus the first repayment was due during the first quarter of 1964. Interest was set at 2.5 per cent and accrued from the date the equipment was first used; that is, on receipt of the consignment or of a voucher for technical services rendered. As is the usual case with Soviet loans, the Russians were to be paid in Egyptian currency, which was to be used for the purchase of Egyptian goods. However, the Soviet Union could demand repayment in a convertible currency if the U.A.R. found itself unable to export the agreed upon goods in six months. The agreement for the second stage contained the same conditions, except that repayment was to begin no later than January 1, 1970.

The Western and the Russian terms each had certain advantages. The simplified Russian plan of construction involved lower costs—$1,165 million versus about $1,300 million. The Russian interest rate was 2.5 per cent as opposed to 5 per cent for the West, although the Western offer allowed forty years instead of twelve for repayment. Further, $70 million of the $480 million offered by the West was to be a gift, whereas all $335 of the Russian loan was to be repaid. However, the Russian plan necessitated a smaller expenditure of foreign currency. In addition, the Russian loan was a soft loan, allowing for repayment in Egyptian currency, whereas the Western loan was repayable in hard currencies of dollars or pounds sterling. Therefore, except for the length of repayment, the Russian loan seemed to be a better arrangement.

By January 9, 1960, when Nasser dramatically inaugurated work on the dam by setting off an explosive charge, the Russians had already had a good taste of how difficult the work ahead would be. The first shiploads of Soviet equipment had been loaded in Odessa in October,

1959. However, after the conclusion of the colorful ceremonies celebrating the arrival of the material at the city of Aswan, the Russians were faced with the unromantic question of how to unload their equipment. The dam site was not serviced by roads, railroads, or adequate ancillary facilities. Thus the Russians had to find some way of moving their supplies from the city of Aswan to the construction site some ten miles away. A West German engineering group, Hochtief-Essen, had already built a railroad spur to their newly opened chemical plant a few miles from the dam site. But to complete the track it was necessary to utilize the construction equipment packed tightly on the barges and railroad cars. Unfortunately the unloading operation required materials handling equipment which, of course, was also packed right alongside the construction equipment, or else was still 400 miles up the Nile. It appeared that there would be endless delays, unless somehow the machinery could be unpacked and moved to the construction site.

After several fruitless appeals to the West German engineers at Hochtief-Essen, the Russians decided to do everything manually. The Egyptian peasants were mobilized, and the railroad spur was built out into the desert in three days. Machinery weighing as much as twenty tons a unit was unloaded and reassembled with only jacks and blocks, eight automobiles, and brute force. Such obstacles were only a sample of what the Russians would have to endure in the years to follow.

With the impenetrability of the granite, the oppressiveness of the 100–120 degree heat, and the bleakness of living conditions, the pace of work on the dam began to lag seriously. Soviet equipment designed for temperate or frigid conditions did not last in the Aswan dust, rock, and heat. Breakdowns were frequent, as any visitor could see from the discarded equipment scattered around the surrounding landscape. Maintenance facilities were overtaxed and incomplete. As a result, big Russian-made trucks had to be sent all the way back to Kharkov for repairs. To cope with the situation, it was necessary to redesign Soviet automotive equipment. The assistant chief of technical control of the Minsk automobile plant was dispatched to the scene. After a year a new model engine was engineered with an enlarged radiator and improved clutch and other modifications intended to contend with the heat and rocky roads.

The work continued to lag, however. Each side blamed the other for the delay. After a sightseeing tour of the dam site, a Russian reporter wrote in the Soviet newspaper *Izvestiia* that the Egyptian guides did not even allude to the fact that the dam was being built with Russian specialists and financial aid.[10] Instead, praise was given to the Swiss, German, English, and Swedish firms which had built the old Aswan

Dam further down the river. Asked why no mention was made of the Russian help, the Egyptian guide had replied that "the new Aswan Dam is not finished yet. We only praise completed projects." This state of affairs continued for another year.

An indication of how far behind schedule the work fell can be seen by comparing the actual work performed with the target. It was planned to pour the first concrete in May, 1962, yet none was poured until September in the intake structure and none until November in the tunnels. The excavation of the diversion canal also fell far behind schedule in the first half of 1962.[11] This set off Russian complaints to Nasser about the quality of Egyptian efforts and Egyptian criticism of the inadequacy of Soviet aid.

The complaints and the obvious difficulties at the dam site had an effect. In the spring of 1962, the work of the fourteen independent Egyptian contractors was superseded by the appointment of a single firm, Osman Ahmed Osman and Company.[12] An experienced firm, it sought to increase the construction efficiency and speed up the work. Seeing that the Soviet equipment was unable to do the job alone, Osman brought in limited amounts of Western equipment. Ten Swedish drills were purchased (reportedly accompanied by Swedish engineers). Between twenty and forty-five Aveling-Barford thirty-ton dump trucks from England were also ordered and quickly painted with Arabic symbols to prevent undue embarrassment. Then when the Russians were unable or unwilling to supply sufficient spare parts for their truck fleet at Aswan (spare parts are generally in short supply in the Soviet Union), the Egyptians put in an order for $125,000-worth of spare parts from General Motors in Detroit. (The Russian trucks had been copied from earlier GM models.) In addition, two American bulldozers and Traxcavators from the Caterpillar Corporation were ordered to supplement the considerably less efficient Russian bulldozers. Since the original agreement on the dam specified that only Russian equipment be used, these actions did not please the Russians: in some instances, the Russians actually demanded the cancellation of orders for other Western machinery. Nevertheless, this equipment helped to produce the desired results.

In response to the Egyptian action, Khrushchev appointed a new project director, Alexei Alexandrov, to replace the original director, Ivan Komzin. About the same time, in September, 1962, Nasser, deciding that even more changes were needed, reorganized the Egyptian staff. Mohammed Sidky Soliman replaced Mussa Arafa as Minister of the Aswan High Dam; this Ministry opened an office in Moscow, and communications were improved considerably.

The effect was immediate. Beginning in October, 1962, activity in all areas reached new heights and finally began to attain the targeted goals. On Nasser's order, labor reinforcements, including army officers, were rushed to the scene. The size of the work force increased from 15,000 in December, 1962, to 34,000 a few months later.[13] The number of Russians in that total increased from 800 to 1,800. But a lot of time had to be made up if the first stage was to be completed on schedule. The diversion tunnels had to be opened by May 15, 1964, before the onset of the spring floods. If the tunnels were not completed by that time, it would be necessary to wait a whole year before it would again be possible to close the river.

As late as fall, 1963, there were few Egyptians or Russians who seriously thought that the tunnels would be completed by mid-May, 1964. The pace of work was accelerated still further. In the race to complete the blasting of the tunnels, safety precautions were relaxed. After the detonation of the dynamite charge, bulldozers would move in immediately to carry out the rubble. Under normal conditions this would never be done. Usually it is deemed essential to send in inspectors to ensure that all the dynamite has been properly exploded. Failure to do this at Aswan inevitably resulted in numerous accidents as the unexploded dynamite was tossed about with the rubble. This practice, and the failure to observe other safety procedures, such as providing steel hats for the bulk of the Egyptian workers, inevitably took its toll. Officially, it was acknowledged that 227 workers' lives were lost (including several that were Russian).[14] Unofficially, some Egyptians admitted that the actual figure was even higher. In contrast to their reaction in China, however, the Russians did not walk off the job.

Despite the loss of life and the difficulties along the way, the diversion tunnels were opened and the course of the Nile was diverted by the deadline. There is no doubt that this was an engineering and physical accomplishment that deserved all the praise it received. The hysterical response of the Egyptian peasants and laborers at the opening of the dam in May, 1964, was indicative of the emotion generated by the changing of history which the diversion of the ancient Nile symbolized. Clearly this was a historic occasion and the Russians had done an impressive job.

Problems of Repayment

In addition to the problems that arose during construction, there were other grievances that must be mentioned if the complete picture is to be appreciated. For even in the case of what appears to be an outstanding success, there are frustrations that try the patience of the lenders and takers.

The events and negotiations accompanying the completion of the first stage of the Aswan Dam reveal much about the difficulties of administering an economic-aid program. In the very midst of the celebrations over the dam, Khrushchev felt it necessary to challenge his hosts. Throughout the week of festivities, the Egyptians and their fellow Arab guests from Iraq, Yemen, and Algeria pointed to the Aswan Dam as a symbol of Arab unity. After several days of this, Khrushchev felt it necessary to complain in a public speech. Asking whether his audience wanted him to say what it would be polite to say or instead what he really thought, he did not wait for an answer, but asked: what does the dam have to do with Arab unity? It was the Russians who had provided the help, and certainly not Arab millionaires.

Furthermore, the opening of the dam coincided with a repayment crisis in Egypt. As stipulated in the original agreement for the first stage of the dam, the first principal and interest payments on the Soviet loan for the dam were due in the first quarter of 1964. Although this meant that the Egyptians had the use of Soviet equipment and manpower for more than four years without any need for repayment, the Egyptians soon discovered that even these liberal terms were not generous enough. There were several reasons for this. First, as is true of most underdeveloped countries, the general balance-of-payments position is very serious in Egypt. The explanation for this problem is familiar by now. In Egypt the population has expanded faster than the increase in food crops, which has meant an even greater reliance on food imports. Cotton exports had not increased enough to compensate for the falling price of cotton and the demand for high priority industrial imports. The ability to repay foreign debts was made even more complex by the mortgaging of the cotton and rice crops for the arms purchased in 1954. Until at least 1961, Egypt seems to have been able to handle this. It had built up a $120.5 million favorable balance of trade with the Soviet Union and $53.5 million surplus with Czechoslovakia. This was of some help in paying off the almost $500-million worth of military aid, which reportedly required about $35 million a year. However, additional arms purchases in mid-1962 for the replacement of the original MIG-19 with MIG-21 jets undoubtedly placed a further strain on the Egyptian ability to pay for the dam and the other economic projects which were then being completed.

A basic assumption in any economic aid program is that the completed projects will generate goods and services that will earn income which in turn will make it possible to repay the loan. However, if a loan is for an unproductive purpose (munitions), or for a project that will not yield direct results for some time (a dam), then repayment is not a simple matter. Since they had both of these types of loans to repay, the financial plight of the Egyptians as of early 1964 and mid-1965 was serious.[15]

Certainly, therefore, the visit of Khrushchev to Egypt in May, 1964, to open the dam aroused mixed emotions on the part of both the creditor and the debtor. Rumors circulated that Khrushchev would offer a new loan to Nasser. Most reports even indicated the amount, $218 million. When Russian economic officials in the Soviet embassy in Cairo were asked about this, they denied emphatically that there would be a new loan. As one official told the author, "The Egyptians pay other countries back, why shouldn't they pay us as well? To do otherwise would establish a bad precedent for other developing countries which have had similar troubles." The Russian officials guessed that the figure of $218 million referred to the amount of the loan already promised for the second and third stages of the Aswan Dam. The rumor about a new loan was due either to a misunderstanding or to wishful thinking. The Soviet Union had already extended $544 million in economic credits (and perhaps an equal amount in military credits), "and that was enough." When this conversation was repeated to Egyptian officials, they reasserted that there *would* be a loan. When the point was pressed, they shrugged their shoulders and said simply that Allah would take care of it. There had to be a renewal of the loan or a postponement of the debt because Egypt simply did not have the $8.33 million for principal and $2 million for interest that was due on the dam loan to the U.S.S.R. in 1964.[16] Originally it was planned to repay the debt with exports of rice that were to be grown on land to be put into cultivation with water from the dam. However, the Nile had only just been diverted, and naturally it was impossible immediately to obtain any rice from this effort. The Egyptians hoped that by 1965 they would be able to export more than $23-million worth of rice from this reclaimed land. Unless food was to be taken from the mouths of the Egyptians themselves, it looked as though Egypt would have to default on a part of its loan, at least temporarily.

As a sidelight, there does seem to be some validity to the criticism that the United States is making it possible for the Egyptians to repay the Russians. The U.S. government has acknowledged that American shipments of surplus grain under Public Law 480 to Egypt, which totaled $125 million in 1963 and $175 million in 1964, made it possible for the Egyptians to divert the rice from the domestic market in order to pay back the Russians. In 1964, the U.A.R. exported about $70-million worth of rice, more than one-half of which went to Communist countries, including about $20 million to the U.S.S.R. The Egyptians had agreed with the United States not to export more than 33 per cent of their rice crop, but there were complaints that the Egyptians had exported up to 40 per cent of it. The United States found itself in an even more embarrassing position in 1959. In May, the United States sent rice to the U.A.R. under a P.L. 480 agreement.[17] By that time it probably had already been agreed that rice and cotton would be the main items with which Egypt would pay back the U.S.S.R. for its help on the Aswan Dam. American rice shipments therefore could have been used directly by the Egyptians to repay their debts, but it is unlikely that they were.

Recognizing that its wheat shipments were indirectly making it possible for the Egyptians to repay their Soviet loans, the United States in 1965 decided to re-evaluate its wheat-loan policy. At the time, the U.A.R.'s food reserves were at a very low point. Seizing the opportunity, and in the hope of soliciting support for Soviet participation in the approaching Algerian Conference of Afro-Asian nations, the Russians decided to provide 300,000 tons of wheat to the U.A.R. Even though the Soviets were still having trouble producing enough wheat for their own needs, they decided to divert the equivalent of $21-million worth of wheat which they themselves had just purchased. The wheat arrived, with great fanfare, just after an American wheat shipment had been unloaded, unnoticed.

To counter the Russian gain, the Chinese, who had even less food available, announced that they were prepared to send 250,000 tons of corn to the U.A.R. Both countries therefore were using their limited reserves of convertible currency to help Egypt in the hope of winning its support at the Algerian conference. The clear winner was the U.A.R., the loser, at least initially, the United States. Since the conference at Algiers had been postponed in the meantime, it is not clear how the Soviet Union and China think they came out.

Whatever his original intention, or the advice of his economic advisers, Khrushchev nonetheless seems to have been influenced by Allah, since the Egyptians did receive a new loan. On May 24, 1964, the Soviet Premier announced a new loan of $277 million. It was expected that this would provide the funds for about 10 per cent of the U.A.R.'s Second Five-Year Plan. It may well be, however, that Khrushchev listened too much to Allah and not enough to his colleagues in Moscow. One of the charges against Khrushchev at the time of his removal in October, 1964, was that he acted unilaterally in granting this loan. Although it was denied, undoubtedly a good portion of this loan was intended as a refunding of existing loans. However, specific new projects were also mentioned.

Other Aid

Among the new projects included in the agreement of May, 1964, were a continuous casting steel mill with a capacity of 1 million tons of steel a year (later increased to one-and-a-half million tons), a coke-chemical works, new thermal and hydroelectric plants, and machine-tool works. Khrushchev also announced a gift of various agricultural machines which would be used on a 10,000-acre state farm. For this the Soviet Union was to provide a variety of agricultural and construction equipment, including 300 trucks and 180 tractors. There were also to be a number of other projects financed on a regular commercial or short-term basis.[18] It is noteworthy, however, that equipment and machinery financed by the $277-million loan was to be repaid within five years after delivery rather than the twelve years normally permitted.

This agreement was a supplement to the original projects announced in January, 1958. At that time, almost a year before the agreement on the Aswan Dam itself, the Russians signed their first aid agreement with the U.A.R. They promised to provide $175 million for twelve years at 2.5 per cent in order to finance sixty-five projects. As of early 1965, all but $9 million of this had been spent. Following the first loan, a second project agreement was negotiated on June 18, 1963. This increased the number of projects to ninety-five. The value of this loan was placed at $44 million. Therefore, as of June, 1965, the Russians had provided the Egyptians with a total of $821 million in loans broken down as follows:[19]

(in millions of dollars)

January, 1958	175	Industrial projects
December 27, 1958	100	Aswan Dam, first stage
August 28, 1960	225	Aswan Dam, second and third stages
June 18, 1963	44	Industrial projects
May 24, 1964	277	Industrial projects and Aswan Dam

The wheat loan of July, 1965, adds another $21 million to the total.

Among the completed industrial projects are the coke plant at Helwan, which was opened in April, 1964, with a capacity of 280,000–300,000 tons of coke a year and numerous by-products including 5,000 tons of ammonium sulphate, phenol, and nitric acid. The Russians have built or are building a rolling mill and a sintering plant at the Helwan steel mill, a machine-tool works and an aluminum cable shop both at Helwan, two oil refineries at Suez and Alexandria, two cotton-spinning mills at Damietta and Mit Chamr, a radio factory at Cairo, a pharmaceutical plant at Abu Zabal, a shipyard at Alexandria, a thermal electric power station at Suez, a milk-processing plant at Tanta Badre and Manzura (built with Czech help), and an onion-dehydrating plant at Sohag (built jointly with the Bulgarians).[20] In the field of education, the Russians have built fifteen vocational-training centers and a nuclear physics laboratory. They had trained nearly 7,000 Egyptians by mid-1964. According to a preliminary estimate in 1961, 32 per cent of all metallurgical products, 36 per cent of all machinery products, and 48 per cent of all mining and petroleum goods produced in the U.A.R. were produced with Soviet-supplied and financed equipment. (See Appendix 5 for the text of the 1958 aid agreement.)

Determining and Dispensing Soviet Aid

From the manner in which the different Soviet aid agreements with Egypt have been announced, it is evident that there is no one way in which the decision is made to give aid. The more important the project and the tenser and brighter the international prospects, the more likely it is that the ultimate decision will be determined by the highest government and party organs. On occasion there apparently has even been a certain amount of spontaneous improvisation by Soviet leaders. The most controversial was Khrushchev's unilateral decision to present the $277-million loan to Nasser in May, 1964. Not only did he disregard the advice of his advisers (a leader's prerogative), but he ignored the counsel of his Presidium colleagues.

Normally, however, decisions to give aid are made within the framework of the bureaucracy created for this purpose. Until 1955—that is, before there was any significant volume of Soviet foreign aid to either the satellites or the developing countries—all questions of technical aid were handled by the Ministry of Foreign Trade. One of its subsidiaries, Tekhnoeksport (technical exports), did the actual operational work. As Soviet interest in foreign aid grew, the Glavnoe Upravlenie po Delam Ekonomicheskeskikh Sviazei so Stranami Narodnoi Demokratii (Chief Administration for Economic Relations with the People's Democracies), or GUES, was created. This indicates the main focus was on the satellite countries. It was only in July, 1957, as aid to the developing countries began to grow at an equally rapid rate, that the GUES was reorganized into the Gosudarstvennyi Komitet Soveta Ministrov U.S.S.R. po Vneshnim Ekonomicheskim Sviaziam (the

Government Committee of the Council of Ministers of the U.S.S.R. for Foreign Economic Relations), or GKES. This administrative agency is in charge of aid to both satellite and neutralist countries. Administration of aid to the nonaligned countries is divided according to geographical location. Not indicated in the diagram are the special units created for particularly important projects such as the Aswan Dam. The present chairman of the GKES is Semen Andrevitch Skatchkov, who replaced M. G. Pervukhin in February, 1958. In recognition of the importance of his position, Skatchkov holds the rank of Minister in the Council of Ministers. This permits him to participate in high-level decisions concerning the political and economic feasibility of various projects.

In addition to its own network of offices, the GKES relies on various outside organizations for advice. Four corporations that have been traditionally attached to the Ministry of Foreign Trade have also been given a special responsibility for foreign aid. Two are especially important: Tekhnopromeksport (technical and industrial exports), which handles irrigation and engineering work and was given initial responsibility for undertaking the work at the Aswan Dam; and Tekhnoeksport, which makes geological surveys, builds industry, and undertakes work connected with transportation. Also involved are Tiazhpromeksport (heavy industrial exports), which is responsible for projects concerned with ferrous and nonferrous metals as well as coal and oil development, and Prommasheksport (industrial machinery exports), which handles machine tools, radios, chemicals, and other machinery exports.

Since the GKES and the various corporations just listed are usually involved only as aid-administering groups, they make use of other foreign trade corporations which in turn make the direct contracts with Soviet factories and engineering institutes. This system has not always functioned smoothly. Khrushchev often criticized Soviet manufacturers for failing to fulfill delivery schedules to foreign customers. In an effort to facilitate operations, a special organization was created in 1960 called the Glavnoe Upravlenie Vneshnikh Snoshenii (Chief Administration for Foreign Relations), which was attached to the Economic Council of the U.S.S.R. Its function was to expedite work on foreign-aid projects by Soviet contractors, especially Soviet factories. However, it is unclear what has happened to this organization after its parent organization was abolished in September, 1965.

When the Soviet Union dispenses large amounts of aid—as it does to Ghana, the U.A.R., India, and Indonesia—negotiations are handled by special branch offices of the GKES in the particular country. Where

Government Committee of the Council of Ministers of the U.S.S.R.
for Foreign Economic Relations (GKES)

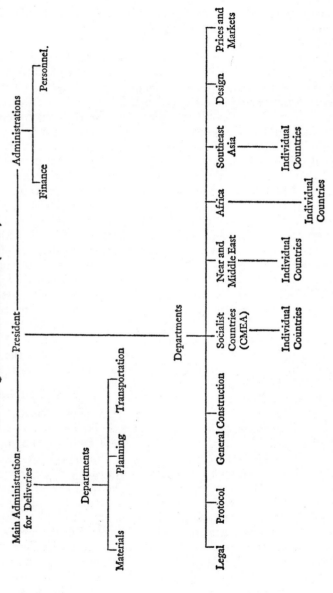

the aid activities are more limited, arrangements are handled by the economic counselor of the Soviet embassy. The whole organizational framework resembles the organization of our own Agency for International Development.

There are several preliminary measures that the Russians usually take before beginning their actual construction work. The procedures are not too different from those followed by Western countries. First, someone must bring up the question of foreign aid. Usually the request comes from the prospective recipient, but the Russians have on occasion initiated an offer on their own. The initial discussion may concern a specific project or just a general monetary commitment. Frequently, the Russians will then pledge assistance in principle to a number of industrial projects without going into details.[21] This tentative list is discussed by both governments. Feasibility studies are then conducted as to the time of construction and type of plant. The next step is to complete the feasibility study, determine the specific site, and draw up the blueprints. Only then is there legal liability, which is reflected in a specific contract for the delivery of equipment on the part of specific corporations in the Soviet Ministry of Foreign Trade. To simplify the contractual procedures, the Russians often utilize a blanket agreement called the *Obshchi Uslovii,* or General Agreement. This sets out the details on such matters as accounting procedures, sending specialists for training to the U.S.S.R., paying Soviet specialists on the job, and arbitrating disputes. (See appendixes for sample agreements.)

With only one or two exceptions, all Soviet aid takes the form of equipment or goods provided by the U.S.S.R. itself. Therefore virtually all Soviet aid is classified as "tied aid," since all purchases are restricted to the Soviet Union. Loans are established for specific projects and are never made available in convertible currency. (Some Russians feel this is one of the reasons why there has been so little scandal or misappropriation of funds associated with Soviet aid projects.) The usual procedure is for Gosbank, the State Bank, or Vneshtorgbank, the Foreign Trade Bank, to set up a special account for each credit approved in the name of the Ministry of Finance or Central Bank of the recipient country. When consignment papers for overseas shipment or letters of authority or guarantees from officials in the developing country are received by the Soviet banks, a debit is entered in the recipient country's account and the money transferred to the Soviet Foreign Trade Corporation, which in turn transfers the funds to the manufacturer. Repayment is usually made by transferring funds (convertible and nonconvertible) to the Gosbank or Vneshtorgbank account, which in turn is opened in the recipient country. Similar procedures and organizational framework are utilized by the satellite countries.

Satellite Aid

Other Communist nations have played an active role in the U.A.R. Table III-1 indicates the loans they have extended, excluding the work being done purely on a commercial basis. For the most part, their record in the U.A.R. is not significantly different from that of the Soviet Union. There are two cases, however, that deserve special comment. An East German loan in 1965 was designed as a wedge to end East Germany's diplomatic isolation. It was expected that in exchange for the loan Nasser would extend full diplomatic recognition to the East German regime. However, West Germany reacted very strongly, and the U.A.R. decided, at least initially, merely to open an East German consulate. Even for this, however, the Egyptians apparently demanded a high price. The early reports of the negotiations indicated that the loan would be for $78.8 million. Ultimately the Germans were induced to increase their offer to $100.8 million.

Also of special interest is the role of China in Egypt's credit program. Until 1965, China made only a token effort. This might have been expected. Egypt is one of the wealthiest recipients of Chinese aid. A loan from Egypt to China is as much to be expected as the reverse, especially since the U.A.R.'s main export is cotton, of which China is a major consumer. The explanation for the unusually large Chinese loan of $80 million made in January, 1965, is found in the Sino-Soviet rivalry. This explanation holds for almost all Chinese loans in 1964–65. In return for his $277-million loan in May, 1964, Khrushchev certainly expected support for the Soviet Union's participation in the Second Afro-Asian Conference. China's loan a few months later clearly was an effort to offset the Soviet move, as was its offer of grain in July, 1965. The same type of competition took place in Algeria, Congo-Brazzaville, Kenya, Tanzania, Nepal, Pakistan, and, to some extent, in Guinea, Mali, and Ghana. (See Chapter 11.)

A large portion of the satellite and the Soviet projects have already been put into operation in Egypt. Paced by the Aswan Dam, it is fair to say that, on the whole, foreign aid from the Communist bloc has been fairly successful. Nonetheless, it is only to be expected that there have been disappointments.

As the Egyptians discovered at Aswan, Soviet equipment is not always of the highest quality. One week after two Soviet bulldozers arrived at Helwan to be used in the construction of the coke oven plant

Table III-1

ECONOMIC LOANS TO EGYPT FROM COMMUNIST NATIONS
(in Millions of Dollars)

Country	Amount	Date	Purpose
Bulgaria	a	March, 1962	
China	5	October, 1956	Ultimately converted into a gift for commodity purchases
	80	January, 1965	Industrial credit
	17.5	July, 1965	Corn loan (or gift)
Czechoslovakia	34[b]	1957	Sugar refinery; cement plant at El Tabbin; bicycle plant; ceramics, textile, and shoe plants; expansion of Talk Ha power station
	56	March, 1962	
	72	March, 1965	
East Germany	21	August, 1958	Thermal electric plant, zinc-coating plant, cold-storage plant, two bridges, cotton-fabric plant, coke freight cars
	6	March, 1961	
	70	March, 1965	Industrial machinery, technical assistance
	30.8	March, 1965	Short-term credit to purchase commodities
Hungary	28	December, 1960; renewed and extended October, 1962	To cover 80 per cent of value of commodities; electric power station at El Tabbin; railroad bridge across the Nile; automatic telephone exchange, surgical equipment; rolling stock
Poland	29	July, 1962	To cover 85 per cent of price of oil storage tanks, bridges, textile dye plants, machine-tool works
	25[a]	1964	
Rumania	70[a]	1964	

Sources: See pages 250-51.

[a]Not officially confirmed.
[b]Only $26 million of this amount has been used.

they collapsed, never to be used again. During my visit to the installation in May, 1964, I could still see them dumped mournfully in the middle of a supply depot. The Arab contractor replaced them with one American Caterpillar bulldozer, which did the work the two Soviet bulldozers were supposed to do. Two hundred feet away, I noticed two broken-down boilers. Only two months after the plant was opened, it was discovered that one Soviet-supplied boiler had been completely scorched. Subsequent inspection revealed that the standby boiler was partially burnt out. It was caught in time so that the whole plant did not have to close down. Similarly one of the two switching engines had been scorched by a premature flushing of coke from the oven.[22] Arab engineers also complained of the inflexibility of the Soviet engineers assigned to the project: no change in the plans, no matter how small, could be made without prior approval directly from Moscow.

Soviet aid officials in Cairo have maintained that the problem was not the quality of the equipment, but the severity of the conditions and the lack of foresight shown by Egyptian planners. The heat, dust, and lack of proper maintenance made it inevitable that even the best equipment would suffer. If the equipment was at fault, then the Egyptians should have returned it. Furthermore, Soviet officials argued, it was difficult to run many of the Egyptian enterprises rationally because decisions were so often based on emotion rather than common sense. As an example, the Russians cited the steel plant built at Helwan by the West Germans. Although it was less than a mile from the Nile River, it had to be serviced almost entirely by rail; the Nile had been destroyed as a waterway by careless officials and colonial railroad interests which had placed low fixed bridges over it. More important, there were no readily accessible supplies of iron ore and coal nearby. In fact, the coal for the Helwan coke plant was first sent from Ukrainian mines by rail to Odessa. From there it was shipped by sea to Alexandria, where it was once again loaded onto freight cars to be sent to Helwan. Such a costly shipping arrangement resulted in a costly steel product. The Russians acknowledged, however, that conditions had improved. Previous to the opening of the coke plant, it was coke that was shipped from the Ukraine, not coal. When the Russian officials were asked whether they would build a second set of blast furnaces at Helwan as was rumored, they replied with mock horror that it would be like putting a jacket on a button. Nevertheless, Khrushchev, in what other Russians described as an irrational moment, agreed to the expansion.[23]

There are other signs that friction developed over the implementation of the Soviet aid program. Russian aid officials in Cairo informed me that they were reappraising their industrial aid schedule with the U.A.R. There was considerable self-criticism over the fact that thus far, except for the Aswan Dam, the Russians had concentrated on some of the smaller projects and had neglected the bigger ones. Although the Russians have been very competitive, they do not always provide the most favorable terms. Thus, it was an American firm, Westinghouse Electric International, that built the West Cairo Power Plant with the help of a $40 million loan from the United States ($30 million of which was in hard currency). The Russians had bid on the project and wanted to build it, since it was bound to have an important economic and psychological impact on Cairo. The Russians explained their loss of the contract by saying that the Egyptians were not willing to undertake their share of the work. The evidence seems to be otherwise. The Russians could not match the American bid in price and efficiency.

The Russians have other complaints about conditions in the U.A.R. With summer temperatures at Aswan in the 120's, it is easy to understand how difficult it must be for people brought up on Russian temperatures and a continental climate. Furthermore, there also seems to be resentment by the Russians over the treatment accorded to Egyptian Communists by the Egyptian government. While they have not been executed, as in Iraq, local Communists have been imprisoned periodically. This happened prior to the spring of 1964 and again in December, 1965. In the latter case, the campaign embarrassed the Russians. They took great pains to show that the guilty parties "were a group of provocateurs calling themselves the 'Arab Communist Party.'" In fact, *Pravda* reported that "not a single Egyptian Marxist has suffered from political repression *recently*." [24] Obviously actions of this sort cause considerable embarrassment for the Russians. It is also awkward that Egyptian law prevents Egyptians from having social contacts with foreigners, especially those from Communist countries. The feeling that Khrushchev had been nicer to Nasser than he should have was intensified when Khrushchev warmly embraced Nasser, calling him "Comrade," during the Aswan visit in 1964. This was a title reserved for the truest supporters of Communist ideals. Without doubt, this undeserved compliment highlighted the clash between the aims of the Soviet foreign aid program and Russia's support of overseas revolution.

Still, the shortcomings of the Soviet Union's aid program to the U.A.R. should not obscure its obvious successes. Next to the burnt-out railroad car at the coke-oven plant, I saw Soviet engineers conversing with their Egyptian counterparts in Arabic or English. Moreover, the plant was operating. Nevertheless, it appears there are still hard days ahead. The Russians, unlike the Americans, expect to be paid back. To the extent that the Soviet industrial growth rate at home slackens or wavers, repayment becomes even more important. As indicated above in the discussion of the unexpected loan of $277 million in May, 1964, the Russians may find it hard to collect on their debts. The Russians themselves estimate that by 1970 the U.A.R. will be saddled with long-term debt repayment to both the East and West that will total about $200 million a year. As Egypt's need for industrial aid continues to grow, and its foreign obligations increase, it is to be expected that there will be periodic dissonance in the harmony that it was hoped Soviet aid to Egypt would produce.

Epilogue

The question that most Americans inevitably ask when they discuss the Aswan Dam is, did we make a mistake in letting the Russians build it rather than ourselves? Such a question is not a simple one to answer. There are strong arguments on both sides.

Those who support the American position argue that the dam was eventually built without the American taxpayer having to pay for it. Considering that it would have cost the United States a minimum of $186 million and that we would have been repaid, if at all, in cotton and rice, the United States may have escaped an unnecessary burden. (Had we taken the $186 million we were prepared to spend at Aswan and made it available to other countries for industrial credits, perhaps the return in international prestige could have been equally impressive; unfortunately there was no such direct diversion of funds.) Then, too, there is nothing to show that the Egyptians have become any more favorably inclined toward Communism and the U.S.S.R. just because the Russians built the dam. It was the original armaments deal that induced the Egyptians' first enthusiasm. Some of the friction that arose over the Dam has already been discussed. Local Communists are still tightly controlled, even though most of them were released from prison, at least temporarily, on the occasion of Khrushchev's visit in 1964.

Finally, it seems fair to say that Americans may not have had the patience and tolerance required for a project of this duration and expense in a country with strong anti-American feelings. In addition to the disagreement over socialism versus capitalism, there are the inflammatory issues of Israel and Africa: the American role in these areas is deeply resented by Nasser. At any moment he was likely to give vent to some criticism of the United States, which would only have produced demands that the United States cease its aid for the dam. In turn this would have produced more resentment in the U.A.R. The end result would hardly have been a feeling of gratitude toward the United States.

Those who feel that the United States made a mistake argue that our withdrawal made possible a Soviet success as significant as the first Sputnik. The Aswan Dam provided a stage for Soviet emergence onto the world economic scene. In addition to the public-relations value, the Russians had a magnificent opportunity to show off their technical and engineering skills. Acceptance by the United States of such a challenge would have done much to offset the colonialist label that the United States often wears. By our withdrawal, we reinforced the view that the Soviet Union is the friend of the oppressed and America the friend of the oppressor. Furthermore, the main shortcoming of American aid has been its diffusiveness. While it may be a mistake to concentrate entirely on impact projects or grandiose schemes, it might be well to promote at least one or two. No American foreign aid project thus far has really caught the imagination of the world—or of the American taxpayer. American projects may win the appreciation of the people in a particular country, but Aswan is a name now known around the world.

Those are the arguments. It is unrealistic to assume that if the United States had undertaken to build the dam, the Egyptians would have broken off relations with the U.S.S.R. or have been significantly less friendly. Certainly they haven't been cooler to the United States because we did not sell them munitions in 1955. If we had built the dam, it is doubtful that present-day relations would have improved enough to warrant the cost. It may be, therefore, just as well that the Russians built the dam. This conclusion would be a little easier to defend, however, if our retreat in the U.A.R. had been offset by a comparable dollar volume in equally exciting industrial projects elsewhere.

4. India: Bhilai, Western Oil Companies, and Bilateral Trade

From the Indian point of view, Soviet economic activity has been a success. Prior to January, 1965, the Russians managed to impress the Indians with one triumph after another. There were minor difficulties, some criticism, and a fear of undue penetration of Soviet foreign trade, but in economic terms the Russians made a spectacular show. Although the amount of Soviet aid is only about one-fifth that of American aid, Russian activities in India seem to have had a greater impact on the consciousness of India and the world than has American aid. Furthermore, India's early advocacy of nonalignment would have been impossible without Soviet financial help, for without the availability of such aid, India would not have been able to risk a stance that was independent of the West. This position ultimately proved awkward to both India and the Soviet Union at the time of the Chinese and Pakistani border disputes, but even these incidents have failed to detract from Russia's over-all accomplishments.

Bhilai

Soviet aid to India began with a flourish. On February 2, 1955, the Russians announced that they would build the Bhilai steel mill. At this time, Russia's only other foreign-aid program was in Afghanistan and involved such relatively unambitious projects as a grain elevator and a flour mill. However, the Indian steel mill, to be located in Madhya Pradesh, turned out to be second only to the Aswan Dam in terms of international impact. What started as a three-way effort by the West Germans, English, and Russians to provide India with a steel industry became a vigorous competitive race in which Russia put its rivals to shame. The Bhilai steel mill provided a demonstration of Soviet technological mastery at German and English expense. It was only in late 1964 that the Russians at Bhilai faltered.

After achieving independence, India immediately decided to industrialize. With pre-independence steel capacity amounting to little more than 1 million tons a year, expansion of domestic steel production became a goal of the highest priority. In 1953, the West German steel firms of Krupp and Demag were approached and asked to draw up a program for the creation of an Indian steel industry. It was recommended that at least three steel mills be constructed, each having a capacity of 1 million tons. These mills would be financed with foreign loans and owned and operated by a state corporation (which ultimately became Hindustan Steel Limited). Negotiations with the Germans and English dragged on for two years without much success. Then came the Soviet decision to build one of the three plants. On March 14, 1955, Bhilai was selected as the site, and by the following year the detailed project report had been prepared and accepted by the Indian government.

In the wake of the Soviet agreement, the West Germans agreed in June, 1955, to construct a plant at Rourkela. Eight months later, the English closed the triangle and undertook to build a third plant at Durgapur. Unfortunately for the English and Germans, there was a natural temptation to compare the three mills. Comparisons were almost certain to be disadvantageous to the English and Germans, because the Russians had chosen the least complex of the three plants. The steel products at Bhilai were less sophisticated in nature, the technical requirements were less demanding, and the skills and machinery needed were therefore less complex. The Bhilai plant produced only merchant steel and rails. Rourkela, the West German plant, manufactured flat steel, a much more complicated process. Furthermore, Rourkela used the LD or oxygen-blowing system, which was a relatively new process at the time and had never been tried before in Asia. Because this system had been devised only a few years prior to the time it was installed in India, not all the technical problems had been eliminated. (It was not until the mid-1960's that U.S. Steel and Bethlehem Steel felt it safe enough to introduce such methods in their own plants.) It is expected that the LD system will eventually produce steel that is at least $6 cheaper per ton than open-hearth steel. This means that Rourkela has a better profit-making potential than Bhilai.[1] But in the meantime, by devoting their resources to a less complex project, the Russians incurred lower construction costs and had fewer immediate operating problems. The Germans, moreover, acting as private contractors, made an inordinate number of mistakes which further served to highlight a superb Soviet performance.

The Russians demonstrated their competitive spirit from the moment they announced their willingness to build the steel mill. They assigned their best people to the Bhilai project, including Venyamin Dymshyts, who was later to become chairman of the State Planning Committee

(Gosplan). Not only did they catch the Germans and English unprepared by their speed in working out the arrangements, but they also offered credit terms that were significantly more favorable. As opposed to an interest rate of 4.5 per cent to 6.3 per cent, and a repayment period that had to be extended periodically, the Russian loan was for 2.5 per cent and was repayable over a twelve-year period, to begin one year after the delivery of the bulk of the equipment.[2] Slightly less advantageous in practice, but attractive on paper, was the Russian willingness to accept repayment in rupees. Despite the fact that this was to create a series of unanticipated problems for the Indians, it generated a more favorable reaction than Western insistence on repayment in convertible currency. Although England and Germany have subsequently extended the repayment period for their loans, the Russian arrangement initially appeared more charitable. Consequently, it made a more enduring impression.

The question of which plant was cheaper is hard to answer. Because the equipment is more sophisticated, it is to be expected that the German plant should be more costly. Furthermore, there are several ways in which cost must be evaluated, i.e., in terms of foreign exchange, the relative size of the foreign loan, and total capital cost. The Russians baldly assert that Bhilai was cheaper. According to their figures, the three steel mills, producing 1 million tons of steel each, were to cost the following:[3]

	Bhilai	Rourkela	Durgapur
		(in millions of dollars)	
Total	275	375	290
Of which foreign exchange	164	256	193

If these projections were correct, the Soviet plant would indeed have been cheaper in terms of both total cost and the foreign exchange required. The official Indian figures, however, show something different. By their figures, the English plant at Durgapur is the cheapest of the three. Cost data of Hindustan Steel Limited and the Ministry of Finance of India show that the cost of each 1-million-ton steel mill was the following:[4]

	Bhilai		Rourkela		Durgapur	
	Actual *	*Planned*	*Actual* *	*Planned*	*Actual* *	*Planned*
			(in millions of dollars)			
Plant township	316		464		331	
Mines	107		55		78	
Total	423	424	519	491	409	430

	Bhilai		Rourkela		Durgapur	
	Actual *	*Planned*	*Actual* *	*Planned*	*Actual* *	*Planned*
			(*in millions of dollars*)			
Foreign exchange *	206–12		274		201	
Portion provided by foreign loan	136		163		74	
Foreign loan as a percentage of foreign exchange	64–66%		60%		37%	

* As of March 31, 1964.

Thus the planned total cost of the English project is approximately the same as, and the actual costs a bit less than, the Bhilai operation. If the steel plants alone are compared, without the cost of subsidiary mines and township construction, then Bhilai is cheaper. Durgapur required a slightly smaller expenditure of foreign exchange, which meant that more domestic resources could be utilized. However, the English provided less of that foreign exchange on a loan basis, which meant that the Indians had to spend their own money. The Russian terms were therefore more beneficial to the Indians only in the sense that the Russians provided a larger proportion of the foreign-exchange requirement in loan form. Whatever the actual costs, the Russians use data which refer to the higher costs of the technologically more complex Rourkela plant when they make their comparisons. They usually ignore Durgapur. They have thus managed to convey the incorrect notion that their plant was the cheapest of the three, and this is the impression that has prevailed.

While the Russians may make unjustified claims about the financial aid they have provided to Bhilai, until recently they have had less trouble finding support for virtually any boast they wanted to make about the operating efficiency of their plant. The Russians excelled in rapid construction and ironing out the production kinks. They not only managed to open the various sectors of their steel plant faster, but they also reached full operating capacity before either the Germans or the English. The first blast furnace at Bhilai was blown in on February 2, 1959, shortly before the blast furnace at Rourkela. The Russians then went on to attain full capacity in early 1962, while Rourkela did not achieve it until mid-1964. The Russian open-hearth steel furnaces were inaugurated in October, 1959, and projected steel ingot capacity was reached by the fall of 1962. Rourkela, which opened shortly after, in January, 1960, did not produce at promised capacity until late 1964. At Durgapur there were delays similar to those at Rourkela. Blast-furnace production had reached its capacity by mid-1963, but steel production continued to lag until 1964.

The Soviet success in production made headlines. Just as important, the Bhilai plant escaped most of the operating breakdowns that plagued Durgapur and, especially, Rourkela. For example, in December, 1961, blast furnace number one at Rourkela, which had been operating poorly, had to be shut down for repairs. The blooming and slabbing mill suffered two breakdowns in 1961, and the dolomite kiln failed to reach operational capacity, which adversely affected the operation of the LD converter. The Indians also complained of a nineteen-month lag between the time of completion of construction and operation of blast furnace number three and coke oven number one. The following year, in April, 1962, a strike closed down blast-furnace operations for more than a week. From January to August, 1962, and again on January 28, 1964, until July 31, 1964, blast furnace number one had to be shut down for repairs; there was also trouble at the blooming and slabbing mill in January, 1963, and a breakdown in the cold rolling mill from January to March, 1963. Just when it appeared that all the equipment had been put into proper working order, civil riots, sparked by the horror tales of Hindu refugees from Pakistan, disrupted operations in March–April, 1964, and caused a final setback. The English at Durgapur had some of the same troubles, although on a smaller scale. These problems at the German and British plants contrasted sharply with the news of success and on-time operations at Bhilai. Naturally, the Russians had some difficulties, but until mid-1964 they were minor in nature and not so persistent. Like Rourkela, Bhilai also has had some labor unrest. At the time of the initial construction, the Bhilai work force consisted of 40,000–45,000 employees. Upon completion of the plant in 1960, it became necessary to cut back the work force. While about 7,000 workers did find jobs on the production line, the remainder did not. This caused considerable resentment. Rallying around the cry, "We built the plant and now you are throwing us out," workers staged a protest and hunger strike lasting several days. Responding to the pressure, the management apparently increased the Bhilai work force more than originally intended.[5] This partially explains the abnormally large labor force at Bhilai: as of early 1965, there were 20,783 employees at Bhilai, 16,973 at Durgapur, and 15,907 at Rourkela.[6] The larger labor force at Bhilai has not meant the elimination of labor unrest. There have been continuous jurisdictional disputes, one of which precipitated a strike scheduled for July 14, 1964.

There were also some minor problems with equipment at Bhilai. Because of poor welding, water leaked into one of the blast furnaces in the spring of 1964. This necessitated a halt in operations. The refractory brick used at Bhilai consumes 20 kilograms of basic brick for every ton of steel produced, compared to 11.5 kilograms at Durgapur and 6 at Rourkela. (The comparable figure in the Soviet Union is 10.2 kilograms per ton, and in the United States, 5.)

Bhilai has had some other shortcomings which are similar to those experienced by steel mills in the U.S.S.R. Employee safety is traditionally a problem in Soviet industry because of the absence of protective safeguards. This is reflected at Bhilai, which had 1,821 accidents in 1964, compared with 1,219 at Durgapur and 619 at Rourkela. As in the Soviet Union, steel mills are designed for prolonged production runs of a particular item. This creates certain economies of scale, but it necessitates large inventory accumulation of some products while others are in short supply. Soviet industry has also not mastered the production of certain industrial items. Thus one finds Otis elevators and Fedders air conditioners in the main Administration Building at Bhilai and that the public relations agency of the Russian-built steel mill is the Indian office of J. Walter Thompson. (See Chapter 7 for a discussion of a similar situation at the Inya Lake Hotel in Burma.)

Obviously, none of these matters is serious enough to detract from the over-all success of the plant and the fact that the mill was operating at 115 per cent of rated capacity in fiscal year 1963–64. Moreover, in October, 1963, Bhilai shipped 12,500 tons of rails to Sudan, one of the first exports of the Indian steel industry. The Indians have also been pleased by the speed with which the Russians have sent their own technicians home and brought in Indian replacements. The total number of foreigners involved in operating the 1 million-ton plant at Bhilai had been reduced from thirty-seven in 1963 to twenty-one early in 1965. At Rourkela, there were 239 foreigners in 1963, but this was reduced to ninety-five (including ten Americans) by January, 1965, and to forty-five by January, 1966. At Durgapur, the reduction was from fifty-seven to forty-three. (Additional technicians were brought in to supervise the expansion programs at all three plants.) However, the Russians have refused to turn over the design decisions and control at Bhilai to the Central Engineering and Design Bureau of Hindustan Steel Limited, as the Germans have done. Like the English, the Russians have used their own design technicians and have thus retained effective operating control over Bhilai. But this is a minor issue. So is the fact that, because of the excessively large labor force, productivity per employee at Bhilai lags behind Rourkela and Durgapur (58 tons per man per year compared to 75 at Rourkela)—this is not significant in a country with such a large and underemployed population. What is important is that Bhilai has been operating longer at rated capacity and came the closest of all the state-owned mills to making a profit during the fiscal years 1961-64.

Russian success changed drastically in late 1964. (By this time, the English had begun to solve their problems, and the Germans actually started to report an average monthly profit of $1 million a month, which resulted in impressive profits in 1965 and 1966.) In contrast, for the first time, a major Soviet component at the mill broke down. As part of a major expansion program that was expected to increase Bhilai's annual capacity to 2.5 million metric tons of steel, a fourth blast furnace had been scheduled for completion in the second quarter of 1964.[7] It was opened belatedly on December 8, 1964. For about three weeks, blast furnace number four, the largest of its kind in Asia, worked well. Production hit 1,643 tons a day, compared to a rated capacity of 1,738 tons. Then in January there was a breakdown, and the furnace had to be closed down for six days. The turbo blower of the furnace had failed to function properly and hot spots had formed on key parts of the furnace. The Russians found it necessary to fly in five experts. As of May, 1965, it was estimated that the breakdown had cost about $10 million in lost production and repair costs. Obviously this was a serious blemish on the record of Russian success in India.

Despite this misfortune, the Russians hope to redeem themselves. To some extent, they were not entirely to blame for what happened. Adhering to their promise to replace Russian technicians with Indians, they employed only one-third as many Russians to build the fourth blast furnace as were used to construct the first three. If the Russians had installed the blast furnace themselves, perhaps there would have been no problem. Two other new blast furnaces were scheduled for 1965-66 and it will be important to see what success they have.

This expansion program is part of a credit agreement of February, 1961, in which the Russians agreed to boost Bhilai steel ingot capacity to 2.5 million tons. That the Indians have tended to favor the Bhilai plant is indicated by the fact that the first expansion programs at Rourkela and Durgapur are more modest than at Bhilai; they call for Rourkela to increase its production to 1.8 million tons and Durgapur to expand to 1.6 million tons.

The Russians also endeared themselves to the Indians because of their agility and receptivity in the Bokaro affair. In addition to the three plants at Bhilai, Durgapur, and Rourkela, the long-range plan for Indian steel called for a fourth plant to be built at Bokaro. This plant would specialize in flat-steel products, critical products which had heretofore been produced in India only at Rourkela. Since the United

States is the world leader in the production of this kind of steel, it was only natural that it would be asked to undertake the construction of the fourth mill. The Indians also reasoned this would be nonalignment at its best, since the United States would find itself sponsoring a plant alongside those of the Soviet Union, West Germany, and England.

Negotiations over the Bokaro plant dragged on for several years. In many ways, this would have been the perfect chance for Americans to improve the prestige and image of their foreign aid. Bokaro could have provided a "flagship" project for the whole American aid effort. It would also have posed an effective counter to Soviet aid, not only in India, but wherever the Russians make the claim that Americans are unwilling to promote industrial projects. Even though the U.S. aid program does in fact encourage industrial projects (including a recently opened $227-million steel plant in Eregli, Turkey), they are little-known either in the United States or abroad.

But to say that a project is an exciting challenge also implies that there are certain costs and pitfalls involved. The costs of the first stage of construction were estimated to be $919 million, including $512 million in foreign exchange. It was anticipated that the completed 4-million ton plant would cost a total of $1.5 billion, including $891 million in foreign exchange. The question of aid for a project more costly than the Aswan Dam came at a time when the whole American foreign-aid program was under sharp attack in the U.S. Congress. Not only was the Bokaro plant to cost about double the capital expenditure per ton of the three other foreign-built plants in India, but there were doubts as to the existence of sufficient demand for that much steel and the availability of adequate raw materials. There was also a demand by the American advisors that the project be built on a "turn-key" basis, i.e., that the Americans construct and operate the plant for a ten-year period at full capacity before turning it over to India. This was to avoid a repetition of the Rourkela experience. While most Indians agreed that some sort of stewardship might be wise, they were unable to understand the need for such a lengthy period of time.

Equally if not more important were the political implications. India's neutralism and open criticism of the United States had caused deep wounds. What was said was bad enough, but the way it was said, by India's acid-tongued Ambassador to the United Nations, Krishna Menon, made it even worse. He alone did more to embitter American-Indian relations than anything short of a direct Indian-Russian alliance. As in the case of Aswan, there was doubt if the American public could tolerate open criticism over the period of time needed for the disbursal of the large sum required at Bokaro. Perhaps if the first Chinese invasion of India had occurred one or two years earlier, and if Menon had been removed from public office sooner, the Americans might have been more receptive. There was also a reluctance to use American money to build up state-owned industry at the expense of the private steel industry. The Indians later agreed that they would if necessary set up a semiprivate corporation in Bokaro, but the proposal came too late. Despite the pleas of Ambassador J. K. Galbraith and President Kennedy, an American steel mission recommended that the project not be supported. Rather than force an awkward vote on the issue in the American Congress, India decided to avoid any more embarrassment and withdrew its request for aid.

Fortunately, the Indians did not respond as emotionally as the Egyptians had. There was resentment and bitterness on both sides, but there was no seizure of property and no violence. Instead, the Indians discreetly looked for an alternative source of aid. The English, Japanese, and Germans all showed some interest. Finally, at the beginning of 1964, the Indians approached the Russians. Again it was the Russians who seized the initiative.

The Russian decision on April 30 was largely unexpected. They had already proven their technical competence at Bhilai. (This was before the fourth blast furnace had broken down, so there was no question of trying to compensate for any shortcomings.) Indeed, many Indians asked why the Russians were not content to leave well enough alone. In any event, the Russians did pick up the offer. However, the Indians had to agree that Bokaro would be designed and built on a "turn-key" basis after all, and by a Soviet firm without American technology.

Nevertheless, the Russian offer had some attractive aspects. The first advantage, just as at Aswan, was that the Russians prepared a set of revised plans that called for a smaller expenditure of foreign exchange. Under the revised plans, the Russians agreed to lend India $211 million for the first stage of construction. This was considerably less than the $512 million in foreign exchange the Americans were expected to lend under the original plan. But the Russians proposed to spend less foreign currency by relying more on India's own resources. The source of supply in this case was to be the Heavy Engineering Corporation Ltd. at Ranchi, a machine-tool project sponsored and financed by Russia and Czechoslovakia.

The use of the Ranchi plants to outfit Bokaro was a clever idea. If the equipment proved to be of good quality, the Russians would be able to complete the erection of two industrial monuments with a single effort. Not only would Bokaro be built with a minimum expenditure of foreign funds, but it would finally provide an outlet for the facilities of Ranchi.

Since December, 1957, the Russians had been involved in the planning and construction of a heavy-machine-building project at Ranchi. Included in this project were the coal-mining machinery plant at Durgapur and two Czech-sponsored units, the foundry forge works and the heavy machine-tool works at Ranchi. The whole complex necessitated a $7.6 million loan from the Soviet Union, $10.5 million from Czechoslovakia, and $23 million from the Indians themselves. Another $8.4 million was put in by the Indians for the construction of the surrounding township and other facilities. Despite the promises of large sums of money and the erection of a fairly effective heavy-machinery industry, there had been no demand for Ranchi's equipment. Other developing countries were unwilling to entrust their equipment needs to a country that was equally underdeveloped. Within India, the demand for heavy equipment had been fairly limited. Even when it was decided to expand the existing steel mills, the foreign sponsor almost always insisted that it be allowed to purchase the necessary equipment from the parent country. It was suggested to the British engineers at Durgapur that they purchase their new blast-furnace equipment at Ranchi. The British replied that this would be done if the Indians insisted, but then there would be no foreign-exchange loan for the other equipment needs which could not be supplied domestically. The Indians decided it would be better to forget Ranchi for the time.

Such reactions seemed to validate some of the earlier criticisms of the Ranchi operation by Indian engineers. They had argued that there was insufficient demand for such products and that the factory would be too large and too costly for India. It seemed unlikely that full use could be made of Ranchi's ability to outfit a complete 1-million-ton steel mill once a year. The Russians eventually complained about the underutilization of Ranchi's facilities, which they pointed out kept the complex from being profitable.[8] In turn the Indians complained that Ranchi's problems were not helped by the Soviet practice of insisting that excessive supplies of refractory equipment and other parts were needed at the plant. This only increased the bill which India would have to pay.[9]

The prospect of being able to supply Bokaro gave the Russians a chance to rescue an impressive but faltering machine-tool complex. At the same time, the Russians were able to embarrass the United States by picking up the pieces of the latest American foreign-aid debacle.

Oil

The second-largest area of Soviet economic activity in India is in the area of petroleum-drilling and refining. Here, too, the Russians have been successful in their over-all performance, although the results have not been as spectacular as in the field of metallurgy or heavy machinery. In terms of competitive effectiveness against the West, Soviet penetration of the Indian oil market is as significant for what it shows about Soviet ingenuity as it is for demonstrating the intransigence, if not greed, of the Western oil companies. Soviet action and Western counteraction follow a pattern that has been duplicated in numerous other areas of the world, including Pakistan, Ceylon, Indonesia, and Cuba.

Until the Russians "interfered," a closely coordinated cartel of three Western firms determined oil prices and products in India. The companies involved were Standard Vacuum Oil Company (Stanvac), California Texas Oil Corporation (Caltex), both of the United States, and Burmah Shell of Great Britain. Stanvac is owned by Standard Oil of New Jersey and Mobil Oil, and Caltex represents the interests of Texaco and the Standard Oil Company of California. The three Western firms purchased crude oil from their parent companies' wells in the Middle East, shipped it (often in their own tankers) to India, processed it in their three refineries, and sold it through private distribution facilities. This complete control effectively reduced competitive threats from either outside or inside organizations, since the members of the cartel refused to process any foreign products in their refineries or to distribute them through their gasoline stations. Various combinations of American, English, and Dutch oil companies have exercised such control in most regions of the world. It was partially because of one of their boycotts that the 1951 nationalization of the oil companies by Mossadegh in Iran failed. While the service provided by the Western firms has usually been of very high quality, their prices always ensured a comfortable margin that often returned annually about 30–50 per cent on the capital invested. More important, however, the Western firms required that all oil purchases be made in convertible currency. Since Western efforts to find oil in many of the poorer countries frequently were futile, there was generally no alternative but to import oil. Depending on the size of the country, such purchases could total more than $200 million annually as they do in India. This was regarded as an onerous expenditure by the developing countries, which found themselves with chronic deficits in their balance of payments and no place else to turn for oil supplies. Because a boycott by the oil cartel and its Western supporters meant virtual disruption of industrial activity, it was practically impossible to overcome such a stranglehold.

If the monopoly profit seemed so secure to the Western oil companies, it also seemed especially attractive to outsiders. Thus various groups decided to risk a competitive struggle even if it meant having to create a completely integrated operation. The most successful challenger was ENI (Ente Nazionale Idrocarburi) of Italy, headed by Enrico Mattei. Painstakingly, Mattei built up his own network of refineries and gas stations throughout the world. With the resources of the Italian government behind him, he also sought his own supply of crude oil. However, he was less successful at oil prospecting than he had anticipated, and he was compelled to turn to the Soviet Union for his oil. Through shrewd bargaining, he often was able to obtain bartered oil from the U.S.S.R. at the exceptionally low price of $1.00 to $1.10 a barrel. This was $.75-.90 cheaper than the posted price for Western-owned oil at Kuwait. The Japanese have also tried to create a similar network.

As long as the Italians and Japanese were the only competitors, the Western oil companies were not too worried. Though they added an element of uncertainty and pressure, both the Japanese and the Italians tended to follow the rules of the game which called for the avoidance of nationalistic rabble-rousing and international muckraking. However, for anyone not willing to adhere to such a code, there were political as well as financial profits to be gained by challenging the powerful oil cartel. These gains could not only embarrass and harm the oil companies, but they would also affect the foreign relations of the governments of the United States and England. These possibilities were not long hidden from the Russians.

In 1960, the Russians offered to supply crude oil to India at $.25 a barrel below the posted industry price. Moreover, the Russians declared their willingness to accept payment in rupees. This appealed to the Indian government and appalled the Western oil companies, which announced that they would refuse to use their facilities to process and distribute Soviet oil. The Russians stood to gain no matter what happened. Ultimately the Western companies were forced to lower their prices by about $.27 a barrel, $.02 less than the Russian bid. This meant a revenue loss to the firms, and a gain to India, of $18–31 million a year.[10] At the same time, India accepted the Soviet offer of crude oil. To process it and break the Western stranglehold, the Indians decided to build their own refinery facilities, the Indian Refineries Ltd., and to set up their own distribution network, the Indian Oil Company. Naturally enough, the Indians turned to the Russians and to the Rumanians for help.

Fortunately, the West seems to have emerged with fewer scars in India than it did in Ceylon and Cuba, where similar tactics by the Russians evoked a more irrational reaction by the oil companies. The counterresponse by Ceylon and Cuba was nationalization of the refineries and distribution systems, and an increased anti-Americanism. It is hard to say how much better relations would have been if the Western oil companies had adopted a more cooperative attitude. It seems fair to conclude, however, that the uninhibited self-interest of these companies seriously damaged the best interests of the United States. After a series of such incidents in several countries, the oil cartel apparently has realized that such policies do not always bring the desired results. Reluctantly, it now markets Soviet oil in Western-owned facilities in Ghana and Guinea. Undoubtedly this action has prevented a more serious reaction in these countries.[11]

The Russians are equally eager to join in the search for domestic oil. Such offers usually follow after a long period of relatively or completely fruitless exploration by Western firms. Then, with embarrassing frequency, the Russians announce the discovery of oil or natural gas basins. In most cases this comes after Western geologists have declared the same areas to be barren. (Once or twice the Russians reportedly were able to obtain the original geological surveys prepared by the Western firms. This allowed them to focus their attention on the most promising areas.) The Russians have been able to claim that they succeeded where the British and the Americans have failed in British Guiana, Pakistan, and India.[12] Furthermore, they often charge that the Western firms did actually discover oil deposits, but kept their finds secret so that they could continue to utilize their existing supplies from the Middle East. Whether or not such charges are true, they do discredit the West, particularly after the Russians do, in fact, find oil. Even if most of the deposits are relatively small in comparison to the Middle East basins, such finds make it possible for India or Pakistan to reduce its expenditure of foreign exchange. In the case of India, the Russian discoveries at Cambay in 1958, and at Ankleshwar, Kaloe, and Rudrasagar in 1960 have provided a potential of 6 million tons of oil a year. By 1966, the eight oil fields in these areas were supplying approximately one-third of India's needs.

Happily for the West, the Russian and Rumanian success in the petroleum field has not been complete. There has been some criticism of their efforts in building refineries. The complaints may have been tempered by the knowledge that the Communist-aided refineries enabled the Indians to break the Western monopoly. Nevertheless, there is a feeling that the Russians and Rumanians did less than their best in pricing and building the refineries.

India first turned to Rumania for help in building a refinery. The Rumanians began construction work at Gauhati in 1959, and operation of a refinery there started in the fall of 1962. The initial cost of the plant was $30 million plus $3.5 million for construction of the township. The foreign-exchange requirements totaled $12.7 million, of which Rumania agreed to provide $11 million with a seven-year credit at an interest rate of 2½ per cent. After several problems, including silt in the water-pumping station that caused a year-and-a-half delay, the refinery finally reached its scheduled production capacity in November, 1963. Subsequently, the Indians asked the Rumanians to expand the capacity of the plant from .75 million tons a year to 1.25 million tons.[13]

In 1961, the Russians agreed to build a refinery in India at Barauni. It was to have a capacity of 2 million tons of oil a year and cost $79 million plus $7 million for the township. The foreign-exchange component totaled $37 million, of which the U.S.S.R. promised initially to provide $25 million. Later this was increased to $47 million. It was subsequently decided to expand the plant's capacity to 3 million tons. The Russians also agreed to build another oil refinery at Koyali in Gujarat with a loan of $21 million. Here, too, plant capacity initially was to be 2 million tons and has been enlarged to 3 million tons.

Work at Barauni also did not always move smoothly. Originally it was anticipated that the refinery would be completed in July, 1962. After half a dozen postponements, the plant was finally opened in July, 1964. Apparently there were similar delays at Koyali. One problem was the need to adapt Soviet and Rumanian equipment to the specifications of Indian oil. But more important was the question of cost. There was considerable evidence to indicate that the Indians had paid an exorbitant price for Russian help. By the time the Indians decided to build their third refinery at Koyali, the Western companies realized the seriousness of the situation and began to make counteroffers. In addition, once the cartel had been broken, other Western firms decided to enter the field. Consequently, Phillips Petroleum Company of Bartlesville, Oklahoma, won the right to build the fourth refinery for the Indian government at Cochin in Madras. Their plan called for an initial capacity of 2.5 million tons. This provoked bids from ENI and other Western firms. Thus, for the first time, India was permitted the luxury of competitive bids. This also made it possible to compare Russian costs with those from the Western companies.

As the Russian Counselor for Economic Affairs in New Delhi, N. M. Silouyanov, explained, it is difficult to compare the costs of refineries because each refinery has different raw materials, transportation, and technological requirements. For instance, the Barauni refinery had a lubricating-oil plant which the other refineries did not have and a poor location which increased the transportation requirements. He also argued that Barauni had a kerosene unit and an electric power plant that made the Soviet-built plant more complete but more costly. Indian critics, however, have pointed out that the cost of the electric power plant would involve an expenditure of no more than about $4 million and that the Cochin plant also had a kerosene unit. Moreover, a poorly located plant is to some extent the responsibility of the builder. In any case, similar dissimilarities did not prevent the Russians from making cost comparisons among the various steel mills that were built in India.

According to official estimates presented in the Indian Parliament, the construction costs and planned capacities of the various refineries were as follows: [14]

Location	Contractor	Planned Capacity (in millions of tons)	Costs (in millions of dollars)
Gauhati	Rumania	.75	32
Barauni	Soviet Union	2.00	76
Koyali	Soviet Union	2.00	60
Cochin	Phillips (U.S.)	2.50	34
Madras and Haldia	various Western firms	2.50	21–25

It will be noted that these figures differ somewhat from those presented earlier in this section. Thus the cost figure for Gauhati is $2 million more, and for Barauni it is $4 million less, than indicated by the other sources. This may be because the Parliamentary figure is a more recent estimate. In any case, the first Russian plant at Barauni cost $16 million (excluding township costs) more than the second at Koyali. Comparison with the Phillips complex at Cochin is even more striking. There, for a capacity higher than that supplied at the Russian plants, the Americans have provided a facility at one-half the price, a saving of $26–34 million. Reportedly, the price of the Phillips plant and the bids of other Western firms were made low in exchange for concessions from India on the price that could be paid the suppliers of crude oil.[15]

The Western plants also were all to be located on the coast, which generally results in cheaper construction costs. Whatever the justification, the gap in costs is sharp enough to be embarrassing.

As a result of a growing number of such disparities, some officials in the Indian government have become disturbed by what they regard as a new trend in Soviet pricing policies. Initially, they had nothing but praise for the competitiveness of Soviet foreign aid projects. Now, they have discovered that where there is no competition, the Russians, like the Western firms before them, are capable of pricing their projects at levels that assure them an excessive return. The reduced charge for the second refinery at Koyali shows the effect of outside competition. Soviet pricing practices in this instance are likened by Indian engineers to their experience with such firms as the Chemical Construction Company of the United States. Because its system was unique, and because the Indians had no one else to turn to, the Chemical Construction Company at first quoted a price of $19 million to build a fertilizer plant at Trombay. Subsequently, the Indians found that the same firm had constructed a similar plant in Florida for $4–5 million. The price of the Indian plant was lowered to $9 million, still double the price of the Florida plant.[16] The Indians complained that this was more than enough to compensate the American firm for the hazards involved in building in India. They asserted that this was the same monopolistic policy used by the Russians.

Other Projects

The other Soviet-aided projects in India do not warrant the depth of analysis devoted to the steel mills and refineries, but they are worth listing. (The Soviet Union's aid to India has been provided under agreements shown in Table IV-1.)

Soviet aid has been extended to almost every sector of heavy industry in India. Equipment has even been provided for agricultural work, and through a gift of $1.6 million, the Russians have supplied material and equipment for a 13,500-hectare state farm in Suratgarh in Rajasthan. They have also donated $856,000-worth of equipment to the Indian Institute of Technology at Bombay. The Indians fully expect such aid to continue in the future. Although no final figure was announced, the Indians anticipate that the Russians will supply them with up to $800-million worth of economic aid for India's Fourth Five-Year Plan. It is unclear whether this includes the $211 million for Bokaro. (See Table IV-1.)

On the whole, the implementation of Soviet economic aid has been relatively successful. As has already been indicated, however, the Russians have also had their share of problems. This is to be expected considering the scale of Soviet activity. In addition to the difficulties encountered in the metallurgical and petroleum industries, the Indians have also criticized the Soviet delay in commissioning the first generator at the Neyveli power station. The Indians complained that the Russians had not delivered the necessary equipment on schedule. When the machinery finally arrived, the Indians found that the Russians had not provided the proper materials-handling equipment so that there was considerable difficulty in unloading the supplies.[17] The initial Soviet design for the Korba coal-washery plant was sent back for reworking because the Indians felt the Soviet plan was not as economical as it might be.[18] Similarly, the Soviet proposal for a glass factory had to be altered by the Indians, who charged that the Russians had not made enough use of India's own resources. The Russians have also been criticized for insisting that all imports must come from the U.S.S.R. and be designated for specific projects. An official government report contrasted Soviet practice in this respect with Western aid, which always consists of some nonproject and untied aid. The Indians found this rule to be particularly cumbersome at one of the Ranchi projects. Western equipment was needed to complete the plant, and bothersome delays ensued before the necessary funds were obtained. This was not an infrequent experience.[19]

The most intriguing criticism of Soviet aid to India comes not from the Indians, but from the Chinese, who in late 1963 complained:

> As for their aid to India, here Soviet ulterior motives are especially clear. India tops the list of newly independent countries to which the Soviet Union gives economic aid. This aid is obviously intended to encourage the Nehru government in its policies directed against Communism, against the people, and against socialist countries. Even the American imperialists have stated that such Soviet aid "is very much to our [U.S.] interest."[20]

Though the Chinese were criticizing only economic aid, undoubtedly they were also disturbed about Soviet military aid.

Military Aid .

Because of India's relatively liberal press policy, it is possible to obtain a little more information than usual about the type of military aid the Russians have provided. While the scope of Soviet military aid to India is considerably more modest than it is in such nations as the U.A.R. and Indonesia, there are several unique features, most of which seem calculated to arouse the Chinese. The most interesting aspect is that the Russians did not withdraw any material or promises of military

Table IV-1

SOVIET AID TO INDIA
(in Millions of Dollars)

Agreement	Purpose	Total Offer	Allocated	Amount Drawn as of December 31, 1963
February, 1955	Bhilai steel mill	136	136	136
November, 1957	Multipurpose	125		
	Ranchi heavy machinery plant		33.4	26.6
	Coal-mining machinery plant		20.8	16.2
	Opthalmic glass factory		2.5	.3
	Korba coal-mining projects		10.3	2.41
	Neyveli lignite thermal power station		29.3	28.9
Total			96.3	74.46
May, 1959	Drug projects	20	19.4	11.2
September, 1959	Multipurpose	375		
	Expansion of Bhilai		117	35.2
	Expansion of Neyveli plant		1.2	.5
	Singrauli power station		1.2	.3
	Expansion of Ranchi plant		12.4	.2
	Kotah precision-instruments projects		.3	.1
	Expansion of coal-mining machinery plant		4.7	.1
	Expansion of Korba thermal power station		29.4	7.4
	Barauni oil refinery		7.3	7.3
	Heavy electrical plant		1.8	1.5
	Exploration for oil and gas		59.8	46
Total			235.1	98.6

Sources: See page 251.

[a]As of October, 1963.

Agreement	Purpose	Total Offer	Allocated	Amount Drawn as of December 31, 1963
September, 1959	Barauni oil refinery	25	25	23.5
February, 1961	Multipurpose	125		
	Bhakra right bank hydro-electric station		12.2	.4
	Oil refinery in Gujarat		16.3	3.2
	Coal washery in Kathara		47.9	.4
	Refractories plant		.1	
	Gas and oil exploration		8.3	
	Production of pumps and compressors, feasibility study		.04	.04
Total			84.84	4.04
Grand Total		806	596.64	347-50

Additional projects agreed to for financing under the savings in the credits

	Kerala precision-instruments projects		.05	
	Expansion of Barauni and Koyali refineries		.01	
	Pumps and compressor plant			
	Steel foundry for railways			
Total			.1	

Future projects anticipated in the Fourth Five-Year Plan: new oil refinery; expansion of coking coal mines; development of new iron-ore mines and expansion of old ones; nitrogen fertilizer plant; aluminum smelter Bokaro; refractory plant; sea fisheries development   up to 800

Grants for mechanized farm at Suratgarh; equipment for Indian Institute of Technology at Bombay; 450 million doses of smallpox vaccine   2.4[a]

help during the 1962 and 1965 conflicts between India and China. If anything, during India's initial dispute with China the tempo of the military aid program was accelerated. Also unusual is the Soviet commitment to build an airplane factory in India. Normally military aid
involves only the sale of armaments, but in India, the Russians have
indicated a willingness to supply not only the finished product, but
facilities for producing such items domestically.

Because of India's close relationship with Great Britain, the Western
powers were surprised when the Indians announced in late 1961 and
early 1962 that it had turned to the U.S.S.R. for military aid. The Indians sought Soviet aid for several reasons. The main factor was that
V. K. Krishna Menon was anxious to strengthen ties with the U.S.S.R.
to end India's complete reliance on the West for military aid. India was
in serious need of helicopters and transport planes to service its mountainous border, especially the Chinese sector. Soviet equipment of this
type was of good quality, and, more important, the Russians were willing to accept payment in rupees or in Indian commodities, which not
all the Western countries were willing to do.

India's first purchase from the U.S.S.R. consisted of ten MI-4 helicopters, twenty-four twin-engine Ilyushin, fourteen piston-driven transport planes, and at least eight AN-12's, a turboprop plane with four
engines and a capacity of 26,500 pounds. In January, 1962, India
ordered another sixteen helicopters and eight more turboprop trans-
ports. It also bought six MIG-19 Soviet jet engines for testing, which it
later hoped to install in its HE-24 jet fighters. When the United
States protested the acceptance of Soviet military aid by India and
threatened to curb American economic aid, the Indians reacted vigor-
ously. They announced that they would accept a Soviet offer to establish a factory to manufacture MIG-21 jet fighters in India. However, to
calm American protests, it was pointed out that the proposed jets
would be used to defend India from China. Moreover, the Indians
announced that the Soviets had agreed to let them manufacture the jet
planes in India, a privilege not extended the Chinese. Presumably this
pleased the Americans more than it did the Chinese.

To produce the MIGs, the Indians formed a state-owned company
called Aeronautics India, Ltd. Two factories were to be set up, one for
the production of MIG jet engines at Koraput in Orissa, and another
to produce the aircraft frames at Nasek near Bombay. However, some
unforeseen problems soon developed. As a test sample, the Russians
had sent the Indians some MIG-21 jets. During a training shakedown
flight in December, 1963, two of the jets crashed and the Indians decided that modifications were needed "to suit Indian conditions." [21]

In May, 1964, the Indians released information which showed that Soviet military aid obtained after the Chinese invasion amounted to about $130 million. In September, they received a new pledge of $140 million. This meant that Soviet military aid was comparable in size, if not greater than, American military aid. In addition to a supplemental shipment of forty-four MIG-21s, the Russians also agreed to supply upwards of fifty surface-to-air missiles, more AN-12s and MI-4 helicopters, about seventy light tanks, six submarines, and an assortment of various infantry weapons.[22] To finance this, the Russians provided a ten-year loan at 2 per cent.

The unfavorable Chinese reaction to military aid to India was anticipated by the Russians, who seem to have accepted the bitter words of the Chinese with a minimum of anguish. Less expected, however, was the displeasure of the Pakistanis. Pakistan's concern became especially evident after the start of hostilities in 1965 over Kashmir. The fact that two Pakistani aircraft (U.S. Jetstar fighters) were shot down by MIG aircraft of the Indian air force meant that Russia found itself, with the United States, in the middle of the dispute. Because the Soviet Union is trying to woo both India and Pakistan, aid to one (especially military aid) is bitterly resented by the other. The same applies to any aid given by the Russians to Ethiopia and Somalia, Algeria and Tunisia, or Cyprus and Turkey. For years this was uniquely an American predicament which the Russians did their best to exploit. As Soviet aid increased in scope, they too found themselves caught between jealous neighbors. At stake is a Soviet investment of close to $1 billion in materials and goodwill in India and $30 million in Pakistan. Under the circumstances, the government of the Soviet Union has become as concerned about preserving peace and quiet in the area as the governments of the United States and Western Europe. This is one of the phenomena the Chinese have in mind when they say that the "Soviet Union is sorely afraid of the revolutionary storm" in Asia, Latin America, and Africa.[23]

The Chinese aid program is still too limited in scope for them to be caught in such a tangle. As their program expands, however, and as they take on vested interests in various governments, it is logical to expect that the Chinese will eventually find themselves caught in similar crossfire.

Satellite Aid

Although some of the aid being provided by Czechoslovakia and Rumania to India has already been discussed, it is worth surveying satellite aid to India in more detail. The initial Czech credit was signed in November, 1959, for $48.5 million, repayable in rupees in eight years at 2½ per cent. There was also a "commercial" credit of about $35 million provided by the Czech export company, Technoexport. Of the government loan, $12 million was assigned for the first stage of construction of the foundry forge and $6 million for the machine-tools building, both at Ranchi. The Czechs also agreed to support the heavy-boiler project at Tiruverumbur with $6 million and the heavy power equipment plant at Ramachandrapuram near Hyderabad with $7.2 million. This meant that the Czechs would pay for one-third of the foreign-exchange costs of the boiler plant and one-fifth of the foreign exchange at the power equipment plant. In addition, the Institute for Machine Tool Technology and Design at Bangalore was to be paid for with a gift from Czechoslovakia, which included $840,000 for equipment and $420,000 for the living expenses of technical personnel.

A second Czech loan was signed on May 11, 1964, for $84 million. Part of this credit is to be repaid in eight years and part in twelve. This loan permits a doubling of the capacity of the boiler factory as well as the further expansion of the heavy power equipment plant. In addition, the Czechs also plan to build two machine-tool plants, a foundry, a forge plant, a thermal electric station, and a factory for the production of small tractors and power tillers.

The only other Communist country that has provided aid in any significant amount is Poland. The Poles have supplied two credits, the first on May 7, 1960, for $30 million, and the second on November 16, 1962, for $32.5 million.[24]

The Hungarians and the East Germans have also offered to provide India with foreign aid. The Hungarian offer was made in 1961, but apparently it was not accepted. East Germany offered the equivalent of $40.4 million, but the Indians rejected the offer out of fear of offending West Germany, which provides about $100 million a year. Nevertheless, East Germany has been helping India prospect for brown coal.

One Soviet source reports that at one time the Chinese were planning to aid India. Apparently China offered to help India expand its railroad network, but that offer, made in the Bandung days of 1955, was not taken up.[25]

Foreign Trade

The economic influence of the Soviet bloc is not limited purely to government loans. In some cases, it is hard to distinguish between a government loan and what would in the West pass for a commercial loan. Thus, in many ways, foreign trade has been as important as foreign aid in the Communist bloc's economic relations with India. As in

Latin America and Ghana, Communist trade has turned out to be a very effective form of economic penetration.

The promise and potential of the Soviet Union as a trading partner whets the appetite of most developing countries. As increasing supply and relatively inelastic demand forces a decline in commodity prices in non-Communist world markets, the attraction of opening new markets in Eastern Europe increases. With a population of over 230 million, the Soviet Union alone could easily absorb whatever commodities a country produces. Moreover, the U.S.S.R. not only has the people, but has a "planned economy," which, it is claimed, makes it possible to project consumption needs in advance. This supposedly assures stable prices and demand. Moreover, the Soviet Union has taken the unprecedented step of unilaterally abolishing all tariffs on goods imported from the developing countries. Accordingly, a trade contract with the Soviet Union often looks like a ready-made solution to a ubiquitous economic problem.

Unfortunately, appearances are deceptive. The abolition of tariffs is meaningless if the government is both the customs collector and the sole importer. Once the retail price for the Soviet consumer is set, the total revenue accruing to the state is the same with or without a tariff. The only difference a tariff makes is that the customs office is credited with some income instead of the total sales value going to the Ministry of Trade. More important, nothing is purchased unless the Ministry of Trade or its agent decides that the goods are necessary. Changes in bookkeeping arrangements affecting internal prices will have little effect on that decision. The promise of a guaranteed price and a stable market for primary products is equally meaningless. Egon Neuberger of the RAND Corporation has shown that prices paid and quantities purchased by the Soviet Union are at best equal to, but generally less stable than, prices and quantities purchased by Western Europe and the United States.[26] While there has been a rapid increase in the over-all volume of trade with the developing countries, this has been offset by more than normal fluctuations in the purchase of a given commodity from particular countries.

Whatever the hazards, India now finds itself the Soviet Union's largest non-Communist trading partner.[27] In 1964, over 13 per cent of India's exports were consigned to members of the East European bloc and some officials estimate the figure could soon reach 25 per cent. The general growth according to Soviet trade sources is shown in Table IV-2. Indian trade figures, at least until 1962, frequently show India, with a favorable balance of trade (column 6 minus column 2). This is a problem common to many of the developing countries and arises be-

Table IV-2

SOVIET TRADE AND AID DRAWDOWNS WITH INDIA
(in Millions of Dollars)

	Russian Exports to India (Russian Figures)	Indian Imports from U.S.S.R. (Indian Figures)	Item 16 Aid Draw-downs (Russian Figures)	Aid Utiliza-tion (Indian Figures)	Russian Imports from India (Russian Figures)	Indian Exports to U.S.S.R. (Indian Figures)
1953	.5				.4	
1954	1.1				3.7	
1955	7.3		.08		4.4	
1956	40	31	5.8		18	26
1957	85	48	43	24	42	37
1958	130	47	98	79	51	49
1959	68	35	34	30	60	64
1960	47	28	18	16	68	63
1961	95	48	40	26	67	69
1962	125	123	65	83	72	75
1963	222	108	81	89	95	103
Total	820.9	468	384.88	347	481.5	486
1964	235	14.5	133	n.a.	156	158
Grand Total	1,055.9	482.5	517.88	347	637.5	644

Sources: See page 251.

cause of Soviet inefficiency in handling the documentation which accompanies their foreign aid shipments. Soviet paper work is almost always slow in arriving. Rather than hold up the materials at the port, most customs authorities in such countries have arranged for the goods to clear the port ahead of the required papers. In India, this is called the "note pass system." [28] Within three months, the Russians are supposed to forward the necessary documentation, but generally it takes considerably longer. The result is that there is more than the normal discrepancy in foreign trade statistics between Soviet export figures and the developing country's import figures (compare columns 1 and 2). Under the circumstances, the Russian statistics are more up to date. Although the gross total makes no distinction between commercial and aid shipments, it is possible to obtain a rough approximation of the yearly expenditures financed by foreign aid by extracting Item 16 from the Soviet statistical handbook on foreign trade. (See Appendix 1.) As indicated in Chapter 2, this item, "Equipment and Materials for Complete Plants," includes expenditures not only for the equipment, but also for technical services. In view of the differences in valuation and time of shipping, the Russian figure of $385 million as of 1963 (Table IV-2, column 3) compares favorably with the Indian figure of $347–50 million of drawdowns (Table IV-1 and Table IV-2, column 4).

Whatever the reservations, an increase in trade with another country is generally a good thing. Clearly there have been benefits for India in its trade with the U.S.S.R. The Soviet Union alone is taking more than $100-million worth of goods off India's markets. As much as one-half of India's imports from the U.S.S.R. are in the form of foreign-aid shipments, but the Russians are now also building plants for private businessmen on the basis of commercial loans. According to the Russian Economic Counselor in New Delhi, Russia is building or about to build an assembly plant for tractors, watches, and electrical power equipment that will be financed outside of the regular stream of governmental foreign aid.

Indian exports to Russia are being used to repay Russian foreign aid. This, too, has its positive and negative aspects. To the extent that prices are rising in India, India is paying less for its aid than intended. On the other hand, repayment of American aid may be made in rupees which are spent only within India. Nothing is purchased for shipment outside of India. Therefore American aid, unlike Russian aid, does not absorb resources that could otherwise be exported and in turn generate hard currency. Furthermore, repayment of Soviet or bloc foreign aid in the form of delayed barter sometimes has secondary effects beyond the immediate one of reducing the commodities that would otherwise be available for commercial export. First, the Russians take not only India's traditional exports, but its newly produced items as well. This includes such items as footwear, household goods, sewing machines, fans, electric appliances, oil engines, rolled ferrous stock, razor blades, and air conditioners.[29] This is a point of pride with both countries: the Indians say this demonstrates their industrial ability and the Russians claim that their purchases testify to the respect they have for India. However, the Indians have begun to realize that there are important shortcomings to such trading activity. The Russians naturally try to purchase those goods for rupees that they cannot obtain elsewhere. But many of the goods just listed contain a high percentage of imported raw materials and components which India can only obtain with foreign currency. This means that, in fact, Russia *is* being repaid in foreign exchange.

The second criticism of commodity repayment is that the Russians frequently resell the bartered merchandise for hard currency at a reduced price. By doing this, the Russians, not the Indians, obtain the hard currency, and the Indians face a reduced world price for the commodities that remain. Burma has had similar problems with its rice, as have Egypt with cotton and Cuba with sugar. In the case of India, the crop most affected is cashew nuts. Although there is little evidence of domestic consumption within the U.S.S.R., the Soviet Union by 1964 had become India's second largest purchaser of cashew nuts, following only the United States. According to official Indian statistics, from April 1, 1963, to March 31, 1964, India exported 28.4 million kilograms of cashew nuts to the United States, 7.8 million kilograms to the Soviet Union, and 3.5 million kilograms to East Germany. The fourth largest importer was the United Kingdom, which purchased 2.6 million kilograms. By April, 1964, East German purchases were about equal to those of the Soviet Union. The Russians made their first purchases in 1960–61, when they helped to stabilize market prices.[30] However, there have been many Indian complaints that subsequent purchases have all too often ended up in American warehouses.[31]

The resale of cashew nuts is conducted as follows: the nuts are placed on board a ship destined for Eastern Europe via Port Said or other intermediate ports. Midway in transit, the goods are rerouted to Rotterdam or sent directly to New York, where they are sold at a 5 per cent discount below the world price. The American importer then opens a credit in dollars for the East European country, which in turn opens a non-dollar letter of credit in favor of the Indian shipper. Naturally, India has strongly protested such practices, which are a violation of its trade agreements with the East European countries. According to Indian customs officials, the Rumanians, at least, have agreed to split any commission they make on such re-exports with the Indians. This is better than nothing, but it hardly solves India's balance-of-payments problem.

Obviously, the more India sells to the Soviet Union, the less it has available to sell to the West. Ultimately, this will precipitate a foreign-exchange crisis, as it did in 1964–65. As happened in Ghana and the U.A.R., the more serious the shortage, the more the affected country is forced to rely on the U.S.S.R. and its satellites for trade and assistance. At the same time, debt repayments have to be made, sometimes in convertible currency, and the crisis becomes even more serious.

Debt Repayment

Debt repayment itself constitutes a serious matter. As of March 31, 1965, India owed the Soviet Union almost $500 million.[32] Based on the loans extended as of December, 1963, India is faced with a critical monetary repayment schedule until at least 1970. (See Table IV-3.) Repayments to the Soviet Union are due to reach a peak in 1967, when they will amount to $57 million. However, actual repayments will be even higher when the loans extended after 1963 are included. Only the repayments to the United States are due to diminish in the near future. This is because a growing proportion of American aid will be in the form of Development Loan Fund loans, which do not require repayments.

Faced with such a repayment schedule, the Indians have complained that the Russian terms of repayment are not as liberal as they appear.[33] The Indians would naturally like more than a twelve-year period in which to repay. Nevertheless, in some cases the Indians have actually been repaying in advance. Thus they prepaid $11 million in 1963–64 on Bhilai.[34] This was ostensibly to enable the Soviet authorities to finance the purchase of Indian goods, although all reports indicated that the Russians already had too many rupees at their disposal.

A more complete breakdown of Soviet loan utilization and repayments is presented in Table IV-4. All loans are for twelve years at 2½ per cent except for the loan for the drug factory, which is for seven years. Interest accumulates from the day the credit is used and payments must be made by March 15 of the following year. Principal repayments are due on March 15 of the year after the equipment or service has been utilized, or as the Indians say, the installments are "payable on the 15th of March of each year following the year in which

Table IV-3

SCHEDULE OF INDIAN DEBT REPAYMENTS
(in Millions of Dollars)

	To All Countries			U.S.A.		U.S.S.R.		Poland		Czechoslovakia	
	P	I	T	P	I	P	I	P	I	P	I
1963/64							6.2				
1964/65	126.5	121.4	247.9	29.4	18.2	18.1	10.4		.3		.2
1965/66	184.2	133.6	317.8	24	19.2	35.9	11.9		.5		.5
1966/67	220.3	134.4	354.7	29.4	18.6	46.7	10.9	3.3	.6	3.2	.6
1967/68	230.2	125	355.2	33.1	19.5	46.7	9.7	3.3	.7	3.2	.6
1968/69	243.4	115.8	359.2	35.5	19.9	44.5	8.4	3.4	.6	3.2	.5
1969/70	237.6	104.7	342.3	34.6	18.1	44.2	7.2	3.3	.5	3.2	.4
1970/71	230.7	94.3	325	34.1	16.5	37.2	6.1	3.3	.4	3.2	.3
1971/72	221.3	83.4	304.7	34.2	14.8	35.6	5.1	3.4	.3	3.2	.2
1972/73	210	74.1	284.1	44.1	13.2	35.5	4.2	3.4	.2	3.2	.1
1973/74	209.8	64.5	274.3	49.1	11.4	32.8	3.2	3.4	.1	3.2	
1974/75	192.4	55.8	248.2	45.4	10.2	32.8	2.4	3.3			
1975/76	179.2	46.6	225.8	44.2	9.2	28.9	1.6				

Sources: See page 251.

P = Principal

I = Interest

T = Total

Table IV-4

COMMUNIST BLOC LOANS TO INDIA AND REPAYMENT SCHEDULE
(in Millions of Dollars)

	Total Authorized	Loans Utilized			Revised Budget Plan 63/64	Budget Plan 64/65	Repayment			
		56/57-60/61	61/62	62/63			1956/57 to October, 1961	61/62	62/63	63/64
Soviet Union										
Bhilai	136	136					35	13	20	11
Industrial enterprises	125	17	28	20	13	19				2
Drug credit	20		.078	.163	11	6				
Barauni	25	.09	.147	16	7					
First credit for Third Plan	375	4	21	29	80	84				3
Second credit for Third Plan	125			.116	6	21				
Miscellaneous					57	41				13
Total	806	158	51	68	174	171	35	13	20	30
Poland										
First credit for Third Plan	30		.006	.120	5	11				
Second crop	33				.021	.105				
Total	63		.006	.120	5	12				
Czechoslovakia	49				2	8				
Rumania	11									

Sources: See page 252.

113

such credit is raised." Close to $80 million of the $136-million Bhilai loan had been repaid by early 1964.

Whatever else may be said about it, Soviet aid to India clearly has had an impact. The Russians are involved in virtually every important branch of heavy industry in India. Even though the United States has made a large commitment of resources, Russian aid on the whole has been of a more enduring nature. American grain shipments are consumed and forgotten. Russian steel mills and oil refineries, despite their imperfections, are of a lasting and monumental character. The United States passed up the one dramatic chance it had to construct an urgently needed steel mill at Bokaro. This would have provided an impact that matched or exceeded any of the Russian projects. Unfortunately, because of so much opposition in the United States, an opportunity was lost. At the same time, for some reason, impressive American projects such as the Sharavathi Dam receive little publicity. Thus, despite numerous shortcomings and a smaller expenditure of money, Soviet projects in India have succeeded better than those of any other country in capturing the admiration and appreciation of the Indians.

5. Afghanistan: Some Lessons for American Aid Policy

It was in Afghanistan that the Soviet foreign-aid program began. Russian foreign aid to Afghanistan dates back to 1927, when the Russians provided a radio telegraph and a cotton gin to their southern neighbor. Other cotton gins were built for Afghanistan in 1938. Russia has also long been one of Afghanistan's major trading partners.[1] It was not surprising, therefore, that Afghanistan became the first beneficiary of the new Soviet program which began after Stalin's death. The first postwar projects undertaken by the Russians in a non-Communist country were the grain elevator and flour mill in Kabul and the grain elevator in Pul-i-Khumri, which the Russians hesitantly but proudly announced on January 27, 1954.[2] This first loan in what was to become a major foreign-aid program was for a modest $3.5 million at an interest rate of 3 per cent. It was to be repaid in eight years, beginning in 1957. This was followed on October 5, 1954, by a second loan for $2.1 million to finance the construction of an asphalt factory and the paving of Kabul's streets.[3] These loans, which came exactly six months after the truce in Korea, preceded by almost a year the Russian loan to India. However, the pattern of Soviet aid had been set; from the beginning, the Soviet Union sought to emphasize impact projects that would not only further the recipient's drive toward industrialization, but would also attract the maximum publicity for the Soviet Union.

Through the cooperation of Afghan officials, a complete schedule of Soviet aid agreements has been made available.[4] The scale and scope of Russian aid to Afghanistan is impressive. (See Table V-1.) As of 1964, the Russians had promised upwards of $500 million in loans and grants, compared with $275 million provided by the United States.[5] This probably represents the highest aid per capita of any country that has obtained a Soviet loan. The Russians seem to have taken a special interest in showing that they can maintain exceptionally friendly relations with a small border state. They are determined to prove not only that they can live in peace, but also that they can encourage economic development without undue Soviet interference.

Table V-1

SOVIET LOANS TO AFGHANISTAN
(in Millions of Dollars)

Date	Amount	Utilized as of December, 1962	Utilized as of December, 1963	Unutilized
January, 1954	3.5	3.5	3.5	
October, 1954	2.1	2.1	2.1	
January, 1956	100	87.8	93.9	6.1
July, 1957	15	13.6	13.6	1.4
October, 1961	81		.2	80.9
October, 1961	116	4	10	106
May, 1962	20	8.7	13.1	6.9
April, 1964	.17			.17
June, 1964	39			39
Total	376.77	119.7	136.4	240.47

Source: See page 252.

After the two initial, relatively small loans in 1954, a major loan was proposed during the visit of Bulganin and Khrushchev to Kabul in December, 1955. Formally signed on January 28, 1956, the $100-million loan was made at an interest rate of 2 per cent for thirty years. Because of Afghanistan's dire poverty, repayments were not to begin until eight years after the delivery of the equipment. The new loan was intended to finance a variety of major projects included in Afghanistan's First Five-Year Plan: Afghanistan's first automobile repair shop at Djangalak, which was opened in May, 1960; hydroelectric plants at Haglu and at Pul-i-Khumri; the port of Quzal Qala on the Oxus River; oil storage tanks outside of Kabul; airports at Bagram and Kabul; the Jalalabad irrigation canal; and the spectacular highway through the Hindu Kush Mountains.

Since it is one of their more impressive aid projects, it is worth saying a little more about the highway through the Hindu Kush Mountain range. Because the site is in such a remote area, it has not received the publicity accorded the Aswan Dam and the Bhilai steel mill. The highway was opened by Alexei Kosygin on September 3, 1964; perhaps the occasion would have attracted more publicity if Khrushchev had been replaced in August rather than in October. Requiring an estimated $38 million to build, the 67-mile road is etched out of one of the most forbidding mountain ranges in Asia. It eliminates 125 miles of highway between Kabul and the northern border, and it permits winter travel through the area for the first time in history. The biggest challenge of the project was the completion of the Salang Tunnel, built through a mountain at an elevation of 11,000 feet and more than two miles in length. Among the unique aspects of the project was the need to ensure that the tunnel could be used by camel and donkey caravans as well as by automobiles. There were some critics who pointed out that there were political and military as well as economic reasons for Soviet aid on the project. They noted that the highway finally provided easy access from the U.S.S.R. to the center of Afghanistan. There were also complaints about the involuntary conscription of workers by the Afghans for their share of the work. Nevertheless, the project must be regarded as one of the major engineering triumphs in the underdeveloped world.

At one time it was also intended that Soviet loans would finance the construction of a nitrate fertilizer plant, a chemical laboratory, auto repair shops in Herat and Pul-i-Khumri, and dams at Palta, Sarg, and Kharvar. However, because of various unspecified difficulties, these projects were dropped on July 16, 1958. The $16 million freed by the cancellation of these projects was then used to pay for the shipment to Afghanistan of Soviet commodities such as oil, sugar, and margarine. Like American counterpart aid, the proceeds from the sale of these products in Afghan currency were used to finance Afghanistan's share of the construction costs on the Djangalak auto repair factory. A similar arrangement by means of a special loan was announced on January 13, 1962, for the delivery of $12 million of such goods. Their sale in domestic markets was intended to supply the local construction funds for use in the Second Five-Year Plan of 1962–66.[6] The Russians also accelerated their shipments of grain after Afghanistan's poor wheat harvest in 1959. They sent 10,000 tons of grain as a gift in 1959 and 30,000 in 1960. As the Russians began to suffer their own crop failures, they substituted sugar and oil for the wheat. This policy continued into 1964.

Another credit was announced on July 30, 1957, for $15 million. The purpose of this credit was to finance geological surveys for oil and gas. Ultimately at least fifty promising petroleum structures were found, some of which are now being exploited. Surveys were also made in a search for other minerals.

On May 28, 1959, the Soviets agreed to undertake another road-building task, the Kush to Herat to Kandahar highway. This is a 425-mile stretch requiring thirty-seven bridges, the largest of which is over the 1,350-foot wide River Hararud. It is estimated that this road will cost about $140 million. Most of the funds for this highway have been provided by a gift of $129 million. This highway will eventually link up with an American-financed and constructed road which is to cover the 312 miles from Kabul south to Kandahar. The American portion is expected to cost about $40 million. Even if it was not intended to work out this way, this is an outstanding example of the cooperative use of foreign aid by the two countries. The Americans subsequently announced that they would build another highway to Qala on the Iranian border, which would link up with the Russian-built road at Herat.

By the end of Afghanistan's First Five-Year Plan, in March, 1961, the Soviet Union had already committed itself to about $120 million in foreign aid. This was almost 70 per cent of all the foreign loans obtained by Afghanistan during its Five-Year Plan. By October, 1961, the Russians were already considering new projects in the Second Five-Year Plan. Ultimately two loans were signed for this purpose, one for $81 million on October 16, 1961, and another for $116 million, approved shortly thereafter. Another credit was provided in May, 1962, for $20 million, apparently to supplement the funds provided in January, 1956. Loans announced since then include a $39-million credit ratified on June 25, 1964, for the exploitation of natural-gas deposits, and a small sum of about $170,000 for the construction of an atomic reactor. The notable feature of the loan for the development of Afghanistan's natural-gas resources is that the principal and 2.5 per cent interest on the loan are to be repaid in gas from the project itself. Beginning in the fourth quarter of 1966, the Afghans are to deliver 1.5 billion cubic meters of gas a year until 1985. This means that no other Afghan resources will have to be utilized to repay the loan.

The new loans are intended to complete some of the proposals originally advanced in the early loan proposals of 1956. Thus the nitrate fertilizer plant is again scheduled for construction at Mazur el Sharif, and a thermal power plant to be fueled by natural gas is also to be built. In addition, there are new plans for a film studio, a home-construction factory in Kabul, a Technical Institute, four state farms at Jalalabad, an oil refinery, and an electric grid from Naglu to Kabul. There is also talk of a massive project on the Oxus River, the demarcation line between the Soviet Union and Afghanistan. Soviet engineers estimate that eight to ten hydroelectric sites could be developed in this area with a capacity of 16-million kilowatts—the equivalent of eight Aswan Dams. Advance calculations indicate that this would require an investment of $280 million and therefore no decision about this project will be made until at least 1967.

For a country as undeveloped as Afghanistan, Soviet foreign aid has been of vital importance. The Russians have spent about twice as many dollars as the United States, and have benefited more per dollar expenditure. Moreover, although the Russians have made mistakes, they have been relatively minor compared to those of the Americans. The Russians have also been considerably more flexible. What explains the poorer American record?

Russian success in Afghanistan has undoubtedly been facilitated by the proximity of the two countries. The closing of the Pakistan-Afghanistan border in 1950, 1953, 1955, and 1961–62 made American communications with Afghanistan even more tenuous. These disruptions severed a supply line that had been stretched halfway around the world. The border blockade is partly responsible for that American white elephant, the Kandahar Airport. This modernistic airport-and-hotel complex on the main air route from Europe to India sits closed because it has been impossible to bring in airplane fuel across the border. A second painful experience has been the Helmand Dam and irrigation project. This was one of Afghanistan's first ventures in seeking foreign technical assistance for which it was actually prepared to pay on a cash basis. Unfortunately, the American contractor, Morrison-Knudsen, was unable to produce, and ultimately the Afghans were forced to turn to the American government for financial aid to complete the project. After more than fifteen years, the Helmand venture is still not completed; neither the United States nor Afghanistan can quite decide what to do with it, and whether it is worth throwing good money after bad. Apparently some of the irrigated land is finally being put to productive use, but there have been serious problems of salination.

As a result of the experiences at Kandahar and Helmand, several Afghan officials have complained that American aid policy in Afghanistan lacks flexibility. As one authority put it, the U.S. "overadministers" its aid. American officials are criticized because of a reluctance to act and to make decisions on the spot and because of their excessive cautiousness. Afghans say that the Russians come in ready to act with a preselected list of suitable projects. (Note that in Egypt the complaints were exactly the opposite.) The Americans defend themselves by saying that it is the Afghans who are slow and who must learn for themselves how to select suitable projects. Learning how to make such decisions is as important as the building of the project itself, they argue. In turn, the Afghans say that although this may be true for more advanced underdeveloped countries, they are so short of qualified personnel that they are incapable as yet of acting on their own initiative.

The American activity that has received the most praise from the Afghans is the sale of secondhand American clothing. Cast-off American clothes are cheap, warm, and of good quality. Not only has this lowered the cost of living, but medical authorities relate the decrease in tuberculosis to the fact that children can be dressed warmly enough to be protected from the cold. But although the sale of secondhand clothing is widely applauded by poor and rich Afghans alike, and although almost everyone (including Afghan officials) considers it to be the best foreign-aid program in the country, the truth remains that it is not a part of the American foreign-aid program at all. It is purely a commercial transaction. Such is the irony of American foreign aid.

Obviously it is unwise to treat all developing countries the same. American officials are doing less and less of this. Yet one way to contend with some of the criticism from the poorer countries such as Afghanistan and to accelerate the decision-making process might be to prepare a series of prototype projects. Such plans might include the specifications for a variety of factories typically needed by growing countries. For example, most countries seem to request lumber mills, sugar refineries, canneries, and furniture factories. The availability of a ready-made plan would eliminate the time usually needed to prepare such plans from scratch. Obviously modifications would be necessary, but it could reduce the time needed for negotiations. For countries which are more advanced and which have the resources to plan independently, there should be less spoon-feeding. As in the case of Afghanistan, however, it is important to recognize that some countries are less capable of acting for themselves than others.

The Afghans complain that the Americans are equally inflexible in extending grants, that is, money and resources that do not have to be paid back. For a long time, the United States provided grants to many countries. However, these countries generally did not show much gratitude. In trying to determine the secret of Soviet success in foreign aid, American officials discovered that most Soviet aid was provided only in the form of loans. This reaffirmed the opinion of those who argued that gifts destroyed the self-respect of the recipient and made him resentful, whereas loans created a sense of mutual respect. American officials therefore decided to abandon the practice of giving gifts and switched to a policy of providing loans. Unfortunately, very few, if any, exceptions have been made to this rule. The Afghans argue that because of their extreme poverty, at least some American foreign aid should be supplied to them as grants. Fifteen per cent of their foreign exports is already being used to service the existing debt. Thus in the year ending March 31, 1963, they had to spend $12.7 million on repayment and interest. Moreover, because the Russian loans to Afghanistan are spread out over a longer period of time than the usual twelve years, the major expenditure for principal repayment is now being made to the United States. Finally, despite their general rule, the Russians have made available to Afghanistan grants totaling about $150 million. While the value of American grants is about the same, no new ones are being offered. In contrast the Russians offer them as the need arises. This inflexibility is what the Afghans have in mind when they say American aid is "overadministered."

The Russian problems in Afghanistan have been negligible by comparison. As already mentioned, some of the initial projects were canceled. Moreover, the bakery and the flour mill did not function properly at first. The bakery was not equipped to manufacture bread in the Afghan style, and American wheat, which the Afghans had to use, did not have the same properties as Russian wheat, therefore necessitating further adjustments in the Soviet bakery equipment. As a result, the bakery lost money and failed to reach its promised capacity. This was acknowledged by the Russians in one of their few public admissions of failure.[7] The flour mill finally earned a profit in 1958, but it still had not reached its specified capacity until after 1960. There are also reports that the silo of the flour mill is built a little like the Tower of Pisa, being eleven inches off center.

Other shortcomings in Russian aid include poor road construction; a number of roads have been washed out by the Afghan rains. Some engineers fear that the Jalalabad irrigation project will suffer from salination just as the Helmand valley does. There are also reports that the Russian-built airport at Kabul was kept locked up for a year after its completion because the Afghans did not like the furniture it contained. But perhaps the strangest criticism of Soviet aid is one that could have easily been avoided. The Russians have been exceptionally generous in training Afghan students in the U.S.S.R. More than 400 have been sent to Soviet schools. Yet the Afghans are frequently treated coldly if not cruelly. The author once observed Soviet customs officials search the luggage of three Afghan students who had just completed an academic year in the Soviet Union. The process took over an hour and was obviously embarrassing to the students. In the end, the officials confiscated a samovar and nearly caused one of the students to miss the plane. It was evident that the goodwill the Russians had attempted to inculcate in the students over many months had been turned to disgust in an hour.

The only other Communist country that has a meaningful aid program in Afghanistan is Czechoslovakia. Afghanistan's ties with Czechoslovakia extend back before World War II; thus it was not entirely unexpected that the prewar relationships were re-established after the war. In August, 1954, the Czechs announced a $5-million loan for eight years. There is an element of confusion surrounding this loan. Russian sources say that the loan was for $5 million. However, official Afghan records indicate that the loan was for £5 million, or $14 million; they show further that by 1962 the Afghans had utilized almost a full $5 million. By December, 1963, they had spent $700,000 more.

The main Czech activity has been the construction of two cement plants, one about forty miles from Kabul at Dzhabel us Siradzh, and a second one at Pul-i-Khumri. The Czechs have also discussed the construction of a cannery at Kandahar. Apparently the cement plants have not functioned properly. The many rumors about the poor quality of Czech cement seem to be substantiated by Soviet actions; in 1960, the Russians had to send 10,000 tons of cement to Afghanistan because of "shortages." [8] Apparently the Russians refused to use the cement produced with Czech equipment and brought in their own instead.

The Czechs have been considerably more successful in purely commercial ventures. An Afghan firm, the Spinzar Cotton Company, erected the Spinzar Hotel at a cost of over $600,000. The building was constructed by Hochtief, the West German contractor, but the Czech agency Politechnika was hired to operate the hotel on a commercial basis. My impression was that the Czechs were running the Spinzar quite efficiently.

Although they trade with Afghanistan, most of the other Communist countries have not extended any meaningful economic aid. In 1957, Poland talked of rebuilding a woolen factory, but no formal loan was ever made. The Chinese have had a trade agreement since July, 1957. As part of the bargaining which preceded the expected opening of the Algerian conference, the Chinese announced a loan of $28 million, but it remains to be seen just what, if anything, will be built.

In summary, Soviet aid to Afghanistan has been immensely successful. The Russians have avoided most forms of political interference. Afghanistan has maintained its neutrality despite the nearness of its imposing neighbor and the remoteness of all forms of countervailing help. The Soviet Union has become Afghanistan's most important trading partner, in many cases out of choice, not compulsion. Russian aid projects on the whole have been well suited to Afghanistan's needs. Even American officials are hard pressed to find major flaws. It would be comforting to ascribe Russian successes in Afghanistan to the proximity of the two countries, but this is not the complete answer. The record indicates that flexibility and determination to show that the Soviet Union can coexist with a smaller nation have been of equal importance.

6. Indonesia: Frustration and Failure

The spectacle of an anti-Communist rally being held in an Indonesian stadium built with Soviet foreign aid is perhaps one of the best examples of Soviet foreign aid gone wrong. It also symbolizes the fact that Soviet foreign aid to Indonesia has been one of Russia's least successful ventures. As the Dutch, Americans, and English could have predicted, the Russians have been unable to cope with the chaos of the Indonesian economy and political system. As of early 1966, the Russians had failed to complete a single industrial project after almost ten years of trying. Instead, they have had to sit back and watch as their unutilized aid supplies have been pilfered and destroyed and as the country has been tossed from one political and economic crisis to another. With nothing being used productively, the Indonesians have been unable to generate any new income and so the Russians have been unable to collect on their debts. American foreign aid in Indonesia has been more successful, industrially, at least, and perhaps eventually, even politically. The dismal and stymied record of Soviet efforts in Indonesia is unique for the Russians: why have they failed so badly there?

To understand the hazards of dispensing foreign aid in Indonesia, it is necessary to know a little about the country's political and economic environment. Despite its rich endowment of oil, rubber trees, and other natural resources, Indonesia has in recent years been so distracted by internal and external political conflicts that the economy has been left to drift for itself. In the immediate postwar era, the initial task was to drive out the Dutch colonialists and declare independence. Once this was done, instead of turning to the problem of economic development, the country concentrated on driving the Dutch out of their last foothold in New Guinea; this necessitated continuous military mobilization and political maneuvering. Under American pressure, the Dutch agreed to terminate their interests. This only encouraged Sukarno, the country's charismatic but impractical leader, to turn his attentions elsewhere. He created a "confrontation with Malaysia," which he swore he would crush. Wearing a military uniform and exhorting the troops and masses was much more exciting and ego-satisfying than planning economic programs and balancing the budget. Thus increased economic investment and improved labor productivity were neglected and made the targets of anarchist or vested-interest groups. As a consequence, no one was willing or able to exert any positive authority or impose the discipline needed for economic development.

Chaotic seems the best word to describe the Indonesian economy. Most foreign companies have been nationalized, but too few Indonesians have been found who can run the firms even semi-efficiently. For many years the oil companies were threatened daily with expropriation. The rubber producers were forced for many months to boycott Malaysian ports. This hurt the Indonesians as much as the Malaysians. Food production fell sharply, and an unwillingness to beg for grain shipments from the United States resulted in starvation in Java until 1966, when the United States and other countries were finally approached to sell grain. Corruption and dishonesty have been widespread. Amidst all of this, inflation has run rampant. Reflecting the debasement of the economy, the official rate of exchange of 500 rupiahs to the dollar contrasted with the black-market rate that at times reached 15,000 rupiahs to the dollar. This was not an environment conducive to a program of foreign aid, whether from a Communist or a capitalist country.

The Russians made their first offers of aid to Indonesia some time before conditions had deteriorated so badly. In an effort to encourage the Bandung spirit of neutralism, the Russians proposed a loan of $100 million on September 15, 1956.[1] The interest rate was 2½ per cent and the loan was to be repaid over a twelve-year period; however, as an extra measure of generosity, repayment was to begin three years after delivery of materials.

From the beginning, there were ominous signs of what lay ahead. Because of internal feuding and, perhaps, U.S. pressure, the Soviet loan was not accepted by the Indonesian Parliament until February 5, 1958, a year and a half after the original proposal. The next problem was to agree on the projects that would be included. As an island economy, Indonesia's first need was for ships. Even before the loan was formally approved, the Indonesians asked the Russians to supply them with ships to replace those withdrawn by the Dutch. The Russians responded immediately to the Indonesian request and by March, 1958, they had sent three ships; nine more followed shortly thereafter. The twelve ships cost $12.5 million. Unfortunately, almost all the ships were secondhand and from two to six years old. They had been built primarily in Belgium, Hungary, and Finland. The Hungarian-built vessels were in particularly poor condition. By December, 1961, the whole fleet had been decommissioned, and Poland was asked to re-equip the ships as part of a new loan.[2]

Except for the ships and some textiles, not much else was agreed upon. After the delivery of the ships it took another year before a supplementary protocol could be obtained. This protocol of January 3, 1959, was followed by a contract on general conditions that required another eight months to negotiate. Not until August, 1959, three years after the original offer, could there be discussion of specific projects. But Russian troubles were just beginning.

Prior to the Soviet offer, a West German consulting firm, Wedexro, had proposed that Indonesia build two steel plants with a capacity of 30,000 and 50,000 tons, respectively. The mills were to rely on scrap metal and Indonesian coal, which it turned out could not be made into coke. After having considered the problems, the Germans wisely refused to provide any credits for such a project. The Russian loan was therefore made to order for the Indonesians, because it provided the financial answer to the question of financing the steel mill. The Russians, however, suggested that not two, but only one, steel mill be built. The Indonesians agreed, but over Russian objections they insisted that the mill be located at Tjilegan. As the Russians predicted, the Tjilegan location caused special problems, since to supply the plant with iron ore and coke, the Russians had to build a road network.

The delay encountered in building the road meant a delay in completing the steel mill. Even with the American tractors that were brought in, the Russians could not finish the road on time. Moreover the supplies for the mill arrived in a haphazard fashion. The Russians have always found it difficult to maintain domestic shipping schedules. Foreign shipping is no easier for them. The Russians do not have access to a merchant marine fleet; thus goods are shipped whenever there is an available freighter. In addition, the Russians are not especially adept at arranging shipping schedules. One of the first pieces of equipment for the steel plant to arrive was the sixty-ton stand for the mill's rollers; it arrived in Jakarta in early 1963, although it will not be installed until 1967 at the earliest. It is true that the mill was originally scheduled for completion in 1965, but it is not difficult to imagine what effect four years on the open docks of Jakarta will have on even a sixty-ton piece of equipment. This is just a part of the $36-million investment (including an extra $10 million for a tin plate mill) that holds great promise, but so far not much else.

Most of the other projects in the first loan agreement have been subjected to similar setbacks. Only the sale of ships and textiles has been carried out—projects that necessitated a minimum of participation by the Indonesians themselves. The Russians have found that anything that involves activity on Indonesian territory or participation by Indonesian workmen seems to falter or collapse. A road-building program in Kalimantan (Borneo) for $11.5 million has met with numerous difficulties. When swamp conditions began to hinder operations, the original construction plans were scrapped. The project was reduced from 300 to about 160 miles of road, and the completion date was pushed back from 1964 to 1967. The Russians have also provided $6.5-million worth of agricultural equipment for two rice farms. As seems to be the case with all Soviet agricultural aid, the Soviet equipment has not been very helpful. As described by one Indonesian, the Soviet machinery "lies idle on its side, sitting there." In the wonderland of Indonesia, even though such equipment was not suited for Indonesian conditions, Sukarno accepted another loan for similar Czechoslovak tractors simply because they were made available on credit terms. The most unfortunate Russian experience has been with the Tjilatjap superphosphate plant. This $9-million plant was agreed to after a quick survey indicated the availability of the necessary raw material. However, a second and more thorough survey after construction had started failed to turn up either phosphate or sulphur, which was also to be refined there. In the words of one disgruntled Indonesian official, "It is like having a hamburger with no meat and no bun."

Because of a series of such mishaps, none of the construction projects anticipated in the original loan were completed by 1966. In a supplemental agreement of July 28, 1959, the Russians agreed to build two new projects, a $5-million Oceanographic Research Institute at Ambon, which was due to open in 1966, and the $12.5-million Asian Games Complex, which is unique in the Indonesian experience in that it has actually been completed.

The story of the stadium is not without its drama. Probably because of its nonindustrial and nonproductive nature, the Russians rejected Indonesia's request to build the Games Complex at least twice. Only after Sukarno personally approached Khrushchev was the loan approved. The stadium, however (as was also true of Russian-built stadiums in Guinea and Mali), has not been a success from an economic point of view. Stadiums simply do not generate much foreign exchange. In addition, the Russians may be having some second thoughts about its political value: while some pulsating rallies have been held in it and while it is lovely to look at, $12.5 million is a lot to pay for a toy (it is five times as expensive as the stadiums in Guinea and Mali). So far, the country has been unable to repay the loans that financed it. The Indonesians have also been disappointed to find that the more practical aspects of the stadium project have not materialized. The cost of the stadium was justified to some extent by the promise that the Soviet heavy equipment used to construct the stadium would subsequently be turned over to the Indonesians for use in road construction. Unfortunately, the equipment was used so intensively and was of such poor quality that there was nothing left by the time the road-building was to begin. Reportedly, it was even necessary to "persuade" the Stanvac Oil Company to release some of its equipment to ensure the last-minute completion of the Games Complex. But the fact remains that that 100,000-seat stadium was completed. The only other construction project the Russians had finished by 1966 was a $2-million hospital. Presented as a gift in a gesture of friendship by the Soviet Union, this is a spacious and airy hospital located on the outskirts of Jakarta. Nevertheless, for some reason, it was only 30 per cent occupied when I visited it.

Even though they were having nothing but bad luck with their first loan, the Russians felt it necessary to maintain their relationship with Indonesia. Accordingly, they agreed to try again with a second loan on February 28, 1960. This credit was for $250 million, with the more traditional twelve-year period of repayment after the lapse of one year. Altogether the Russians had loaned a total of $367.5 million as of 1964.[3] The following projects were included in the second loan: an experimental atomic reactor ($1.1–2.2 million); a mineral survey ($3 million); an iron-and-steel project at Kalimantan, provided the raw materials can be found ($166 million); a sulphur-refining plant addition to the Tjilatjap superphosphate factory ($1.5 million of the original $9 million allocation); a soda-ash plant ($2 million; the expenditure for this project may ultimately reach $30 million); the Asahan River hydroelectric and aluminum plant ($120 million). Except for some work on the atomic reactor, little or nothing has been completed on any of the other projects and most work is far behind schedule.

A specialist on Indonesia, Dr. Alexander Shakov, reports that in addition to the two formal credits, there was another loan for $8.4 million in February, 1957, to finance the sale of jeeps. Although Russian data does not include such a loan, Shakov says that the Russian jeeps were purchased, despite the fact that they cost $1,867 each (compared to $1,490 for an American jeep) and were not suited to Indonesian conditions (the carburetors were too small and there was not enough protection from the humidity).[4]

Indonesia has received considerable aid from other Communist countries, including China. Generally this aid has been no more successful than Soviet aid. One of East Germany's projects seems inept even by

Indonesian standards. The Germans reportedly built and completed an $8.6 million beet-sugar mill at Djogjakarta before discovering that the Indonesians grow only sugar cane. However, the plant was eventually refitted to process sugar cane and the Indonesians agreed to accept German apologies. To make amends, in January, 1964, the Germans presented a plan to build a cotton-spinning mill for $5.65 million. They have also offered to build a planetarium, which is scheduled for completion in November, 1966. More practical is the German offer to build five printing presses, but this was arranged on a commercial basis rather than as an aid arrangement.

Czechoslovakia has done considerably better. Offering a $27-million loan in 1956 and a $33.6 million loan in July, 1960, the Czechs have even managed to carry out some of the things they promised to do. Under the 1956 loan, the Czechs sent a shipment of enamelware intended for resale in Indonesia and they completed the construction of the Intirub tire plant. The Intirub factory has been expanded by the Czechs and a sugar mill at Sulawesi has also been erected. By mid-1964, Indonesia had received about 2,500 badly needed Czech railroad cars out of an order for 4,500. Plans were also being made for the construction of a hydroelectric plant at Tjurung and a diesel-engine assembly plant. The Czechs had also agreed to undertake some geological surveys. But the Czechs have also had their troubles. The unsuitability of their agricultural machinery has already been mentioned. In addition, a cement plant planned for Macassar is reported to be the Czech counterpart of the Tjilatjap superphosphate plant. As at the Russian plant, the Czechs have been unable to find the necessary raw materials. Similarly, the Czech plant also lacks electricity, water, roads, and a port. Apparently, roads which have been used thus far have been unable to carry the necessary equipment. Consequently much of the equipment cannot be moved from the harbor area.

In the usual Indonesian pattern of incompleted or inappropriate aid projects, the only part of the aid promised by Poland which has materialized is that which could be produced in Poland and sent to Indonesia. The Indonesians have received twenty-four freighters worth $39 million under a $39-million loan announced on June 26, 1958. Other projects planned for the future include four shipyards financed by a $5.6-million loan on July 20, 1959. In August, 1961, a $30-million loan was provided to support the construction of a $10-million cement plant in North Sumatra, a $10-million coal mine at Sawahlunte, a carbide plant at Padang, a light-aircraft plant at Bandung, a sugar mill at Atjah, a building-materials plant, an iron-casting plant, and a reinforcing bar plant. The interest rate on at least two of the three Polish loans was set at 5 per cent—perhaps a reflection of the risk of doing business with Indonesia.

Hungary also charged a rate of 5 per cent on its August, 1959, loan for $22 million. This was followed by a second loan at 2½ per cent for $28 million. Even if not all the money has been or will be used, the fact that the Hungarians have committed themselves to the large sum of $50 million is surprising in view of Hungary's own domestic difficulties. Thus far, however, Hungary has produced very little of a concrete nature in Indonesia. A shipment of diesel buses was completed, but as of mid-1964, a promised light-bulb factory and an oxygen plant had not been finished. The Hungarians did deliver a shipment of telephones to be used in Jakarta. However, three weeks after the telephones had been installed, the Indonesians decided to replace them all with Siemens phones from West Germany. They came to the conclusion that the Hungarian telephones simply would not work in Indonesia. The Indonesian telephone system is still in a state of chaos, but what little communication it does provide is a source of pride.

To make it unanimous among the East European countries, even Rumania and Bulgaria have promised Indonesia some form of help. On June 7, 1961, Rumania promised to provide $35 million for the development of Indonesia's oil industry and $15 million for the cost of 2,100 railroad cars. As of mid-1964, some geologists had done some exploring and 600 railroad cars had arrived in Indonesia. But not much else had been accomplished. Even little Bulgaria has provided a loan of $6 million, which is ultimately intended for a $5-million electric-motor factory, and $500,000 for a citronella-oil plant. Thus far, like the projects promised by most of the other satellites, few have gone beyond the planning stage and nothing has been completed.

Reflecting the competition for Indonesia's political affections, the Chinese have also been extremely generous in promising economic aid. The only project completed is the delivery of $11.2–$16.4-million worth of rice and textile products for sale inside Indonesia. In April, 1959, a loan of $30 million was extended for six textile mills and a spare-parts factory, but nothing tangible has been done. During the maneuvering before the scheduled 1965 Algerian conference, when they were trying to win support against the Russians, the Chinese were reported to have promised new loans. Initial indications were that the loans would total $50 million, of which $10 million was to be in foreign exchange. At the time of the deterioration of Sino-Indonesian relations in late 1965, the Chinese were forced to abandon their work on a $16-million center for the Conference of New Emerging Forces.

The combined total of economic aid to Indonesia from members of the East European bloc and China amounted to about $725 million as of 1965.[5] (See Table VI-1.) This is exclusive of military credits. Even more significant than the size of the credit is the fact that every one of the East European countries has promised something. This is unparalleled anywhere else except in Cuba. Although information is not complete about military aid, inclusion of Soviet military credits would probably boost the total to considerably more than $1 billion, including about $40 million in military aid from Czechoslovakia. With this exceptionally large sum, the Indonesians have built up a navy containing at least twenty submarines, two cruisers, four destroyers, and several motor torpedo boats. In addition their air force includes at least ninety MIG-15's and MIG-17's plus an undisclosed number of MIG-19's along with some bombers and helicopters. The Indonesians apparently received another $50 to $100 million of military credits in 1964. This was sought by Indonesia for its campaign against Malaysia and agreed to by Russia in an effort to win support at the Algerian Conference.

Clearly, the amount of Communist aid, both economic and military,

Table VI-1

ECONOMIC LOANS TO INDONESIA FROM COMMUNIST COUNTRIES
(in Millions of Dollars)

Lender	Amount
Bulgaria	6
China	100-108*
Czechoslovakia	60*
East Germany	15
Hungary	50
Poland	74-78
Rumania	50
U.S.S.R.	367-76
Total	722-741

Sources: See page 252.

*Approximate

has been very high. Equally evident is the fact that there is little to show for it. Only the military aid seems to have made an impact—yet it was the armed forces that led the attack on the Communists. Therein may lie the explanation for the difficulties with the economic projects. Political and military activities are much more appealing to revolutionary leaders like Sukarno than economic development. As a result, for almost a decade a country like Indonesia diverted most of its budgetary and human resources from economic to military projects. Whenever an undue proportion of a country's resources are diverted from productive to military activities, the economy suffers. The investment needed for future growth is squandered elsewhere. At the same time, the increased expenditures for military personnel and equipment create an enlarged wage fund but no consumer goods for the wage fund to absorb. This is the prime explanation for the soaring inflation that racked Indonesia.

Inflation has made economic development still more difficult. With constantly changing prices, the value relationship between goods and resources has become hopelessly distorted. It is difficult to ascertain just how much goods are really worth. Similarly, as Indonesian currency loses its value, foreign traders and investors lose faith in the country and are reluctant to commit any of their own resources. Such phenomena are not unique to Indonesia. They arise in all inflationary crises. But Indonesia has not been content to suffer as others suffer; things always seem to be a little worse in Indonesia than they are elsewhere. Even though the Indonesian rupiah had badly depreciated, Indonesia under Sukarno consistently refused to release enough local currency for the completion of its share of its foreign-aid projects. For some reason, monetary discipline was enforced only when it came to allocating rupiahs for domestic manpower and resources that had been promised for use on economic projects being built with foreign aid. The Indonesians claimed that they could not provide the necessary rupiahs because this would have made the inflation worse.

The rationality of such a situation completely escaped the Russians. They saw thousands of people hungry and unemployed. They saw a valueless rupiah and their equipment rusting on the docks, being cannibalized and resold on the black market. Most responsible Indonesians acknowledged that the failure of foreign aid in Indonesia was largely their own fault, although Indonesian ineptness also seems to bring out the worst in the aid-giver, witness the Russians and their superphosphate plant, the Czechs and their cement plant, and the Germans and their beet-sugar mill.

The rupiah "shortage" explains why the U.S.S.R. and Czechoslovakia have included commodities for sale in Indonesia in their foreign-aid packages. Only by selling consumer goods on Indonesian markets could they obtain the necessary local currency. It also explains why the Poles were unable to construct their shipyards in time. According to a reliable source, Sukarno's refusal to release sufficient rupiahs for the aid projects was one of the main reasons for Mikoyan's trip to Indonesia in the summer of 1964. Mikoyan was particularly disturbed over the lack of Indonesian cooperation at the Tjilegan steel mill.

The failure to complete any productive projects has not facilitated the process of repayment. The Russians have completed the delivery of large quantities of goods, both economic and military, and they expect repayment whether or not the projects are self-liquidating. Inevitably, there have been serious repayment problems. According to Indonesian sources, the Indonesians were forced to seek a rescheduling of from $70 to $90 million in debt due to the Communist bloc. About $43 million of this amount was for economic aid. The Poles and Russians agreed to a rescheduling, but apparently the Czechs did not. Nevertheless they were not paid. Debt repayment was even higher in 1964. Reports indicated that $100 million was to have been paid, $50 million of it for economic aid. Total debt owed to all creditors and due in 1964 reportedly totaled $230–$250 million, equal to about one-third of Indonesia's exports each year.

Not one Communist country has a record it can be proud of in Indonesia. Even those countries that have managed to complete a project have also made at least one major mistake. Ironically, the United States is one of the few countries that has anything to show for its efforts, and for a long time it appeared that it was only in economic, not political, terms. It was only in late 1965, after the abortive Communist revolution, that political relations with the United States were anything but unpleasant. Yet despite its share of uncompleted and ill-fated proposals, the United States has had three successful, even profitable projects: the Gresik cement plant, the Sriwidjaja urea-fertilizer plant (both built by Morrison-Knudsen, the firm that did so poorly in Afghanistan), and the Jakarta highway bypass. (A fourth project, the Surabaja thermal electric power plant, was scheduled for opening in 1965.) Despite various construction problems and mistakes in other aid projects, all three projects are operating at promised capacity. Nikolai Elizariev, the Assistant Economic Counselor of the Soviet Embassy in Jakarta, criticized the three American efforts as "turn-key" projects, i.e., built primarily with American, not Indonesian, technicians. But this negative view was disputed by some Indonesians weary of waiting for the non-"turn-key" Soviet projects to be completed.

Indonesia has proved too much of a challenge not only for Communist countries, but for almost every donor of economic aid. With only a few exceptions, even those projects that have been completed seem to be failures. Given the conditions that existed under Sukarno, it was highly unlikely that a constructive foreign-aid program could ever be developed. As a wise but discreet and perhaps prophetic Indonesia official told me during the last few months of Sukarno's rule, "Nothing can be done to salvage Indonesia's aid program until *you* have a new form of government." More than any other country, Indonesia reveals the difficulties of administering a foreign-aid program in conditions of underdevelopment.

7. Asia: The Ubiquitous Chinese

Although the present foreign-aid program of the Soviet Union began in Asia, only in Afghanistan have the Russians been the largest donor of aid. In Asia, the Russians have found themselves competing not only with the capitalist countries of the West but with a particularly sensitive and jealous power, China. Initially the Chinese showed little concern over Russian involvement in Asian affairs. There was no noticeable protest about the early loans to Afghanistan, India, and Indonesia. Gradually, however, the Chinese began to react not only with promises of economic loans, but with scathing criticism of Soviet intentions. Asia, after all, was within China's historical sphere of influence. Russia was basically a European power and therefore an interloper. This was China's contention during the maneuvering prior to the ill-fated Algerian Conference of Afro-Asian Countries in 1965. It also seems to have determined the aid policy of the Chinese in Asia. We have already discussed the Sino-Soviet economic rivalry in Afghanistan and Indonesia. Only in India, China's main opponent in Southeast Asia, were the Russians left to themselves. Now we shall examine Soviet and Chinese aid to other countries in Asia, including Nepal, Burma, Cambodia, Ceylon, Pakistan, and Laos. This will provide an insight into the particular problems the Chinese have created for the Russians.

Nepal

Strategically located between India and China, mountainous Nepal is unique among the recipients of foreign aid. It is wooed not only by the rich nations of the world, but by the poor. Thus along with aid from the United States, the U.S.S.R., and Great Britain, the Nepalese are busy trying to use Chinese and Indian aid as well. Nepal's problem is not so much a shortage of funds, but whether or not it can successfully absorb all the help directed its way. As of February, 1964, the United States had committed itself to $71.6 million in grants and loans, India was second with $60.6 million, China third with $43.4 million, the Soviet Union fourth with $14 million, and Great Britain last with

$5 million.[1] Considering that all three of the richer countries channel hundreds of millions of dollars' worth of aid to India and that the Soviet Union has provided large sums to China, it is likely that the richer countries have mixed emotions as they watch India and China competing with them for favor.

Compared to the aid promises of the Chinese, Soviet aid to Nepal has been relatively minor in scope, especially in the early stage of the aid-giving rivalry that has developed between the two countries. On April 24, 1959, the Soviet Union signed an agreement for economic and technical aid to Nepal. (The text of the official aid agreement appears in Appendix 6.) The aid was to be provided in grant form, which it was estimated would total about $7.5 mllion. The Russians obtained funds for local construction costs by importing and selling Soviet goods on local markets. In this way a sixty-bed hospital was completed in Katmandu in early 1963. Subsequently $4.2 million in additional grants and $2.7 million in loans were made. This money was used to finance a small hydroelectric dam at Panauti with a maximum capacity of 1,200 kilowatts that was subsequently increased to 2,400 kilowatts, a cigarette factory at Janakpur, and a sugar refinery at Birgunj. The latter two plants were opened in January, 1965. In April, 1964, the Russians also agreed to build half of the east-west highway across the country. Their seventy-mile portion will run from Janakpur to Simra. Some officials estimate this road through mountainous terrain will cost as much as $31 million. The Russians have also committed themselves to the construction of an agricultural implement plant and perhaps a cement factory.

Soviet aid to Nepal has been something less than a complete success. The Russians have had to call on the Czechs to provide them with the equipment for both the sugar mill and the cigarette factory. The Russians are used to dealing only with sugar beets, not sugar cane, and the Russian equivalent of a cigarette, the *papirossi,* is half filter and half tobacco, not all tobacco and a little filter, as are cigarettes in Nepal. Therefore Russian equipment was of no use in Nepal. Furthermore, there is now concern that the two plants have excessive capacity. Nepal grows little sugar cane and may have to import sugar cane from India if the factory is to be fully utilized. There is also some dismay over the fact that the agricultural implement factory will make old-fashioned equipment designed for use with horses rather than newer and more modern instruments. The Nepalese are not entirely convinced that these are the kind of tools best suited for the present stage of their development. As for the Soviet hospital in Katmandu, there is some indication that it is not being fully utilized. During the beginning of the

1964 monsoon, when disease is usually at a peak because of the flood-ing, I found that only about fifteen out of the sixty beds were being utilized, whereas the other hospitals in town were jammed. It is unwise to base any generalization on one visit, but it is worth noting that the Russian-built hospital in Jakarta was similarly empty. The reasons for the lack of full use are the same in both countries. Apparently there is some distrust of Russian doctors and equipment.

Russian efforts at Panauti deserve special mention. In a most ingenious manner, the Russians have managed to replace capital, which is relatively expensive and in short supply, with an intensive use of hand labor, which is cheap and readily available. Almost all of the lumber is prepared in a primitive but highly effective hand-operated saw mill. Until a rock-crushing machine was brought in, all the gravel was prepared by having hundreds of laborers hammer the rock into little pebbles. Nevertheless, in comparison with the water resources available in Nepal and the imagination shown by the Russians with their other hydroelectric projects around the world, the dam at Panauti is an expensive but highly unproductive gadget. The main storage reservoir is contained by a small dam across the Panauti River that stretches a mere forty to fifty feet. Moreover, all three generators of the dam can be utilized only during the four months of the monsoon; only two generators can be used during the following four months; and only one generator will be in operation in the four months of the dry season. Thus it is estimated that on some days the dam will be able to produce only about 500 Kilowatts of power. When asked why the Russians chose to build such a project, Nepalese officials replied that the Russians wanted to be the first to bring in hydroelectric power to Katmandu. The Indians were building a similar but more rationally located project, and the Russians were determined to beat them— another illustration of the strange things that are done in the name of foreign aid!

Chinese aid was initially much grander in scale and concept than Soviet aid. It was made available at first in the form of two loans. The first loan, for $12.5 million, in October, 1965, was intended for budgetary support. The Chinese agreed to supply goods for resale in Nepal with the proceeds to go to the Nepalese government so that it could balance its budget. Unfortunately, no one wanted to buy the Chinese goods, so the Chinese agreed reluctantly to provide $8 million in cash. As of 1964, the Nepalese had obtained only about $3 million from this loan.

China expected to make its major impact, however, with industrial projects. In March, 1960, it provided a second loan of $21 million for the construction of three factories: a cement factory at Hetaura, with a capacity of 50,000 tons of cement a year; a paper plant, with its own power plant at Nepalganj, with a capacity of twenty tons a day; and a tannery and shoe factory at Katmandu. The Chinese compared their projects with the "light" sugar mill and cigarette factory that were being built by the Russians. As they were to repeat many times, the nature of their projects demonstrated that they, and not the Russians, were willing to help with the basic needs of industrialization.

When such statements were repeated to Soviet economic officials in Nepal, the immediate retort was that the Chinese were lying. The Russians never questioned whether the American interviewer was distorting the Chinese statement. It was obviously the kind of thing the Russians had heard and expected the Chinese to say. As proof of the meaninglessness of the Chinese boast, the Russians were quick to point out that in fact the Chinese had abandoned their two "heaviest" projects, the cement plant and the paper plant, in 1963. The Russians then went on to express their own interest in building the cement plant at Hetaura. The Russians were attempting to top the Chinese just as they had taken advantage of the United States at Aswan and Bokaro. However, their offer was subsequently overshadowed when Alfred Krupp of West Germany announced, in February, 1964, that he too was interested in building a cement plant at Hetaura.

The Russian assertion was correct. The Chinese had indeed had to alter their plans. The Russians did not point out, however, that the reason for the cancellation of the original plans was that Czechoslovakia refused to sell China the equipment needed in the cement plant. It will be remembered that the Russian cigarette and sugar-cane plants were also dependent on Czech equipment. The Russians, however, have better relations with the Czechs.

The Chinese were therefore forced to switch to other projects, those that could be built with Chinese-made equipment or with large quantities of labor. Since equipment for the tannery and shoe factory was available in China, this project was not dropped. In addition, the Chinese also promised to build a brick and tile factory, two warehouses, and a rice and flour mill. However, since the only existing supply route for this equipment ran through Calcutta, the Chinese could not count on full cooperation in moving their goods. The opening of the tannery plant was postponed several times. Food shortages in both India and Nepal in 1964 made it even more difficult to obtain the necessary transport facilities. However, even though the Indians were doing their best to frustrate the completion of the tannery, their own aid program oddly enough will eventually make possible the operation of the tannery. The tannery's supply of water will come from a water reservoir being built in a nearby town by the Indians, a further example of what strange bedfellows foreign aid sometimes makes.

Because of its lack of capital resources, China traditionally has favored projects that are labor intensive. Therefore, as we shall also see in Yemen, China offered to finance and supervise the construction of some vital highway links. In October, 1961, the Chinese provided another loan of $9.8 million for a highway to be built from the Katmandu Valley to Kodari on the Tibetan frontier. For Nepal, this highway, which was opened to one-lane traffic in December, 1964, held the promise of restoring Katmandu as a main juncture on the ancient trade route to the interior of Asia and Tibet. For China, the road would bring the rich grain plains of southeastern Nepal within trading distance of Chinese-ruled Tibet. For the Indians, it would mean new competition for rice in one of their traditional granaries. The Chinese also wanted to build an extension of the Katmandu-Kodari road to the Indian border. The Indians put pressure on Nepal to keep the Chinese out of that area. Instead, the Chinese agreed to build half of the east-west highway, to link up with the Russian half. The Nepalese envisaged a furious competition to see which country would finish its half first. Once again the Indians protested, since this work, too, would have placed the Chinese too close to Indian territory. As compensation, the Indians agreed to build the road instead. The Chinese then offered to build a 140-mile highway in the interior from Katmandu to Pokhara. For this, they made available $28 million, although it is unclear whether this was a new loan or a transfer of funds from earlier Chinese loans that had not been utilized.

The Nepalese have been quite adroit in playing off one aid donor against another. As should be evident by now, the rivalry between China and the Soviet Union has been especially intense in Nepal. In addition to the examples already cited, in at least one other instance the bitter rivalry has come into the open. Again, it concerns the construction of a highway. For about fifteen to twenty miles, the Katmandu to Kodari road that the Chinese are building parallels an older road that serves as the only supply link between Katmandu and the construction site of the Russian dam at Panauti. This is a three-hour trip by automobile over unbelievably rugged territory. On May 10, 1964, the following comment, under the headline "Chinese Deliberately Damaging Katmandu," appeared in the *Naya Sandesh* (*Nepali Weekly*) published in Katmandu: "According to a Soviet technician working at the Panauti Hydroelectric project, the Chinese are trying to damage the Katmandu-Panauti road by taking out stones from it." The Soviet complaint stemmed from the fact that damage to the road served to cut off their sole supply line to the dam.

The Chinese protested that the article had slandered them and had damaged relations between Nepal and China. This led to the suspension of the paper two weeks later by the Nepalese government. As for the truth of the matter, the Russians in Katmandu refused to comment. After my own trip over the road to the dam in July, 1964, I found it easy to believe the Russian charges.

Generally, Chinese attacks on Soviet aid have emphasized that Russia, as a "rich" nation, is no different from the United States or the countries of Western Europe in its treatment of poorer nations.

To speak plainly, the policy and the purpose of the leaders of the Communist Party of the U.S.S.R. are open to suspicion. They often take an attitude of great power chauvinism and national egoism in matters concerning aid to newly independent countries, harm the economic and political interests of the receiving countries and as a result discredit the socialist countries.[2]

Thus, according to the Chinese, the Russians, like the other neocolonialists, are reluctant to aid basic industry in poorer countries. Although the Russians fiercely deny this, it is true that they usually help only the richer members of the Afro-Asian bloc with their heavy industries. There is some logic in this, since it is only the richer members of the Afro-Asian bloc that have the infrastructure upon which to base such industry. But whatever the record, the Chinese try to ignore what the Russians have done to help basic industry elsewhere in the world. On those occasions when they are forced to acknowledge that the Soviet Union has provided help, they accuse the Russians of tying strings to their aid and of withholding key spare parts. The Chinese also maintain that such aid is sometimes provided in order to build up countries, like India, that are China's enemies.

The Chinese argue that poor countries must "rely on one's own forces or on those of allies who are equally poor" to bring about industrialization without strings. As expressed in a joint Chinese-Tanzanian communiqué of June 21, 1964:

In order to lift themselves from poverty and backwardness, the Asian-African countries must first of all rely on their own people and resources for the work of national construction and secondly they also need mutual aid and economic cooperation among themselves on the basis of equality and mutual benefit. This is the reliable way for the Asian-African countries to attain economic independence and common prosperity.[3]

The Chinese argue that this was how they brought about their own industrialization. The Russians, of course, are quick to remind the Chinese of the aid they received from the U.S.S.R. and that the strength of the Chinese economy and its foreign-aid program leave much to be desired. The Soviet press reported that Chinese aid to developing countries equaled only 8 per cent of the aid supplied by the U.S.S.R. and Eastern Europe. Furthermore, they pointed out that as of mid-1964, the Chinese had agreed to 108 projects in Africa and Asia, but had completed only five factories, three hospitals, and a few other smaller projects.[4] Not much more has been completed since then. Chinese criticism of Soviet aid may be just, but until Chinese resources grow enough for them to counter with a meaningful aid program of their own, their complaints are not likely to have much impact.

Burma

Burma's xenophobia creates more than the usual number of problems for the donor of foreign aid. Burma's distrust of foreigners is reflected in its decision of 1964 that no foreigner, without very special permission, including many on official business, be permitted to stay more than twenty-four hours in the country.

This ruling has had an especially serious effect on one of the Soviet aid projects. Included in the original foreign-aid agreement of January 17, 1957, was provision for a luxury hotel.[5] Naturally, if tourists are discouraged from visiting the country, it follows that a luxury hotel is not the wisest investment. Completed in late 1962, the 206-room complex on the shores of Lake Inya was built with all the latest facilities. The Burmese insisted that the hotel be made suitable for tropical conditions, but since the Russians do not manufacture air-conditioning equipment, they did not plan to install any. When the Burmese discovered this, they forced the Russians to buy Westinghouse air conditioners from the United States. They also insisted on Otis elevators. Then came the question of who would operate the hotel. Because the Russians have trouble operating hotels outside (or even inside) their own country, the Burmese sought the services of an American firm. However, the vision of a Hilton- or Sheraton-run Soviet foreign-aid project was too much for the Russians. They insisted that the Burmese look elsewhere. After trying a few Japanese firms, the Burmese finally ended up with a two-year contract with the Israeli firm of Federmann Brothers. Despite several years of exceptionally cordial relations, the Burmese decided in 1964 that the Israelis were also imperialists, and the Federmann firm was expelled from the country. The Burmese themselves took over the operation of the hotel. The Federmanns were lucky. Because of the obstacles confronting a tourist who wants to stay more than twenty-four hours in Burma, the hotel is normally less than one-quarter full. Thus through no fault of the Soviet Union, a Soviet foreign-aid project has become an extra burden for an already over-burdened country.

Because the hotel, the Technological Institute of Rangoon, and a 200-bed hospital in Taunggi were technically presented to Burma as gifts (valued at $5–10 million), Burma should have had no cause to worry about the earning capacity of these projects. However, the Burmese had insisted that they be allowed to make a reciprocal gift of rice, also worth $5–10 million. Beginning in 1963, Burma began to send 5,000 tons of rice a year as its part of the bargain. Since 1957, when the arrangement was made, the price of rice has climbed from $85 a ton to $100. Consequently the Soviet gift is in fact a loan, and one that ended up costing Burma more than it had anticipated.

The 1957 agreement also called for the Russians to build a stadium, an 1,800-seat theater, a 1,000-seat conference hall, and an agricultural and industrial exhibition grounds. These other projects never materialized. The Russians have subsequently agreed to build a dam and irrigation system on the Kyetmarektaung for about $4–5 million; there was also talk of a fertilizer plant.[6] The Russians have also provided the Burmese with a gift of 4 million doses of smallpox vaccine and provided them with credits to purchase 100 tractors.[7]

One of the more publicized Soviet endeavors in Burma was a shipment of Russian cement that hardened on the docks of Rangoon. The combination of poor packaging, inadequate warehousing facilities, and rainy weather was responsible. Failure to improve the packaging has led to similar consequences in Guinea, Ghana, and the Sudan. When *The Wall Street Journal* of May 16, 1962, cited the hardened cement as an example of the poor quality of Soviet economic aid, the Russians for some reason defended themselves and the quality of their aid by replying, "Even nonspecialists in the building trade know that if cement hardens on contact with water, it means that it is good cement: and if it doesn't harden it is bad."[8]

The Chinese have also been active in Burma. Until 1965, however, most of the action involved promises rather than deeds. Despite the promise of a loan for $84 million in 1961, by 1964 the Chinese had done little except conduct surveys. A visit by Chou En-lai to Rangoon in July, 1964, produced yet another promise of eventual performance. Ultimately, the Burmese expect to receive small-machine works, a sugar mill, a paper factory, a plywood mill at Mupum, a tire factory at Danyingon, and a textile plant at Okkyin. The Chinese have also promised to build several bridges and a hydroelectric project. The Soviets have again pointed to the difference between Chinese promise and performance in Burma.[9] The only other bloc country that has promised aid to Burma is Czechoslovakia, which in 1964 offered a credit for 2,000 tractors.[10]

Cambodia

As in the case of Burma, the promises of Chinese aid to Cambodia are larger than those of the Russians. In Cambodia, however, the Chinese have managed to complete some of their projects. There have been at least three Chinese loans, the first in June, 1956, for $23 million, the second in December, 1960, for $26.5 million, and the third in November, 1964, for either $5 million or $10 million, for a total of $54.5 million or $59.5 million. The Russians, as of mid-1963, had provided only $6 million in gifts. This financed a 500-bed hospital and a technological institute in Phnom Penh. In 1963, Cambodia accepted a credit for $12 million to build a dam and power station on the River Camachai. When completed, the dam will have a capacity of 50,000 kilowatts.[11] The Russians have also supplied military equipment to Cambodia, including two MIG-17 and four other jet fighters.

China has completed more projects in Cambodia than in any other nonaligned country. Three factories and a radio station have been completed, and the fourth factory, a cement plant at Chakrey Ting, is nearing completion.[12] However, although this is more than the Chinese have been able to do elsewhere, there are many reports that the plants are far from satisfactory. For example, the Sihanouk–Chou En-lai Plywood Factory at Dey Eth has been particularly unsuccessful. Situated outside the forest area, the plant has not been able to obtain adequate supplies of lumber. The trees can be cut only during the dry season, and then must be stored until the arrival of the monsoon, when the rivers rise high enough to carry the logs to the mill. Moreover, because the locally produced glue used in the plywood is of such poor quality, the plywood falls apart in the humid Cambodian climate. Also, faulty maintenance has resulted in the breakdown of the plant's boiler. As a result of such mishaps, the plant's plywood sells at a price three times that of plywood smuggled from Hong Kong. Understandably, the factory has had a difficult time selling its product. Even a ban on plywood imports has not helped. The plant has run at a loss since its opening in 1961, and there was talk of closing it down. Conditions at the paper mill at Chhlong and the textile mill at Kompong Cham are considerably better. Even though the level of technology is not very advanced, the plants were reported to be operating at full capacity and with some efficiency.

Czechoslovakia is again the only other Communist country that has provided aid of any importance. The Czechs have built a sugar refinery at Kompong Speu, a tire factory at Kandal, and a tractor assembly plant at Sihanoukville.

Ceylon

In the discussion of Soviet success with the oil industry of India, it was noted that the Russians had scored similar successes in Ceylon. After the Western oil companies refused to take any more local currency for their oil, or to match the price of crude-oil imports quoted by the U.S.S.R., Ceylon decided to buy as much as 80 per cent of its oil from the Soviet Union and process and distribute it through Western-owned facilities. The Western companies balked at such arrangements, and Ceylon countered by nationalizing oil company property in early 1963. In December, 1963, the gasoline stations were nationalized. When Ceylon rejected demands of the oil companies for additional compensation, the oil companies appealed to the American government for support. Accordingly the United States suspended economic aid to Ceylon. This amounted to about $4 million a year. A change in government ultimately led to an agreement over compensation and the American government resumed economic aid to Ceylon.

It should be noted that the nationalization of the oil companies was not working to the complete satisfaction of the Ceylonese. Because Soviet oil deliveries to Ceylon did not arrive with regularity, the state-owned oil companies had to buy oil from the Western oil companies anyway. As a result of this unexpected situation, and of mismanagement, the Ceylon Petroleum Corporation showed a slight loss in its first month of operation. This happened despite the fact that as a result of nationalization the company had been freed of all capital costs and charges.

The Russians have been equally active in the purchase and sale of other goods to Ceylon. Large quantities of cocoa have been purchased by the Russians, along with rubber, cocoanut oil, and tea. To facilitate additional purchases by the Ceylonese of Russian goods, the commercial line of credit was increased by the Russians from $840,000 to $1,400,000. A longer-term credit of $30 million was made February 25, 1958.[13] The Russians agreed to build a steel mill capable of producing 35,000 tons of rolled steel a year, a tire plant with an output of 360,000 tires, a peat factory, a flour mill, a factory for the production of prefabricated housing, a cold-storage warehouse, and an expanded fishing industry. Russian help in providing geological surveys and irrigation work was also mentioned.

The exact amount of Chinese aid to Ceylon is difficult to ascertain. A loan for $16 million was extended in September, 1957, another for $10.5 million was offered in September, 1958, and a third for $4.2 million to buy Chinese textiles was provided in March, 1964. In addition a fourth loan of $10.5 million may have been provided in October, 1960, but there is no firm evidence about this. Aid from other Communist countries includes a loan for a cold-storage plant from Bulgaria, the joint construction of a sugar mill by Poland and Czechoslovakia, and the erection of an agricultural-implement factory by the Poles under a $6-million credit.[14]

Pakistan

As a member of the CENTO and SEATO alliances and the recipient of $4.5 billion in economic and military aid from the United States, Pakistan resisted tempting Soviet foreign-aid offers for almost ten years. In March, 1961, when its patience was tried by difficulties with the Western oil companies, Pakistan finally agreed to accept a Soviet loan of $30 million for oil and gas exploration. As Pakistan became increasingly disturbed over American aid to India, it also signed a barter agreement with the Soviet Union for $1-million worth of railroad ties in exchange for raw jute in August, 1963, and accepted a commercial loan in July, 1964, for $11-million worth of agricultural machinery and other equipment to be used for irrigation work. Just before the outbreak of hostilities between Pakistan and India, the Russians also announced they were prepared to extend another loan for $50–70 million. Apparently the fighting caused a reassessment of the offer.

To some extent the February, 1965, offer to Pakistan was stimulated by Russia's concern about Pakistan's growing alignment with China. In a move that caught the West by surprise, Pakistan revealed that it had accepted a $60-million interest-free loan from China in July, 1964. The money was intended to pay for imports of machinery, cement, sugar mills, and other goods. This initial loan was followed up by the offer of a second loan in January, 1965, for $30-million worth of goods and equipment. If this loan succeeds in attracting Pakistan into China's orbit, the ramifications of this move on the balance of power in Asia will be felt for a long time.

Among the other Communist countries that have extended aid to Pakistan are Czechoslovakia, which offered a loan of $40 million for the establishment of various sectors of heavy industry, and Rumania, which has offered to build an oil refinery.[15] The status of all such loans will undoubtedly be affected by the political and military moves yet to be made by China and India.

Laos

Laos has also received a promise of economic help from the Soviet Union. In April, 1963, the Russians agreed to build a dam on the river Nam Niep, financed by a loan of $4 million.[16] In addition the Russians declared they would build a hospital and radio station as a gift for the people of Laos. There had been earlier reports that China, too, had supplied Laos with a long-term loan, but the terms and projects of such a loan have not as yet been made public.

Conclusion

Although we shall find other examples of Sino-Soviet rivalry, notably in East Africa, it is in Asia that the competition is most intense. It is in Nepal that the Russian economic counselor eagerly seeks information about the Chinese leather and shoe factory from his American guest who has just visited the factory site. The Russian himself has never been allowed near the plant. It is in Asia that the Chinese outdo themselves with promises of aid. With the exception of Laos, every country surveyed in this chapter has received a larger promise of aid from China than it has from the U.S.S.R.; in Burma, Cambodia, and Nepal, Chinese promises were double and triple those of the Russians. Although Chinese promises may be larger than Chinese deliveries, the Chinese have managed to derive considerable propaganda from their promises alone. This is quite similar to the conditions the Americans had to deal with in their early competition with the Russians. It is likely, however, that China will take much longer to fulfill its promises than it took the Russians to fulfill theirs. Sino-Soviet rivalry is a not entirely anticipated dimension in the foreign-aid derby. The future developments promise to be as fascinating as those of the past.

8. The Middle East: Changing Fortunes

Soviet economic relations with the countries of the Middle East have been especially mercurial. Partly because of the antagonism of the Moslem religion to the Communist movement, and partly because several of the countries share a common border with the U.S.S.R., the Russians have had difficulty in establishing friendly relations with the Middle Eastern nations. Periodically, however, whether because of some mistake by a Western government or because of a domestic coup, the attitude toward the Soviet Union in a particular country changes. The Russians have usually reacted with considerable agility. But just as there are revolutionary coups that bring to power friends of the U.S.S.R., so there are rebellions that throw them out.

The Russians have discovered that such governmental switch-overs can be troublesome, especially after economic loans have been provided. Equally disconcerting is the periodic assertion by the Arab League that all Communist Party activity in the Arab world is illegal. Inevitably repression of domestic Communist Party activity creates concern about the wisdom of having provided long-term investment funds. Like foreign investors the world over, the Russians have been embarrassed by former "friends" who become unappreciative and threaten to default on their loans. As we have seen, such an occurrence is not limited to countries in the Middle East. However, these turnabouts have been especially common in this area of the world. As the Soviet commitment to the underdeveloped world increases, it is inevitable that such reverses will occur with increasing frequency. Soviet experience in the countries of the Middle East may give an indication of what lies ahead.

Algeria

Among the Arab countries in Northern Africa and the Middle East, Algeria stands second only to Egypt in the amount of aid it has been promised by the Soviet Union. Algeria, however, was a late starter. Its first aid commitment of $100 million from the U.S.S.R. was received in September, 1963, fifteen months after Algeria obtained its independence from France. Until that time, despite Algeria's great need and the political gains to be made from providing more aid, the Russian contribution to Algeria consisted of clearing some land mines left over from the revolutionary war with France, and a gift of wheat and some helicopters.

However, Russia's affection for Algerian President Ben Bella grew rapidly as he became more critical of the West. Accordingly, in May, 1964, an additional $127.6 million in economic aid was presented. By the time of Ben Bella's ouster, on June 19, 1965, Soviet-Algerian economic relations were exceptionally cordial. Foreign aid to Algeria since that time has continued, but the post–Ben Bella government has so far been a little more conservative than the U.S.S.R. would like, and it remains to be seen just how much of their promised aid the Russians will actually provide.

The major project scheduled under the Soviet aid program is a $125-million steel mill at Bone. It is anticipated that the new steel mill, if and when it is built, will have a capacity of 300,000–350,000 tons of rolled steel a year.[1] Even though it is assumed that the plant will rely almost entirely on domestic raw materials, the same project was turned down by the French, West German, and Swedish groups for economic reasons. The Russians have also talked of building an aluminum-processing plant as part of the loan arrangement. Other Soviet projects are to include an Oil and Gas Institute and a Textile Institute. The former is to be presented as a gift. In conjunction with the institutes, the Russians plan to build several vocational schools to train oil and textile technicians; an agricultural school is also planned. Three hundred Algerian doctors have been sent to the U.S.S.R. for advanced training. The Russians are also conducting surveys for minerals and irrigation. Algeria has received over 500 self-propelled grain-harvesting combines and tractors made in the U.S.S.R., and has been promised several ocean-going freighters and tankers. Similarly, the Algerian airline, Air Algeria, has received two Ilyushin-18's on credit.[2] Large quantities of military aid have also been supplied. By mid-1965, the Algerian armed forces had obtained at least 300 Soviet tanks, 9 MIG-21's, 12 Il-28 jet bombers, and 7 AN-12 transports.

In addition to the two Il-18 planes provided on credit to Algeria, the U.S.S.R. made a gift to former President Ben Bella of a third plane, which was delivered at the time of Chou En-lai's visit to Algeria in January, 1964. This was one more manifestation of the competitive battle with China. After the initial $100-million loan from the Soviet Union in September, 1963, the Chinese countered with an offer of $50 million on October 28 of the same year. The Soviet bid was raised by the May, 1964, loan of $127.6 million, but the financially strapped

Chinese could raise their bid no higher. As of this writing, the only sign of any economic aid from China has been the delivery of a 13,000-ton cargo ship in February, 1965. The Chinese had also promised to supply an undisclosed amount of material for Algeria's Popular Militia. This was regarded as a move to counter the effect of Soviet military aid. With the overthrow of Ben Bella, the Popular Militia was disbanded, and it is not known what has happened to the Chinese equipment. Both the economic and military rivalry represented attempts by the U.S.S.R. and China to win Algerian support for particular policies, such as the inclusion or exclusion of the U.S.S.R. in the Afro-Asian Conference. The only other satellites reported to have offered aid to Algeria are Bulgaria and Rumania.[3]

Iraq

Iraq is the third largest recipient of Soviet aid in the Arab world. Relations between the U.S.S.R. and Iraq, however, have not always been the warmest. The several years of close cooperation with the government of Abdul Karim Kassim were followed by a revolutionary coup that brought the Ba'th Party to power in February, 1963. One of the first acts of the new regime was to suppress the Iraqi Communist Party. Hundreds of its members were killed, and many more were arrested. Simultaneously, Iraq criticized the Soviet Union for its interference in domestic affairs, specifically its support of the Kurdish rebellion in the north. With economic aid promises totaling $183 million and a military aid agreement amounting to about $300 million, the Russians found themselves providing substantial help to a government that had become openly hostile. Undoubtedly ingratitude of this sort has led to criticism within the Soviet Union of its foreign aid program. This is indicated in A. M. Rumyantsev's attack on those who argue that "the aid of the socialist states to economically underdeveloped countries objectively leads to the preservation in these countries of the status quo or even strengthens the forces of reaction."[4] Such sentiments must have been reinforced when a second roundup of Iraqi Communists took place in late 1965.

The initial loan agreement with Iraq was signed on March 16, 1959, for the amount of $137.5 million.[5] Among the projects mentioned were factories producing steel and pig-iron, nitric fertilizer, sulphur, drugs, agricultural machinery, electrical equipment, light bulbs, glass, cotton and wool textiles, knitwear, ready-to-wear clothing, and canned goods. Also promised were a radio station, a geological survey, a grain-storage elevator, a sugar-beet farm, agricultural machinery, an irrigation system, a nuclear reactor, and the rebuilding of the narrow-gauge railroad between Bagdad and Basra. The loan was supplemented with another $45 million in 1960 to provide facilities for building and maintaining the railroad and its equipment. By the spring of 1965, only the railroad, the cannery, radio station, nuclear reactor, clothing factory, and a few agricultural projects had been completed.[6] Work on some of the projects has gone so poorly that some of the remaining projects, such as the drug plant, equipment factories, knitwear plant, and the grain-storage elevator, have apparently been canceled. However, in March, 1965, in a renewed display of mutual friendship, both sides announced plans for the construction of a large dam and hydroelectric station on the Euphrates. Unofficial estimates of the cost of the project were placed at $140 million, although it was not clear whether this figure represented the cost of the whole project or only the Soviet loan for their portion of the work. The Russians have also declared their willingness to build a tractor-assembly plant and three training institutes.

The Russians have also sent a large shipment of military equipment to Iraq. Prior to the 1963 *coup d'état,* Western newspapers reported the presence in Iraq of 80 to 100 jet aircraft, including 12 MIG-21's, 10 TU-16 bombers, a variety of MIG-17 and -19 fighters and Il-28 light bombers, air-defense missiles, naval vessels, and 250–300 medium and light tanks. The Russians were reportedly distressed to see this equipment directed against the Kurds, whom they had been supporting.

Among the other Communist countries, only Czechoslovakia appears to have been involved in Iraq in any significant way. It has lent Iraq $34 million for such projects as an oil refinery, petrochemical works, and an electric power station.

Syria

Soviet loans to Syria have been cloaked in more than the usual amount of mystery. Initially, this may have been due to the confusion that resulted from Syria's vacillating attitude toward partnership with Egypt in the United Arab Republic. Also, the Ba'th Party in Syria has not always been on the best of terms with the U.S.S.R. The hot-and-cold relations between the two countries have affected the disbursal of foreign aid as well as the bestowal of political favor.

As of late 1964, Western sources estimated that total bloc aid to Syria had amounted to $193 million and that Soviet aid alone totaled $150 million.[7] Then in May, 1965, the Russians announced that their original agreement of October 28, 1957, had been for only $87 million.[8] Another Soviet source placed total aid of the Communist bloc to Syria at about $90 million;[9] this apparently included a Bulgarian loan for the Rastam Dam completed in 1961. However, this figure makes no provision for a Czech loan of $15–20 million and an East German loan of $3 million, which have been reported by the U.S. State Department. It also excludes a Polish loan of $16.7 million and a $20-million loan offered by China in March, 1963, before the Ba'th takeover.

The original 1957 list of Russian projects provided for construction of a 450-mile railroad between Kamishli and Latakia, a nitrogen-fertilizer plant at Homs (built with Czech help), equipment for the Rastam Dam, irrigation, highway bridges, geological surveys, oil prospecting, and three agricultural-research centers.[10]

As an anti-Communist faction gained control of the government, relations deteriorated. Among other setbacks, the Russians lost out to the West Germans, at least temporarily, on a bid to construct a major dam on the Euphrates. Then, in 1963, as government attitudes changed again, Syria urged the Russians to reactivate some of their earlier projects. By mid-1965, relations had improved considerably. By mid-1966, after the February revolution, they were even better. The Russians were busy assembling forty-three oil storage tanks and conducting surveys for oil and water and power stations on the Euphrates. They also agreed to help reconstruct the railroad from Aleppo to Khois and Akkara. In a major move in April, 1966, the Russians also offered to finance the construction of the Euphrates River Dam, which had been included under the original 1957 aid agreement. The cost of the Russian share was estimated at $150 million, almost double the amount originally specified in the total aid agreements.

Tunisia

Soviet aid to Tunisia was made public in a most dramatic fashion. Although France had readily agreed to give Tunisia its independence, it had continued to hold on to the air and naval base at Bizerte. Fighting broke out in mid-July, 1961, between French and Tunisian forces. Both sides finally agreed to a cease-fire on July 22, but by then almost 700 Tunisians had been killed and a thousand wounded. Feelings were running high. On August 4, the Russians announced that they had extended Tunisia a loan of $28.5 million. Although negotiations had actually been going on since April, the Soviet move was taken as an indication of Russia's ability to profit from any dispute between NATO powers and the third world. The original terms of the loan obligated the Russians to build dams and power stations with a capacity of 2,000 kilowatts each, irrigation systems on the Kesseb, Dzhushin, and Serzhenan rivers, and a technological institute for 700 people to be attached to the University of Tunis. Shortly thereafter, the Czechs agreed to a loan of $10 million and the Poles provided another $10 million. Although Tunisia has been one of the most pro-Western of the Arab League countries, the Russians so far seem to have avoided the in-and-out situation we found in Algeria, Iraq, and Syria.

Yemen

Because of its strategic location as a steppingstone between Asia Minor and Africa, Soviet activity in Yemen has been watched closely by Western authorities. This was especially true, because of its military potential, of an 11,500-foot runway built at Rakhav, ten miles from Sana, the capital of the country.[11] This project was financed out of an initial $20-million loan extended before the Nasser-sponsored revolution of 1962. The same loan financed the construction of a port at Hodeida which was put into operation in April, 1961. Along with the port the Russians built a power house, a gas station, a radio station, and nearly 500 homes. In a preliminary maneuver before the Afro-Asian conference, in March, 1964, the Soviet Union offered Yemen another $72-million credit. This loan was to finance the construction of a major road from Hodeida to Taiz, a cement factory, a fish cannery, a hospital, and two secondary schools. The Russians have provided ships for Yemen's fishing and agreed to explore for oil. Despite their unfortunate experiences in Guinea, Mali, and Indonesia, they are also planning to build a stadium in Sana.

Like other countries in the Middle East, Yemen has also received military aid from the U.S.S.R. A Soviet military mission has been helping the Egyptians train the Yemenite army. Along with other equipment, the Russians provided about fifty airplanes in 1959. Unfortunately, they were not properly cared for and the government ultimately decided to scrap the planes. The metal has been melted down and converted into automobile license plates.

The Chinese have been especially active in Yemen. They built a highway, over shifting sand dunes, from Hodeida to Sana. Subsequently they agreed to build another road from Sana to Sada, a distance of 125 miles. The Hodeida to Sana road was financed out of a $16.3-million loan extended in January, 1958, which was also to be used to finance a fish cannery at Hodeida, a textile mill in Sana, and a glass factory at Taiz. A second Chinese loan for $28 million, presented in May, 1964, partially as a countermove to the Soviet loan extended in March, was for the Sana to Sada highway.[12] At the same time, the Chinese agreed to make $5-million worth of repairs on their original road.

As we have seen in numerous other countries, the rivalry between China and Russia has resembled a big poker game with foreign aid being used for the chips. But, because of their inability to match Soviet financial resources, the Chinese have had to resort to propaganda. They noted that their work on the Hodeida-Sana highway had required extraordinary sacrifices. Help of this sort to a fellow developing country, the Chinese continued, could only be rendered selflessly by the "men of the East." [13]

This is not the only time the issue of racism has been raised in the competition between the Soviet Union and China. Although both the Chinese and the Russians have been accused of prejudice by African students in Moscow and Peking, the Chinese have attempted to mobilize resentment against the white man and direct it against the U.S.S.R. In protest over the Chinese assertion that the "East wind would prevail over the West wind," a Russian critic complained at a meeting in Moshi, Tanganyika, in February, 1963, that "some of the chauvinistically inclined leaders would like to direct the solidarity movement not against imperialism, colonialism, and its agents, but against all white people." [14] The Chinese in turn demanded that the Russians should desist from referring to the "yellow hordes." [15] The racial issue could have effects that extend far beyond the question of economic development.

Turkey

For historical and geographical reasons, Turkey has been one of the most anti-Russian nations in the world. While it did accept Russian economic aid in 1932 for textile mills, it has generally viewed all Soviet overtures with more than a moderate degree of suspicion. [16] Border incidents and Turkey's membership in CENTO and NATO have increased these tensions. Furthermore, Turkey has seemed content with its $2 billion of economic and food aid from the United States, including $130 million for the $285-million steel mill at Eregli plus another $2.3 billion in military aid. However Turkey's bitterness toward the United States and the other NATO powers for failing to support Turkey in Cyprus provoked the Turks to a more independent foreign political and economic policy. Ironically this switch was made despite the fact that Russia's attitude toward Turkey had been even less sympathetic than that of NATO.

Hence, in April, 1964, Turkish and Soviet officials met together for the first time in many years, and the announcement of a Soviet loan was made shortly thereafter. Included in the $168-million loan is a $15 million dam on the Arpa Chai River, which divides the U.S.S.R. and Turkey. The Russians have also agreed to submit bids for a steel mill, an oil refinery, a vodka distillery, a tractor factory, a sheet glass factory, and four other plants. However, a change in government in 1965 brought to power a more conservative faction, which has been somewhat more cautious about the advisability of accepting Soviet aid and has sought counteroffers from the West. The Turks have also reportedly signed loan agreements with Czechoslovakia for $6.4 million and Hungary for $1 million.

Iran

Like Turkey, Iran is a member of the CENTO alliance and a victim of border incursions by the U.S.S.R.; it, too, has exercised extreme caution in taking economic aid from the Russians. This policy was modified in July, 1963, when it was announced that both parties would cooperate in the construction of a hydroelectric plant on the river Arak at Tabriz.[17] Also planned are a 500,000–600,000 ton steel mill at Isfahan, eleven grain-storage elevators, and a caviar-processing plant. To finance at least a part of this, the Russians have supplied Iran with a $39-million loan. Poland has also lent Iran about $9 million for sugar refineries.

Other Countries

Jordan announced in October, 1963, that it might seek aid from the U.S.S.R., but evidently nothing came of it. While it has apparently received no economic aid, Morocco has obtained Soviet military aid. Although the deal was attacked by the left-wing parties in Morocco, the government obtained artillery, tanks, and other vehicles in April, 1962. Ironically, there have been negotiations between Kuwait and the U.S.S.R. Since Kuwait is in a better position to lend money to the U.S.S.R. than vice versa, it is uncertain whether the agreement signed on November 9, 1964, called for a Soviet loan or direct cash payment for the projects in Kuwait. Most likely, Kuwait will have to pay immediately for what it is to receive.[18] Finally, Libya was presented with a gift of two Soviet hospitals.[19]

Conclusion

As the number and size of Soviet loans to the developing nations increase, the U.S.S.R. is finding itself with vested interests in a large number of countries in the Afro-Asian world. Although the Russians do not own shares of stock in enterprises they have helped to establish, they are owed a long-term debt that they expected would be repaid. The vested interest that such a debt creates helps to account for the Soviet concern over events in Algeria, Iraq, and Syria, and also partially explains Soviet moderation in the disputes over India's border. As it does for their counterparts in the Western world, this should induce an increasingly conservative attitude toward any radical change in areas where the Russians have provided loans of significance.

9. *Latin America: Opportunism and Pragmatism*

Until the advent of Fidel Castro, Soviet involvement in Latin America was relatively insignificant. After Castro came to power, the Russians took a greater interest in certain Latin American countries, but their distance from Latin America still makes it difficult for them to have too much influence. The Russians do not seem overly eager to create any serious confrontations in Latin America. They seem to accept this area as the American sphere of influence. The disappointing and embarrassing aftermath of the Russian build-up of missile bases in Cuba and the failure to support a promised campaign of industrialization are examples of the problems that any major Soviet penetration must face.

In its economic relations with Latin America, the Soviet Union has not been particularly concerned with ideological considerations. Whenever there was money to be made, a product to be bought, or a political inroad to be established, the Russians have not hesitated to make whatever political compromises might be necessary; for example, they had major dealings with dictators Perón of Argentina and Batista of Cuba, without regard for their political coloration.

Usually foreign aid, short-term loans, and trade agreements are viewed by the Communist bloc as a means of obtaining economic entree into a tight market clearly under the American sphere of influence. Until 1962, the Communist bloc invariably had a deficit trade balance with the few Latin American countries with which it dealt. This seems to be an inevitable part of Communist economic strategy. The usual Soviet pattern is to place an order for a particular country's major export commodity. The purchase may be paid for in convertible currency. Occasionally, an attempt may be made immediately to pay with barter, usually Soviet oil. (The Russians used to exchange wheat before they had to start importing it themselves.) Either way, the Russians build up a deficit balance of trade. (See Table IX-1.) If they have been paying in cash, they tell the country that, if Soviet purchases are to continue, more Soviet goods must be accepted in exchange. But, as we shall see, whether the Russians have been paying in cash or oil, the country often finds that it has more ruble credits at its disposal

Table IX-1

SOVIET FOREIGN TRADE WITH LATIN AMERICA
(in Millions of Dollars)

Country	1955	1956	1957	1958	1959	1960	1961	1962	1963	1964	1965
Argentina											
Export	24	19	4.7	17	17	14	11	8	1	4	20
Import	28	13	21	16	28	22	20	10	18	20	72
Brazil											
Export	0	.1	0	0	1	16	18	30	30	24	28
Import	2	3	2	1	5	9	24	36	43	37	33
Cuba											
Export	0	0	0	0	0	71	276	366	400	366	375
Import	36	15	47	16	7	104	312	234	164	288	342
Jamaica											
Export				0					0	0	
Import				.2					.1	3	
Mexico											
Export	0	.1	.2	.6	.4	1	0	0	.1	.3	
Import	2	.1	.2	.2	1.3	3	.5	7	8	2.1	
Peru											
Export					0	0	0	0	0	0	
Import					.5	0	2.2	6	0	0	
Uruguay											
Export	0	3	0	6	9	1.5	1	0	0	.2	.4
Import	10	12	18	25	15	1.5	4	15	5	1.	3.

Sources: See page 252.

than it would like. At the same time, its supply of convertible currency is often adversely affected because it has less coffee, sugar, meat, or mineral output available for sale to the West. Consequently, the smaller country often finds itself more and more dependent on Soviet trade. This strategy has worked exceptionally well in such countries as India, Egypt, and Ghana. However, except for Brazil and Cuba, the Latin American countries have been unusually wary of such deals and have managed to maintain a cash relationship in most of their negotiations (perhaps a lesson learned from their dealings with Hitler's Germany in the 1930's). The Soviet pattern of trade is remarkably similar.

The Pattern

The first country to establish significant economic relations with the U.S.S.R. was Argentina, which signed a trade agreement with the Soviet Union as early as August, 1953. This was several months before the U.S.S.R. decided to seek the friendship of the developing countries. With Perón's backing, there was an exchange of trade delegations in 1954. The summer of the following year, Perón allowed the Russians to present an industrial exhibition in Buenos Aires, one of the first such shows outside the Soviet bloc. With the overthrow of Perón in September, 1955, the growing rapprochement was temporarily halted. It was not until October 27, 1958, that the Russians presented Argentina with a credit for $100 million. This was the first Russian loan to a Latin American country, but it has been largely unutilized.

Except in 1956 and 1958, Soviet imports from Argentina have always exceeded Soviet exports. Argentina's own trade figures show less of a trade imbalance and a slight Soviet export balance for 1958–60. Because of the wheat shortages in the U.S.S.R. in 1963–65, and Soviet purchases of Argentinian wheat, the Soviet imbalance in trade has increased with no offsetting economic or political advantage for Argentina. Initially, the imbalance was financed with convertible currency, which was to Argentina's advantage. But the Russians have subsequently tied their purchase of Argentina's wheat to a reciprocal purchase of Soviet oil: one ton of wheat for one ton of oil. In 1965, the Russians ordered the equivalent of $170-million worth of wheat, most of it in exchange for petroleum.[1]

Uruguay was also an early trading partner of the Soviet Union, although political relations between the two seem to have been much less significant than was the case with Argentina. Financial and trade negotiations were first conducted in July, 1954. On August 11, 1956, a trade and shipping agreement was signed. Until 1960, Soviet purchases of wool in Uruguay were important. In fact, in 1959, Russia was one of

Uruguay's largest wool customers. In 1960, the Russians attempted to switch from a convertible cash basis to a barter basis as a means of financing their trade. They wanted to pay for all of their purchases with Soviet oil. The Uruguayans refused. They insisted on cash or no deal, obviously a dangerous way to treat one of your largest customers. Fortunately for Uruguay, it found other cash customers and actually managed to sell its full wool output in 1961 for the first time in several years. Export revenues hit a peak and Uruguay was able to avoid becoming unduly dependent on the U.S.S.R. In recent years, the Russians have returned to purchase Uruguayan wool with cash.

Chile was subjected to similar pressures by the Russians. When Chile sent a trade delegation to the Soviet Union in January, 1960, the Russians offered to buy 60,000 metric tons of Chile's copper a year for a five-year period if Chile would agree to a barter deal. Like Uruguay, Chile refused. The Russians finally agreed to pay in sterling, and in September, 1962, they bought 1,000 metric tons of copper for $644,000. Chile resisted the Russian demand for barter at least for the time, but it lost a sizable sales opportunity. The Chinese have also entered the copper market, and in mid-1965 purchased 6,000 metric tons, apparently for cash.

Mexico's relations with the Soviet Union go back to 1942. However, Soviet interest in Mexico was minimal until Castro took control of Cuba; Soviet purchases from and attention toward Mexico immediately increased. The high point was reached in November, 1959, with Mikoyan's flying trip to Mexico to visit the Soviet trade fair. In recent years, the Russians have started to expand their purchase of Mexican goods. Poland sent a trade delegation to Mexico in early 1961 and China and Mexico signed a trade agreement in late 1963.

Brazil has received more attention from the Communist bloc than any other Latin American country except Cuba. As was true with Mexico and Chile, Soviet interest in Brazil increased with Castro's accession to power. For what appeared to be political rather than economic reasons, Russia, a tea-drinking country, announced the purchase of large quantities of Brazilian coffee. In the widely publicized trade agreement of December 9, 1959, the Soviet Union agreed to purchase $25 million in coffee in 1960, $37 million in 1961, and $45 million in 1962. There was some disagreement whether this amount was to be spent solely on coffee or on other goods as well. In return, the Russians were to provide Brazil with wheat. In 1964, when the Russians found themselves short of wheat, they switched their exchange offering to petroleum. They arranged to supply one-third of Brazil's needed oil (about 4 million tons), worth about $21 million. As the Soviet trade

figures in Table IX-1 indicate, the Russians did not buy as much coffee as they had promised. (Brazilian statistics show the same shortfall.)
Still, there was a significant increase in trade after the signing of the
pact. But except for 1960, the Soviet Union bought more than it sold to
Brazil, and once again the country with the export surplus found itself
in a dilemma. What could it buy with the rubles? It could buy more oil,
but Brazil, especially after the 1964 revolution, was reluctant to buy
more than one-third of its petroleum from the U.S.S.R. for fear of becoming even more dependent. In order to generate more flexibility and
prevent a curtailment of trading arrangements, both sides agreed to extend each other a $10-million commercial loan to permit temporary
imbalances of trade.[2] Finally, in an attempt to salvage something from
its favorable but nonliquid trade balance with the U.S.S.R., Minister of
Planning Roberto Campos asked the Russians in the summer of 1965
to finance the construction of a dam on the Parana River. The Russians agreed instead, in August, 1966, to provide $100 million in credit
for industrial equipment—a move that was indicative of their newly
commercial approach. In contrast to the usual pattern, the credit was
extended for only eight years at the commercial rate of 4 per cent. It is
in such ways that trade and aid are often interconnected.

The Brazilians have also developed extensive trading relations with
other countries in Eastern Europe. A Brazilian trade delegation was
sent to Eastern Europe to seek loans and promote trade in April, 1961.
By the time they had returned home they had managed to obtain promises of loans from everyone but Bulgaria and the Soviet Union itself.
Rumania offered $50 million, Hungary $60 million, Czechoslovakia $60
million, Poland $26 million, and East Germany $40 million. Subsequently, East Germany apparently offered another $50 million. It is un-
clear how many if any of these loans have been accepted by Brazil. Except for Poland, whose offer was not accepted by Brazil, these offers
were all larger than the formal loans the same countries made to Cuba.
Similarly, the trade of the various East European countries with Brazil
was almost as large as it was with Cuba. Obviously Brazil was considered to be an important area for economic penetration.

The Special Case of Cuba

The Latin country most involved with the Soviet bloc is Cuba. Cer-
tainly Soviet activity in Cuba does not follow the usual pattern. It is to
Cuba that the world has directed its attention and it is here that the
U.S.S.R. has had its biggest successes and perhaps its greatest problems.
It is not clear what role, if any, the U.S.S.R. played in bringing about
Castro's victory in 1959. There is evidence to indicate that the local

Communist Party actually opposed Castro for some time.[3] Certainly, it cannot be said that Soviet economic aid caused Cuba to turn Communist. Russia's purchases of sugar in the 1950's actually strengthened Batista's government. However, there is no doubt that the U.S.S.R. did benefit after Castro took over, largely because of the strong nationalistic and anti-Yankee feelings he generated throughout Latin America. In asserting his independence from the United States, he sought an alliance with the only other world power that would then support him in this endeavor. As was true in Argentina and Brazil, anti-Americanism, as much as attraction for Communism, has facilitated Soviet inroads into Latin America.

Soviet ties with Cuba date back to World War II. Diplomatic relations between the two countries were established in 1942, when both were members of the Allied Powers. Relations were broken in 1952 during the Korean War and re-established by Castro on January 10, 1959. However, the Soviet Union was a major purchaser of Cuban sugar as early as 1955. In 1957, it bought about $50-million worth. (See Table IX-1.) With Castro settled in power, sugar sales increased rapidly and reached more than $100 million in 1960. In 1961, sugar sales to the U.S.S.R. exceeded $300 million. Since this was at a time when the U.S.S.R. was not seriously short of sugar, some wags have suggested that after the coffee deal with Brazil in December, 1959, the Russians decided they had better buy some extra sugar.

Cuba's financial arrangement with the Soviet Union is complicated. It is made even more confusing by the sale of military equipment. Because the details of the military transactions are not known, it is harder to isolate the purely commercial dealings from the export-import information. Sugar exports are probably being used to repay not only commercial debts, but also military purchases. Thus the existence of a trade surplus does not necessarily mean that the Cubans still have claims on Soviet commercial commodities. These surpluses may have been previously pre-empted to pay for military imports.

The first Soviet loan to Cuba, announced in February, 1960, was for $100 million to finance the construction of two thermal electric plants, an oil refinery, a fertilizer plant, an auto repair shop, a housing project, and the refitting or construction of three metallurgical plants. The Russians also agreed to make a geological survey and build a fishing port.[4] Shortly thereafter, virtually all the European satellites and China followed Russia's lead and offered formal loans. In June, 1960, Czechoslovakia offered $40 million for a tractor and truck factory and agricultural machinery; Bulgaria offered a total of $6 million in two loans made in October, 1960, and January, 1961; China offered $60 million,

Table IX-2

SOVIET-CUBAN SUGAR TRANSACTIONS

	Production	Actual Delivery	Sales Plan (May, 1960) (in Millions of Tons)	Sales Revised (December, 1960)	Sales Revised (October, 1961)	Sales Revised (December, 1962)	Sales Revised (January, 1964)	Soviet Price (in Dollars)	World Price per Pound (in Dollars)
1960	6	1.5	.425			a		.03[b]	.03
1961	6.7	3.3[c]	1	2.7	3.2			.04	.02-.03
1962	4.8	2.2	1		3.2				.02-.03
1963	3.882	1	1		3.2			.06[d]	.09-.12
1964	4.398	1	1		3.2				.11-.02
1965	6.050				3.2		2.1		.02
1966	4.5[e]						3		
1967							4		
1968							5		
1969							5		
1970	10[f]						5		

Sources: See pages 252-53.

[a] No new figures given.
[b] The Soviets paid the world price of $.03 until December, 1960.
[c] Includes .5 to China.
[d] As of June, 1963.
[e] Preliminary.
[f] Plan.

and was followed by East Germany with $10 million, Hungary with $15 million, Rumania with $15 million, and Poland with $27 million.[5]

The most important financial negotiations were not the credits, but the sugar agreements. The Russians demanded that Cuba pay in sugar for almost all the equipment it received. In early 1960, the Russians agreed to purchase 425,000 tons of sugar. (See Table IX-2.) The agreement also stipulated that from 1961 to 1964, the Russians were to step up their purchases to 1 million tons a year. It was decided that this sugar would be purchased at the prevailing world price, then about $.03 a pound. Twenty per cent of the bill would be paid in cash and the rest in goods. The initial plans were revised in December, 1960, when the Soviet Union contracted to take up to 2.7 million tons a year in the event that the United States boycotted the Cuban sugar market. The Cubans were also able to win a price increase to $.04, a subsidy close to what Cuba had previously been receiving from the United States. The following year, in October, 1961, Cuba apparently found it increasingly difficult to find adequate outlets for sugar and again prevailed upon the Soviet Union to increase its purchases. This the Soviet Union did. It agreed to step up its orders to 3.2 million tons and committed the whole bloc to 4.86 million tons annually for the five-year period 1961–65. The Soviet Union did in fact buy 3.3 million tons in 1961, its largest acquisition until at least 1965. However, as a charitable gesture, the Soviet Union rerouted 500,000 tons of sugar to China during the time of China's food shortages. (Because the Chinese had their own Cuban sugar, the Russians generously gave the Chinese until 1964–67 to repay them.) The Soviet Union ordered 2.2 million tons of sugar for 1962, but a new problem arose when the Cuban sugar harvest fell to one-half the 1961 level.

Castro had long complained that the United States had dominated Cuba and restricted it to a monoculture based on sugar. In an effort to break out of this enslavement, he embarked on a crash program of industrialization and crop diversification. As a result, sugar was neglected. In fact, no new sugar was planted in 1960 and 1961. Sugar output was further affected by the uncooperative reaction of the peasants to Castro's land reform edicts. Thus the sugar harvest fell sharply in 1962, and reserve stocks were quickly exhausted. As a result, Cuba found itself with inadequate supplies of convertible and ruble currency to pay for its imports of heavy equipment. To obtain convertible currency, it sought to divert some of its sugar crop to non-Communist countries. This could be done only if the Soviets agreed to revise their October, 1961, purchase agreement for the period 1962 and after. This the Russians did in December, 1962. Although the specific adjustment agreed to was not made public, Russian imports in both 1963 and 1964 were about 1 million tons.

Soon after the revision of the purchase agreement, there was another difficulty. As Cuba's sugar crop diminished, the price in the world market rose sharply. From a price of $.02–$.03 per pound, it reached a peak of $.09–$.12 in late 1962 and early 1963. Because the Russians were paying only $.04 a pound, what had once been a Soviet subsidy now became a Cuban subsidy. The Russians agreed in June, 1963, to raise their price to $.06 a pound. This may have been partial compensation for Soviet mistakes in the missile crisis of October, 1962. In any case, the Russians refused to accede fully to Cuban requests to pay a higher price for the sugar. Ironically, the world price in sugar then fell again during 1964 to about $.02 a pound, and the Russians ended up paying a subsidy after all.

When sugar production began to rise, the Cubans asked the Russians to revise their plans again and to increase their purchases. This was arranged in January, 1964. The Soviets promised to buy 2.1 million tons in 1965, 3 million in 1966, 4 million in 1967, and 5 million tons annually from 1968 to 1970. (The 1965 commitment was in fact more than 1 million tons less than the earlier agreement of October, 1961.) If Cuba is able to increase its sugar output, it is likely that it will request that the Soviet Union buy even more. The bargaining that produced these rapidly changing agreements has not always been harmonious. Clearly, relations between the two countries must have been badly strained at times, especially during the delay between the time the underlying conditions were altered and the time the agreements were revised.

The state of credit negotiations is a further indication that relations between the U.S.S.R. and Cuba have not always been smooth. As the sugar crop suffered and exports to Russia diminished, the export balance which Cuba had maintained from 1955 to 1961 changed into an import balance. Since the Russians had provided a loan of $100 million and a swing credit that permitted a deficit or surplus in trade of $10 million without any interest charge, there appears to have been no problem until 1963. Then, for reasons that are not entirely clear, the earlier export balance in Cuba's favor for 1960 was not added in the ongoing calculations. In 1963, it was announced that the Cuban trade deficit had become excessive and that a new loan would be necessary. Thus, it was agreed on February 6, 1963, but not officially approved until almost a year later (December 26, 1963), that the Soviet Union would provide a loan of $403 million at 2 per cent solely for the purpose of covering the trade deficit.[6] There seems to have been no allowance in the calculation for the credit of February, 1960. Furthermore, instead of a positive balance of trade in 1961 of $24 million, as indicated in the Soviet trade figures shown in Table IX-1, the agreement mentions a negative balance of $31 million; similarly, instead of a negative balance of $132 million in 1962, the agreement cites the figure $185 million. It was estimated that the 1963 deficit would be $187 million; it turned out to be $236 million. These discrepancies could mean several things. The calculations could have been based on Cuban trade records, although this is not the normal Soviet practice. The discrepancy is too great in any case. It is more likely that some of the exports of Cuban sugar were being used to pay for military goods. Neither one of these suppositions indicates how, if at all, the original $100-million loan was entered into the calculations. The $403 million of the "second loan" exactly equals the revised trade deficits for 1961–63. It appears likely that the original $100 million was included in the $403 million so that only $303 million should be considered as a new loan. Even then, the $303 million was more in the form of a refunding of already created short-term credit. A third loan, announced in February, 1966, must be regarded in the same way. The Russians reported that they had provided Cuba with $89 million to offset Cuba's negative balance of trade.

According to Soviet trade figures, the trade deficit for 1964 amounted to about $80 million. This was considerably less than the deficit of either $187 million or $236 million officially reported for 1963. However, the trade deficit was reduced at the cost of increasing the burden on Cuba's economy. Despite Cuba's pressing needs, the Russians cut back their exports to Cuba. In 1964, Russian exports fell by $33 million, while the Soviets insisted on an increase in Cuban exports. Thus the Cubans exported $124 million more to Russia in 1964 than they did in 1963, despite the fact that the sugar harvest in 1963 and 1964 was the lowest in modern times. The Russians did the same thing to the Chinese in 1962. Although China at the time was confronted with serious economic difficulties, Chinese exports to Russia exceeded imports by $283 million, the highest surplus in Sino-Soviet history. This, too, was accomplished by the reduction of Soviet exports to the lowest level ever recorded up to that year. The Russians also insisted that the Chinese repay the interest that had accumulated on the loans. In Cuba the pattern was repeated. The first interest payment on the 1963 loan was due in the first quarter of 1964, and principal repayments were due to begin in 1965, when the trade balance fell to a low $33 million. Just as the Chinese were infuriated by such treatment, it is fair to assume that the Cubans were also.

There are indications that Cuban relations with the other satellites have also had their less rapturous moments. At least one of the satellites, Rumania, has apparently decided it has taken enough. Rumanian trade volume fell from $20 million in 1963 to $5 million in 1964, and to $33,000 in the first half of 1965. After waiting for Cuba to pay its bills, Rumania apparently refused to export without obtaining imports in payment. Since the Soviet reaction was in the same vein, it is fair to assume that some of the other satellites also had the same inclinations.

Additional evidence of this is the embarrassing public split that occurred between China and Cuba. After what seemed like a particularly warm romance, sometimes in obvious defiance of Soviet wishes, Castro in January, 1966, suddenly launched a violent attack on China. He accused the Chinese of cutting off vital rice exports to Cuba. This, Castro charged, had necessitated a slash in the basic rice ration of every Cuban citizen. He also claimed that the Chinese were trying to propagandize Cuban military officers against the wishes of the Cuban government. In reply, the Chinese claimed that they needed the rice themselves and that they no longer had any use for the sugar (they had paid back the Russian loan of sugar). Like the Rumanians, the Chinese also insisted that trade with Cuba should be balanced. In the dispute that followed, the Cubans openly linked Chinese efforts at interference and economic imperialism with those of the United States. Certainly underlying the Cuban complaint was the knowledge that food shortages at home had not previously prevented the Chinese from helping more cooperative countries with rice shipments in the past. Castro argued that the turn in events was politically inspired, specifically, that China resented Cuba's increased reliance on the U.S.S.R. Whatever the provocation, this was an incredible spectacle for the non-Communist world.

In addition to the tension already evidenced between Cuba and some of the satellite countries, there have been problems in connection with providing adequate transportation from Eastern Europe to Cuba. Cuba's remoteness from Eastern Europe, the general inadequacy of the Soviet merchant-marine fleet, and the shipping boycott imposed by the United States have not only made it difficult for the bloc to supply Cuba adequately, but have adversely affected the bloc's trade relations and balance of payments with both Western and developing countries. Because of the shipping boycott, those ships at the disposal of the Soviet Union must frequently be taken off their normal commercial runs in order to ensure transportation service to Cuba. Soviet commerce with other countries must then be sent in foreign ships, which costs Russia convertible currency. Occasionally the magnitude of Cuba's needs has even caused difficulty within the U.S.S.R. There were reports that dockworkers in Odessa in 1961 had refused to load Soviet butter on a ship destined for Cuba.[7] It was not that the Russians disliked Castro; on the contrary, they idolized him. But they resented the fact that there was no butter in Odessa's shops.

On Cuba's side, a fundamental source of resentment is the realization that a switch in allegiance from the United States to the Soviet Union did not bring immediate economic independence. Like China, Cuba has had to postpone its dream of industrialization. In 1963, Castro announced that Cuba's first priority was again sugar and the development of agriculture. Hence the plan to build a Cuban steel mill has been scrapped. Even more ironic, agricultural efficiency and reform is usually the greatest shortcoming in every Communist country. After winning peasant support with the promise of land, the land is nationalized after the revolution. The peasant generally becomes more alienated and less productive than before. At considerable cost, Cuba managed to increase its 1965 production of sugar to nearly the levels that prevailed in 1960 and 1961. But it must pain the Cubans to ship raw sugar to the U.S.S.R. and see the Russians process it and re-export it in the form of refined sugar. There is not much difference between this and traditional colonial exploitation. Like any imperialist country, the Russians are not averse to imposing economic pressure if there is no possibility of alternative help. In many respects, Cuba is faced with the same basic economic problems as before Castro.

It would be incorrect to leave the impression that there are no advantages to the alliance between Cuba and the Soviet bloc. Castro could not have remained independent of the United States without Soviet support and supplies. Since the alliance has not been broken, the Cubans must find that the advantages of such a relationship outweigh the disadvantages. Nevertheless, it is easy to see that it has not been free of strains.

10. Africa: Repayment Problems and the African Mystique

Economic development in Africa has a mystique of its own. Operating conditions and what passes for economic rationality in Africa are often significantly different from those that prevail in the developed areas of the world. There are even major differences between some of the concepts of economic development in Africa and those that predominate in other developing areas. This presents special problems for an outside country that hopes to make an impression with its foreign aid. Africa is rich in natural resources and national dreams, but poor in operational know-how. The colonialists from Western Europe long ago realized the hazards of trying to win over the Africans. The Soviets in sub-Saharan Africa today are encountering experiences similar to those of their West European predecessors.

Guinea

A study of Soviet experience in Guinea provides the ideal tonic for those who believe that history is on the side of the Communists. In 1958, after Guinea voted to leave the French family of nations, the French, in anger, ripped out the phones and tossed most of the country's machinery into the sea. Simultaneously, France induced the rest of the Western world to boycott Guinea in the hope that the country would be forced to turn again to the French for assistance. Instead, Guinea turned to the members of the Communist bloc for economic and political help. The U.S.S.R. signed a trade agreement in February, 1959, and an aid agreement in August, 1959. These agreements gave the Soviet Union its first opportunity for economic and political penetration of sub-Saharan Africa.[1] In the years that followed, Guinea became an ardent admirer of the Russians. There was little doubt that Guinea was on the verge of becoming an African Cuba. By December, 1960, there were reports that the Russians had obtained an agreement to establish a submarine base on Guinea's coast. Yet, only twelve months later, on December 16, 1961, Sékou Touré, the President of Guinea, accused Soviet Ambassador Daniel Solod of meddling in Guinea's internal affairs. This was the same man who, six years earlier, had been so adroit at winning a Soviet foothold in Egypt and Aswan. Charged with fomenting a strike and encouraging a coup, he was expelled from Guinea.

To understand what had precipitated such an unanticipated reversal, it is necessary to learn more about what the Russians did in Guinea. The aid agreement of August, 1959, provided Guinea with a loan of $35 million. The specific projects to be financed under this loan were spelled out in a detailed protocol of March 1, 1960. This first loan was later supplemented by a second loan, which raised the total amount of credits to $61–75 million. In addition there was a gift of $7–8 million for a radio station and another gift of a 500-bed hospital.[2] A military loan of about $3 million was also arranged.

At first, the Russians were eager to answer Guinea's every need. They agreed to build a large sawmill at N'Zerekore, a shoe factory in Kindia (able to produce 500,000 pairs of shoes a year), a fruit and vegetable cannery at Mamou (with an output of 5 million cans a year), and a cold-storage plant in Conakry (with a 3,000-ton capacity). They promised to conduct geological studies for cement, gold, and diamonds, and at one time they spoke of building a cement plant. To aid agriculture, the Russians sent in agricultural machinery to help operate a state rice farm of 7,000 hectares. They shipped Soviet cattle to a dairy farm at Dittnn with the intention of opening a dairy. They completed the airport and runway begun by the French at Conakry. Since Guinea had few airplanes capable of using the airport, the Russians agreed to supply Air Guinea with 4 Ilyushin-18's and 6 Ilyushin-14's. The initial cost of the aircraft, as well as the annual operating expense of $5–10 million a year, was financed by Soviet funds which apparently were above and beyond the basic $75-million loan. They also provided aid for the construction of a railroad from Conakry to Mamou. Finally, in Conakry, the Russians built a 25,000-seat Olympic stadium and swimming pool, the modernistic Polytechnic Institute, and the 120-room Camayenne Hotel.

As the Russians started to complete their projects, numerous shortcomings became readily apparent. The Russian-built factories were generally too large in both size and productive capacity for a small country with a population of about 3 million. The Russians are accustomed to building for a population of over 200 million. Of course, it is anticipated that the excess capacity in Guinea will be utilized for export sales. But it is questionable whether it is wise to produce for foreign markets before it is proven that the plant is efficient enough to compete in domestic markets. There is also some question about how much trade might be realized when Guinea's neighbors are often producers of the same kind of food and clothing products. A large but underutilized plant usually costs more money than a small but fully utilized factory. Moreover each year the creditor becomes more insistent that the debt be repaid, whether or not the plant is self-liquidating. Virtually every Soviet project in Guinea has been criticized because none of them provided for the repayment of Soviet loans. The factories are too large and do not earn a profit, much less foreign exchange. Because the secondary schools within the country do not produce enough graduates, the Polytechnic Institute as of mid-1964 had only 100 students with accommodations for 1,400 more. The airline, with its inefficient Ilyushins, has required a steady flow of financial support. Engine overhauls were necessary every 700 hours and major repairs could be undertaken only in Moscow. Excessive operating costs made profitable operation impossible. Consequently, in 1965, Guinea sent back more than one-half of its Soviet airfleet and replaced the planes with American DC-4's, which need overhauling only every 1,800 hours.[3] They also signed a servicing and training agreement with Pan American Airways to replace an earlier one with Aeroflot.

Many of the other projects were equally unproductive. The $2.5-million stadium brought in no foreign exchange or goods that could be used for repayment. Even the hotel, which had the potential for generating foreign exchange from tourists, was a burden for a long time because Guinea could find no one to operate it. As in Burma, the Russians were unwilling to take over the running of the hotel. Consequently, the completed hotel was empty from at least April, 1964, until October of the same year. When asked about this, the Soviet Ambassador to Guinea replied that he would prefer to have a Swiss firm run the hotel but would, if necessary, settle for an American operator. Even the radio station, which was presented as a gift, was criticized. It seems that Mount Kakoulima on which it was located is rich in iron ore and therefore poor in radio transmission.

Besides their excessive scale, Soviet projects were not always designed for the rigors of Guinea's climatic conditions. In tropical weather a piece of equipment that is not used regularly rusts or deteriorates. The remoteness of Guinea and the difficulty of supplying equipment with Russia's inadequate merchant marine fleet are added handicaps. As a result, the docks and even the streets of Conakry, the main port, are crammed with equipment waiting for installation. That which has been there for weeks or years is obviously no longer in suitable condition. Soviet machinery is primarily intended for temperate or Arctic conditions. Only belatedly did the Russians realize that a tractor with the exhaust pipe passing through the enclosed cab for extra heat is inappropriate in Guinea. Similarly, Soviet technicians find it hard to adjust to year-round tropical heat. While initially travel to Africa may have been regarded as an exotic opportunity, the thrill soon turned into discomfort and boredom for most Russians. When the author asked the Assistant Director of the modern Polytechnic Institute how long he had been in Conakry, he instantly replied, "394 days!"

Everyone (including the Russians) agrees that it has not been easy for the U.S.S.R. in Guinea. Because of dissatisfaction on the part of both parties, work on all Russian projects was halted from the spring to the fall of 1963. Construction was then resumed, and some of the projects (the hotel, the institute, and the stadium) have been completed. But completion also brings a bill for services rendered. Unfortunately, although Guinea has tremendous economic potential, at present its resources are seriously underdeveloped and overtaxed. Thus Guinea finds itself unable to repay the Russian debt of about $10 million, which is due in both 1965 and again in 1966. What resources it could export to the U.S.S.R. it now finds it can sell in the West for convertible currency, which it naturally prefers to do. When the Russians complain about overdue repayments, the Guineans respond by criticizing the Russians for allowing Guinea to build projects that do nothing to increase the country's export or productive potential. The Russians point out that to restore Guinea's self-confidence after the French withdrawal, they agreed to do virtually anything Guinea wanted. As the Soviet Ambassador told me, "Guinea was in such a state of economic and psychological shock, we felt we could not refuse her requests." To this Guinea officials have retorted, "But the Russians were more experienced than we and should have known better." Privately, many Russians in Guinea acknowledge their errors.

There are many lessons for Americans to learn from the Guinean experience. One of the more obvious is that it is easier to let someone else make the first mistakes. Usually the Russians begin their foreign-aid program only after the Americans have had a chance to make the first blunders. In Guinea, the situation was reversed and the United States had a chance to profit from Soviet errors. Furthermore, Guinea shows the value of a flexible foreign policy. With an adaptability not often found in American diplomacy, the United States tried to maintain communications and friendship with Guinea for several months, even though there was no reason to expect anything but the worst in Guinean-American relations. After Ambassador Solod's expulsion, the United States quietly followed up the incident with an offer of American aid and an invitation for Sékou Touré to visit President Kennedy.

The U.S. aid program was inaugurated in May, 1962, and Touré's visit followed in October. By late 1965, American aid to Guinea totaled $65 million, half of which had been in the form of food. This is about $10 million short of what the Russians have promised, but from all appearances, American aid will shortly surpass Soviet aid in quantity and impact.

Guinea has by no means become a lackey of the United States, but it has reasserted its independence from the Communist countries. Two disparate examples indicate just how independent Guinea has become. At the time of the Cuban missile crisis, in the fall of 1962, Guinea denied a Russian request to land Cuban-bound planes at the Conakry airport. This created more than the usual dismay in the Soviet Union since it was the Russians who had reconstructed the airport only a few months before. In another case, the Conakry office of the Russian news agency Novosti was closed down after it attacked the work of the U.S. Peace Corps in Guinea.

It would be incorrect to say that the honeymoon had been spoiled solely by a bungled foreign-aid program. Obviously, Ambassador Solod's interference in domestic politics was the major reason. Furthermore, despite blunders, the fact remains that some of the Soviets' projects have made a positive contribution; certainly their mistakes cannot be compared with their failures in Indonesia. Nevertheless, Guinea's relations with the Soviet Union have taken a turn for the worse. Dissatisfaction with Soviet foreign aid has been at least partially responsible.

The efforts of some of the other Communist countries in Guinea have not been too much more successful than those of the Soviet Union. The Czechs have promised about $10 million in aid, but they walked out on a telecommunications project they were building at Kipe.[4] East German aid totals about $5 million. One of the major projects is an outdoor theater, situated on a busy corner in Conakry, which is only a quarter complete; the structure has taken on the appearance of the Roman Coliseum. Some Guineans have complained to the Germans that the theater is an eyesore and that if some way can be found to protect the neighboring buildings, it should be blown up. A somewhat more successful venture has been the Patrice Lumumba Printing Press. The press is reported to be larger than what Guinea needs, and there is some question whether enough printing work can be brought in from outside the country to keep it busy. The Hungarians started to build a glass factory as part of a $2.5-million loan, but stopped. Guinea announced it would refuse to repay the loan after the Hungarians increased the cost of the plant to as much as three or four times the original estimate. The Hungarians were also reported to be constructing a waterworks at Dingiuraya. Poland has made an offer of $5 million and Bulgaria has promised $2 million, but both countries are apparently having trouble finding projects on which they can agree with the Guineans.

Guinea is one of the few countries in Africa where the Chinese have completed the construction of an industrial-aid project. As part of a $24 million loan, the Chinese have built a cigarette and match factory for an estimated $3 million. While it too seems rather large for Guinea's needs, it does indicate what China can do when it considers a project important enough. The Guineans have been appreciative of Chinese efforts; sometimes more appreciative than they are of Russia's. An issue of the Conakry paper included an article about the Russian sawmill being built at N'Zerekore. No mention was made of the fact that it was being built by the Russians. On the opposite page, an article about the cigarette factory was extremely complimentary to the Chinese. Subsequently, however, there were reports that the Chinese factory had to be closed down because of the lack of foreign currency to buy imported tobacco. The Chinese have undertaken operation of a tea plantation near Macenta, and they were making surveys for a dam site at Kin Kon, on which work had begun in July, 1964.[5] The Chinese have also supplied goods as a form of foreign aid, including 15,000 tons of rice delivered in May and August, 1960. Finally, China provided Guinea with a loan of $7 million in convertible currency. Reportedly, the Guineans used some of this to buy some 250 Mercedes Benz automobiles for Guinean officials. The ones that have not already been cannibalized still may be seen on Conakry's bumpy streets.

Ghana

Communist efforts in other parts of sub-Saharan Africa have not been much more rewarding than in Guinea. The expulsion of Russian officials from the Congo is a well-known story. Soviet foreign-aid experience in Ghana, until February, 1966, while politically more effective, was not very successful in economic terms. After the ouster of President Kwame Nkrumah in February, 1966, there were major questions about the political successes.

Russia's first loan to Ghana was announced on August 4, 1960. Initially for $40 million, it was subsequently increased to $82 million.[6] Nevertheless, as of 1966 no Soviet aid projects of any significance had been completed. The most impressive project in Ghana has been the Volta Dam, sponsored by the United States government and Edgar Kaiser Industries and completed in 1965. The Soviets have no projects, completed or planned, to compare with this $200-million dam, with its lake of nearly 3,500 square miles and its 768 megawatts of power.

The Russians at one time planned to build a competing dam on the Volta at Boui. Located upstream of the Volta Dam, the Boui Dam was scheduled to produce 200 kilowatts and was to be completed by 1966. Cost estimates ranged as high as $75 million. As of 1964, the Russians had spent $3 million on equipment and surveys for the project, and Ghanaians were being trained in the Soviet Union for the eventual construction work. But with the completion of the Volta Dam, there seemed to be little need for additional electrical power until at least the mid-1970's. Thus the project is at a standstill. The same is true of the other projects connected with the dam, including an electrical grid system which without the dam is useless.

Other, smaller Soviet projects include a fish-processing plant, a dry-dock at Tema, and a metal foundry capable of producing 2,500 tons of pig iron a year. A prefabricated housing project at Tema was started in October, 1963. The Russians have also promised to build an atomic reactor worth about $5 million; three technical schools for machine-tool work, technical engineering, and agriculture; a gold-refining factory; a textile mill; and a 200-bed hospital; [7] plans for a paper mill have apparently been abandoned. On a cash basis, Ghana purchased twenty-one fishing ships from the U.S.S.R.

As in Afghanistan, the Russians have been conducting their own form of P.L. 480 aid. In March, 1963, they apparently shipped in $22-million worth of Soviet goods for sale on local markets. The proceeds were used to finance the local currency needs of the Russians. Ghana has also been one of the few countries to receive agricultural help from the U.S.S.R. Four state farms were built and equipped with Soviet aid. It was intended that these farms would produce rice, corn, and cotton. As might be expected, given Soviet experience with tropical agriculture, all of the farms have thus far been unsuccessful and unprofitable. Finally, the Russians have provided aid to the Ghanaian airline in the form of nine Il-18 planes and have promised to build an aircraft maintenance workshop. The planes proved to be too costly to operate, and in late 1963, five of them were returned; the workshop has not yet been built.

Military aid to Ghana is classified information, but the Russians had apparently delivered at least $1 million in equipment by 1961. In mid-1964, there were reliable reports that Ghana had sought about $10 million for the construction of an airport with an 11,000-foot runway, one of the largest of its kind in Africa. Since it was to be located about 400 miles from Accra and most commercial activity, it was believed that the airport would be built primarily for military purposes.

Soviet commercial activity in Ghana has had a considerably greater impact than foreign aid. Like most developing countries, Ghana has had serious balance-of-payment problems with the Western world. Although foreign reserves amounted to almost $500 million in 1959, they were squandered at a rapid rate so that they had fallen to less than $100 million in 1964. Simultaneously, foreign debt rose from about $55 million in 1960 to over $500 million in 1964. Finding themselves unable to finance their ever-increasing imports from the West and seeing that they earned less and less as the price of cocoa continued to fall, the Ghanaians increasingly turned to Russia and Eastern Europe for their imports. By 1963, Russia had an accumulated trade deficit with Ghana of over $700 million. This meant that although Ghana had been selling large quantities of its cocoa crop to the U.S.S.R., it had been unable to find enough suitable goods to buy in the U.S.S.R. At the same time, less and less of its cocoa crop was left over for sale to Western Europe and the United States. In 1963, 22 per cent of Ghana's cocoa crop was sold to the bloc. This is even more serious than it appears, since not only are the Ghanaians selling more and more of their crop to the Communist countries, but they are receiving less and less convertible currency for their products and receiving rubles instead. In 1962, the Soviet Union agreed to pay for 55 per cent of its purchases in pounds sterling. In 1963, this was to fall to 50 per cent, in 1964 to 40 per cent, in 1965 to 30 per cent, and in 1966 to 20 per cent. As in Latin America and India, the commercial penetration of the U.S.S.R. and the resulting trade surpluses which accrue to the developing countries are more of a danger than succumbing to Soviet foreign aid. There was some indication that just before his overthrow, President Nkrumah had finally realized the hazards in such a situation and was trying to reduce such barter sales to Eastern Europe.[8] As an indication of Ghana's financial plight, two days before Nkrumah's fall from power it was announced that Russia had agreed to a moratorium on the repayment of Soviet credits and short-term loans.

Aid to Ghana had also been promised by some other Communist countries. In 1961, Hungary extended a loan of $14 million, mostly in export credits.[9] This was to include the construction of an electric light-bulb factory and a pharmaceutical plant. Czechoslovakia agreed to build a sugar refinery at Amudome, a hydroelectric station near Pra, and a shoe factory, at a total cost of about $7 million. Poland provided a loan of $14 million for a power project and a metallurgical factory. It also agreed to build a sugar refinery to process sugar cane. It was planned that the cane would be grown on land to be irrigated by the American-built Volta Dam at Akosombo, an example of international cooperation between aid-giving countries. East Germany had committed itself to providing a printing press at Tema at a cost of about $2 million and Bulgaria agreed to develop some of Accra's beaches for use as a resort.

As a challenge to the U.S.S.R., China increased its initial December, 1961, loan of $20 million by another $22 million in July, 1964. Except for sending three agricultural technicians in 1964, however, the Chinese have done little for Ghana. The supplemental loan in mid-1964 was probably intended to influence Ghana at the Algerian conference.

Mali

The nature of Soviet aid to landlocked Mali is not too much different from what it is in Ghana. The initial aid agreement was signed on March 18, 1961, and involved a loan of $44 million. The loan was subsequently increased to $61 million.[10] The main project was the construction of a 200-mile railroad link between Bomako, the capital of Mali, and Kouroussa, the rail terminal in Guinea. Completion of this line would have provided an alternative link to the sea for Mali, making it independent of its traditional port at Dakar in Senegal. But the need for the new railroad line became less urgent as relations between Mali and Senegal gradually improved from the low point reached at the breakup of their federation. Thus, even though Soviet engineers had completed a survey of the prospective roadbed, the project apparently has been postponed.

The Soviet Union spent about $10 million on geological surveys for oil, gold, and cement. The cement explorations were evidently successful since the Russians agreed to build a 50,000-ton cement plant in 1965. This represented a reduction in the 100,000-ton capacity originally intended.[11] The Russians also aided with surveys and development along 125 miles of the River Niger and built a school for 300 students. Another $10 million was allocated for agricultural work. Included in this figure were funds for agricultural equipment and a Polytechnic and Agricultural Institute at Katibougov.[12]

As in Guinea, the Russians were also involved in constructing a 25,000-seat stadium. Since Bomako already had two suitable stadiums, a loan for a third stadium hardly seemed like the best expenditure of funds. Russian engineers working on the project were openly annoyed at having to build such an unnecessary project. A native engineer working with the Russians mischievously answered, when asked why the new stadium was being built, "The other two stadiums are out of date; they were built by the imperialist French. We need a new and modern stadium; one that is built by the Communist Russians."

As in Guinea and Ghana, the Russians have also provided aid to Mali's airline. And as elsewhere, this help has been of a continuing nature with little indication when it will be self-liquidating. According to official reports, an initial subsidy of $6.4 million was increased to $11 million the following year. There has also been an unspecified amount of military aid in the form of Russian trucks, jeeps, and artillery.

While Mali seems to be firmly committed to the Soviet Union, it seems clear that Russian aid has not been as helpful as anticipated. Many of the projects did nothing to increase the country's productive capacity. Some of the others were abandoned or were poorly planned. For instance, some of the prospecting work of the Russians has proved to be so unsatisfactory that Mali has had to call in the Winston Diamond Company of the United States to take over from the Russians. The Russian exhibition held in Mali in 1964 suffered from faulty planning. The Russians included in their exhibition a model of their justly famous atomic ice-breaker *Lenin* and a display of Soviet furs—two exhibits which did not arouse much enthusiasm in the 105-degree heat of the country.

The Chinese seem to have come off considerably better. Their exhibition consisted of consumer goods which were then offered for sale (duty-free to the fair visitors). They also had a display of rice produced on Mali farms with Chinese assistance. The Chinese thus were able to show that something had been accomplished with at least a portion of their $20 million, and that in fact they had helped Mali produce an item which at one time had been a traditional Chinese export. The Chinese claimed that their good intentions were demonstrated by their willingness to aid other countries in the mastery of economic activities that could compete with their products. Actually, since China had been so short of food, the possibility of China producing for the rice market in Mali was unlikely, but it was a nice gesture. In addition to the Chinese loan, there were also loans of $10–12 million from the Czechs, $7 million from Poland, and an unspecified sum from Bulgaria.

Sudan

Total promises of aid to Sudan from the Soviet Union are relatively small in amount. Only $22 million has been offered. Most of the projects are related to the food industry. The Soviet Union is building grain elevators at Gedaref and Port Sudan. Also scheduled for construction are a milk plant at Babanoosa, an onion-dedydrating plant at Kassela, and fruit canneries at Wau and at Kirina. Proposals for future projects include some fish canneries, another grain elevator, and a cement plant. As of mid-1963, it was estimated that only about $2-million worth of credits had actually been utilized. The Russians have also built a veterinary laboratory and an agricultural research station. Both the laboratory and research station were presented to Sudan as gifts worth about $1 million.

Some Sudanese have complained that the Soviet projects were built on too large a scale for Sudanese purposes. As in other countries, this has resulted in excess capacity. As the location of various projects suggests, the Russian projects have been kept out of major urban locations so they and the Soviet technicians would have as little impact as possible. Sudan has been cautious in its relations with the U.S.S.R. It apparently accepted Soviet aid to demonstrate its neutrality.

No other Communist country at this writing has offered a loan to the Sudan. It is worth noting, however, that the Russians and Chinese apparently have had some difficulties with each other over trade concessions. This rivalry dates back to 1958, long before the start of overt feuding. In 1958, Sudan allowed a private Sudanese trader to barter almost $3-million worth of Sudanese cotton to China. In 1959, virtually the same package was sold instead to the U.S.S.R., and the Chinese were apparently frozen out.[13] It is logical to assume that the Chinese were not entirely pleased with the Soviet encroachment.

Ethiopia

Russia was offering assistance to Ethiopia as early as the 1890's. At that time, a group of Russians on their own initiative sent a Red Cross medical team to provide help to disease-ridden Ethiopians. This medical interest was renewed in 1947, when the Soviet Red Cross Hospital was opened in Addis Ababa. Since its opening, the Russian-sponsored hospital has provided medical aid to more than half a million people.[14] The hospital in Addis Ababa stands in contrast to the considerably less successful Soviet-built hospitals in Katmandu and Jakarta.

The modern Soviet aid program began with Emperor Haile Selassie's trip to Moscow in 1959. At that time, the Russians made an offer of $100 million for a series of economic undertakings. No projects were agreed upon until the summer of 1962, when a contract was finally signed for the construction of an oil refinery at Assab. Designed for a capacity of 500,000 tons of crude oil, the project provoked considerable criticism because of its cost and location. Most concerned were the

Western oil firms, which for a long time had vested interests in Ethiopia. These interests proved beneficial to Ethiopia when the Russians ultimately were forced to reduce their price for the refinery. Initially, the Russians claimed the refinery would cost about $20 million. Western counterproposals forced the Russians to lower their price to about $12 million, plus an additional $3 million for a power station. The Russians also agreed to process Western oil in their refinery. Some Westerners expect the Russians eventually to lower their bids on Russian crude oil to induce Ethiopia to use only Russian oil. In mid-1964, Russian officials in Addis Ababa assured me that they were fully prepared to handle any Western-owned oil from the Middle East. If in fact this does happen, it will reverse the usual procedure whereby Western refineries are forced to process Russian oil.

The only other Soviet project completed in Ethiopia as of 1965 was a technical school at Bahr Dar, which was presented as a gift. Opened in 1963 at a cost of about $2 million, this school for 1,000 boys has been staffed primarily by Peace Corps teachers from the United States—the Russians lack enough teachers with a knowledge of English. Again, this offers the spectacle of the commingling of Soviet and American aid with the Americans apparently reaping most of the glory.

Thus of the $100 million in credits that has been made available to Ethiopia, only about $15 million has been committed to specific aid projects. Actual drawings for project and nonproject aid were reported by Soviet officials in Addis Ababa to total about $15 million. This covered work on the refinery and deliveries of Soviet trucks and tractors. A rumor that $1 million or so of this sum had promptly been invested by Ethiopia in the New York money market probably was a factor in the decision of the Soviet Union to send an economic mission in the summer of 1963 to seek out new projects. Ethiopia and the U.S.S.R. agreed to build a tanning factory, a leather and a shoe plant, a meat plant, and vegetable and fruit canneries. As in the Sudan, there are reports that Ethiopia accepted Soviet aid only to show that it too was neutral.

Czechoslovakia is reported to have offered $10 million in 1959 for help in building a canvas shoe (tennis shoe) factory and cotton and sugar plantations. It provided another $1.8 million for the purchase of hospital equipment.

The modest aid provided by the U.S.S.R. to Ethiopia has not been without its difficulties. Ethiopia has been in a periodic state of war with Somalia, which has also received aid from the Russians. Naturally whatever the Russians offer to one country is resented by the other. As we found, similar situations exist in Pakistan and India and Turkey and Cyprus. Ethiopia is a little more sensitive about the matter than Somalia, because Soviet aid to Somalia includes military equipment and technicians reportedly worth about $30 million. Acknowledging the delicacy of their position, the Russians sent Deputy Foreign Minister Yakob Malik to Ethiopia in March, 1964, and again in May, 1966, to explain and reassure Ethiopia about Soviet military aid to Somalia.

Somalia

The bulk of Soviet aid to Somalia derives from a Soviet loan agreement for $52 million made in June, 1961.[15] The agreement includes $8-million worth of goods to be sold in local Somali markets to finance construction expenditures in local currency. Among the projects to be built are a cotton gin, a dairy in Mogadishu, a meat-packing plant and tannery in Chisimaio, and a fish cannery in Lascora. Three state farms were to be built, one for vegetable-oil crops near the Scebeli River, one for cotton near the Guiba River, and one for grain and cattle near Taquagiale. There were also to be dam and irrigation projects. A supplemental protocol in 1964 added a flour mill and a grain elevator. The Russians were also engaged in the construction of a major seaport at Berbera. In addition the Russians made Somalia a gift of a radio transmitter, a printing press, a high school, and a fifty-bed hospital at Wajid.[16]

Not all of the Soviet projects have been appropriate for Somalia's conditions. According to an article in *The New York Times,* the dairy plant at Mogadishu is not near enough to the cows.[17] The first shipment of Soviet flour mildewed when it was not stored properly. The meat-packing plant at Chisimaio was built with a capacity which, if fully utilized, would have totally consumed the nation's supply of livestock.

Yet the Russians in Somalia have apparently been more warmly received than the Chinese. The Chinese have promised loans of $20 million and a grant of $3 million to help balance the budget. However, only half the grant was provided in cash, the rest was in the form of Chinese-made goods which were to be sold in local markets for local currency. Furthermore, although there have been reports that the Chinese would utilize their $20-million loan for a 100-mile road and agricultural scheme, construction has not begun on a single project. The only other Communist country which has offered to help Somalia is Czechoslovakia, which is reported to have offered $30 million for a cement plant and a technological institute.

Other Areas of Sino-Soviet Influence

One notable aspect about much of the aid to Africa is the competitive rivalry between the U.S.S.R. and China. Each one vies with the other to see which can provide the most aid. As we have already seen in Guinea and Ghana, this competitiveness reached a peak just before the scheduled meeting of the Bandung nations in Algeria. Thus in the Congo Republic (Brazzaville), China offered a loan of $5 million in July, 1964, to help balance the budget. This was followed by a Soviet offer of $9 million in late 1964. The Soviet loan was intended for a hydroelectric dam, geological surveys, and a 120-room luxury hotel.[18] In response, the Chinese countered in March, 1965, with yet another offer of $20 million for a variety of small industrial operations.

A similar rivalry in Kenya has been heightened by intrigue over military aid and the establishment of a school for political affairs. The Chinese apparently started off the bidding with the promise of $18–$28 million in aid. This was followed by a rare open-ended promise from the Russians for a series of yet to be chosen projects. The Russians said they would specify the exact amount of their loans when the preliminary feasibility surveys had been completed. However it was estimated that the loan would total at least $2.8 million. It was to cover the approximate cost of such probable projects as textile, fish-canning, fruit-processing, and sugar-refining factories, as well as a radio station.[19] In addition, the Russians offered to build a 200-bed hospital at Kisumu and a technical college for 1,000 students. The Russians ran into a barrage of criticism, however, after they opened the Lumumba Political Affairs Institute in December, 1964. Jomo Kenyatta, the President of Kenya, criticized the school's political nature and its orientation toward the far left. All of its students seem to support Oginga Odinga, Kenya's leftist Vice President until March, 1966. In July, 1965, two months after the school had been shut down, twenty-seven students from the Institute attempted to take over the headquarters of the governing party. Russia was further embarrassed when President Kenyatta in a bitter public statement rejected a shipment of military equipment and technicians from the U.S.S.R. The equipment was criticized because it was obsolete, but there were also rumors that Kenyatta was primarily disturbed because the material had been consigned to Vice President Odinga for his own purposes.

Kenya's displeasure with the Soviet Union was soon matched by its criticism of the Chinese. In May, it was discovered that seventy-five tons of Chinese weapons in eleven trucks had been sent from Tanzania across Kenya's territory to Uganda without official permission. There was concern that the ultimate destination may not have been Uganda, as claimed, but again Vice President Odinga.

The Chinese were also attacked for allegedly trying to bribe the new state of Malawi. According to Hastings Banda, the Prime Minister, the Malawi Embassy in Tanzania had been offered $50 million if Malawi would agree to recognize Communist China. The Chinese are suspected of having conducted similar activities in Burundi, from which they were ultimately expelled, and in Tanzania, where they were considerably more successful. Initially, the Chinese found their welcome warmest on the island of Zanzibar. Before the merger of Tanganyika and Zanzibar in the spring of 1964, China had committed itself to a series of small loans to Zanzibar. Shortly thereafter, China announced a loan of $14.5 million to Zanzibar and another loan of $28 million to the union.[20] Included in the various projects were a textile mill at Dar es Salaam, a radio station at Kunduchi, a farm training center at Mwanza, a food-processing plant at Arusha and a rice-planting program in the south. The Chinese have also been selling large quantities of consumer goods in Tanzania markets to earn money for local developmental costs. This has hurt Kenya, which now finds that one of its traditional sales outlets for consumer goods has been closed off. The combination of all these activities makes Tanzania one of the focal points of Chinese effort in sub-Saharan Africa. Topping off the economic aid is a shipment of at least 1,000 tons of arms and ammunition.

The Chinese have also sought to encourage the construction of a 1,300 mile railroad from Zambia to the port at Dar es Salaam. This would allow Zambia to bypass Rhodesia. If the Chinese do finance this project, it is expected that it will cost them approximately $200 million, although some estimates run closer to $300 million. It remains to be seen if Tanzania will actually go through with such a large undertaking and, if so, whether China can really afford to finance it.

Soviet aid to Tanzania has been much less impressive. After an initial burst of promises in August, 1964, the Russians found that the Tanzanians had virtually excluded them from any meaningful activity. Tanzania did accept 1,100 tons of Soviet military equipment, some military advisors, and some Russian veterinarians, but the Russians have been unable to implement any other aspects of their planned loan of almost $42 million. The reasons for this cold reception are unclear. It may be simply that Tanzania does not want to become involved with a European power. In any case, virtually no work has been done on the fisheries, technical college, telephone network, the cold-storage, milk-processing and cement plants, or geological and hydroelectric surveys that have been promised.[21] Together with the Americans, whose aid program has been cut back to about $4 million a year, the Russians have been outmaneuvered by the Chinese.

Some of the other East European countries have extended economic aid to Tanzania. The East Germans have offered to build a hospital, a radio transmitter, and houses. Poland has formed a joint sugar company with Tanzania and will help develop a fishing fleet. Czechoslovakia has also agreed to provide some industrial and agricultural aid. It is not known just how successful these efforts by the satellites have been.

To complete the picture, Soviet aid to sub-Saharan Africa includes a $6.7-million loan to Senegal. As yet, no specific projects have been announced. The Russians have also provided $15.5 million to Uganda.[22] The Chinese reportedly offered a similar sum. The Russian loan was to cover the cost of building the usual cotton textile plant, agricultural institute, cold-storage plants, a dairy plant, and the delivery of a batch of tractors and bulldozers. Trade agreements, but apparently no aid agreements, have been signed with Cameroon, Niger, Nigeria, and Sierra Leone.[23] Finally, it was reported that China had made a loan of $518,000 to Zambia.

Conclusion

How do the quantities of Soviet and Chinese foreign aid in Africa compare with each other and how do both in turn compare with American aid? (See Appendix, Table 2.) Chinese aid exceeds Russian aid in Congo-Brazzaville, Kenya, and Tanzania. Soviet and Chinese aid exceeds American aid in Congo-Brazzaville, Guinea, Mali, Somalia, Tanzania, and Uganda. Moreover, much of the American aid is in the form of food, not industrial aid. In addition, whereas the American presence in Africa is strongly felt in a few selected countries, such as Nigeria, the Russians have devoted more economic aid than has the United States in a surprisingly large number of other important areas. It is evident that despite the mistakes they have made, the Russians consider sub-Saharan Africa a major area of interest and of promise. In terms of the relative amount of resources devoted to the area, the Russians have attached more importance to the area than have the Americans. Historically, this represents a new area of influence for the Russians, one that was beyond the reach of the Czars. In many ways, Soviet efforts in this region are reminiscent of the activities of the Western European powers in the era prior to World War I. The Soviet Union, as the European powers before it, seems to be trying to carve out a sphere of influence. The Russians, however, have encountered Chinese competition, although not as severely as in Asia. Soviet and

Chinese mistakes in Africa, combined with African nationalism, may counterbalance the apparent lack of American interest and the continued withdrawal of the governments of Western Europe. Perhaps, the mystique of Africa will generate its own protective covering in the struggle for world influence.

11. Conclusion

Although Soviet economic relations with the less developed countries have varied according to time, place, and politics, certain conclusions may be drawn by posing four major questions: What has been the Russian purpose in undertaking economic relations with the less developed countries? What has the Soviet Union accomplished with its aid and trade programs? What has it failed to do? What lessons can Americans draw from the Soviet experience?

The Reasons for Soviet Aid and Trade

The Russians have had many reasons for undertaking economic relations with the less developed countries. Their motives are not very different from those of any large country. In fact, the Soviet experience with the less developed countries of the world differs only in emphasis from that of the United States. This means, therefore, that the motives are mixed and not entirely consistent.

1. One of the earliest stimuli for Soviet interest in less developed nations was the desire and need to maintain trade relations. In some cases, these areas possessed vital raw materials. In the years following World War II, Russia relied heavily on the East European countries for coal, oil, uranium, and other commodities. The technologically more advanced countries, such as Czechoslovakia and East Germany, also supplied the Soviets with machinery. Eventually, the Russians cultivated trade relations with the non-Communist developing countries as well; even here, trade often preceded aid and diplomatic activity. Through such trade, the Russians were able to obtain rubber, cotton, sugar, cocoa, and coffee.

Before long, the Russians had other reasons for promoting trade. By the late 1950's, the export side of trade became almost as important to the Russians and their East European allies as the import side. As Communist Europe passed through the initial agony of industrialization, it found that much of its industrial capacity had been overdeveloped in terms of basic heavy industry and unsophisticated consumer goods. After a time, many markets in Eastern Europe and the U.S.S.R.

had become saturated. When trade relations with China were drastically curtailed in 1960, the problem became especially serious, for China had been a major market for such products. Since the goods affected were not readily salable in the more advanced countries of the West, it became necessary to cultivate the markets of the developing countries.

With a few exceptions, however, the newly developing areas continued to rely on the West for merchandise and machinery. In some cases, the Soviet Union and East Europe were able to penetrate such markets by entering into all-encompassing barter agreements. This approach was successful in the case of countries that experienced a drop in the price of their primary export commodities. In the absence of such a barter arrangement, it was usually very difficult for Communist countries to make any inroads. About the only other way local businessmen in the developing countries could be weaned from the habit of trading with the West was through the use of credit or the inducement of repayment in soft currency. Hence, for the Soviet Union and its allies, aid became a very important means of displacing Western merchandise from its traditional markets. At the same time, it provided an outlet for the excess goods produced by Communist Europe's industry. In the words of a senior Polish trade official. "The West no longer has a monopoly on foreign trade. But to compete, the Communist countries, especially the smaller ones, have to provide the sweetener of credit. Without credit the developing countries would naturally buy from the West. This is important to Poland, since we now have to worry about securing markets for our own domestic industry. Our heavy industrial sector is overbuilt and we are now unable to sell all we produce within Poland or even to other Communist countries."

In 1965–66, the Russians openly began to revert to the imperialist position that foreign aid should be used to stimulate the flow of raw materials to the Soviet Union. Articles in *Voprosy Ekonomiki* of November, 1965, February, 1966, and April, 1966, argued that Russian aid should be channeled so that it promoted the flow of tin, copper, zinc, aluminum, oil, rubber, iron ore and cotton to the Soviet Union.

2. A second motive for foreign aid has nothing to do with conventional commercial considerations. For some Russians, just as for some Americans, the prime motivation for allocating one's own resources for the benefit of another country is a humanitarian one. Helping someone poorer than oneself has always appealed to man's nobler instincts. Moreover, many Russians believe that the countries in Africa, Asia, and Latin America are poor today because of their exploitation by the capitalistic West. Therefore, even though their own country is relatively poor, the Russians feel they have an obligation as Communists and human beings to facilitate the industrialization of these areas.

The Russians had much the same feeling about China until the late 1950's. China, too, had been plundered by the imperialists—including Czarist Russia. As a consequence, the Russians made a sincere effort in the early 1950's to provide economic aid. In terms of present Russian capabilities, Soviet aid to China may not appear to have been so generous, but in relation to Soviet potential at the time, it was a major effort and undoubtedly reflected Russian compassion for the poverty of China.

3. Perhaps the most important consideration underlying Soviet actions is the one of political self-interest. It can be argued that all Soviet economic relations with the less developed countries are subservient to political calculations—whether or not an action will advance the interests of the U.S.S.R. It is only when confronted with pressure in the form of unrest, as in Europe in 1956, or competition for prestige or influence, as in India, that the Russians will respond with any meaningful help.

In evaluating Soviet motives, it would be an oversimplification to assert that a particular decision was made solely for political, economic, or humanitarian reasons. Certainly behind every action there are mixed motives. It is true, however, that the U.S.S.R.'s relations with its satellites until 1956 were governed by the determination to promote Soviet national interests and to take as much out of Eastern Europe as possible. All other considerations were secondary. Stalin felt that the cause of world Communism could best be served by reconstructing and strengthening the U.S.S.R. and by maintaining tight control over Eastern Europe and China. The growth and fortification of the Soviet bloc in relation to the United States and the NATO countries was viewed as an urgent necessity. The best way to assure such a goal was to promote the development of a strong Soviet state.

In the mid-1950's, as the field of East-West contention shifted to the non-Communist world, the Russians sought to increase their prestige and well-being by making inroads in areas long under the influence of the United States and its West European allies. As a challenger of the status quo, the Russians had to adopt a much more generous policy than was necessary in Eastern Europe. Wherever possible, the Russians encouraged anticolonial sentiment and the formation of independent states. It was anticipated that ultimately these governments would be transformed into Communist regimes—the goal foreseen by Lenin and others who argued that the road to London and Paris lay through Asia and Africa. Soviet trade and aid could help produce this desired result.

The Russians soon found, however, that it was often much wiser, at least in the short run, to settle for independent but anticolonial governments in the Afro-Asian bloc than for Communist governments. In the case of the Communist regime in Cuba, the Russians discovered that supporting Castro was very costly. The Russians simply lacked the necessary materials and logistical facilities. With a non-Communist but anticolonialist regime, the Russians could provide whatever aid they thought appropriate and then watch as the Western countries paid the bulk of the bills but continued to face the wrath of the embittered new nations. In this way the Russians could have their cake without having to assume complete responsibility for training and supplying the cooks. While gaining national prestige and appreciation for their foreign aid, the Russians could wait contentedly for the Communist revolution they were confident would come one day—when they would be better able to support it.

It was not too long, however, before it became apparent that furthering Russian national prestige sometimes ran at cross purposes with the long-range goal of spreading international Communism. To the extent that Soviet foreign aid did in fact facilitate the industrialization of developing countries, and to the extent that these countries became economically viable, a Communist revolution became less likely. While the Aswan Dam brought immense international prestige for the Soviet Union, there was no satisfactory answer for those who asked what, if anything, the millions of rubles spent on the dam had done for the Communist movement in Egypt. Such questions became especially embarrassing when Nasser decided to jail members of the local Communist Party. More than anything else, such actions by aid-receiving countries highlighted the conflict between the national self-interest of the Soviet government and its commitment to revolution and the spread of Communism. This was especially disturbing to those in the Communist movement who resented the fact that the Russians usually subordinated the international movement to purely national aims. Thus in Latin America, the Russians extended official diplomatic recognition to Eduardo Frei's government in Chile at the same time that Fidel Castro was calling for a revolt in the country. Castro's supporters charged that such "Soviet actions in Chile and Brazil hold back the struggle for liberation."[1] These activities also upset the Chinese, who seized upon such dilemmas to embarrass and attack the Russians.

As the feud between China and the Soviet Union intensified, foreign aid was used for a new political purpose: both countries used it to increase their national prestige at the other's expense. Although both were still anxious to outperform the NATO countries, they were often more concerned about competing with each other. The climax of this competition occurred prior to the cancellation of the second Bandung

Conference in Algeria, which after many earlier postponements was scheduled for June, 1965. A comparison of the aid commitments of both countries for the months preceding this meeting indicates how much like a poker game the foreign aid negotiations had become. (See Table XI-1.) Numerous offers of long-term credit were given in the hope that the donor would thereby gain support for either the inclusion or the exclusion of the Russians at the forthcoming conference. These loans in turn were generally met by counterbids from the other country. In Cambodia and Algeria, the counterbids were followed by yet a third offer. At this stage, neither the Russians nor the Chinese appeared to be seriously interested in the furtherance of international Communism; behind the ideological camouflage it was essentially a question of Soviet national interest versus Chinese national interest.

What Has Soviet Aid Accomplished?

The purposes of Soviet aid, then, are complex, although generally not much different from those of other providers of foreign aid, but what has this foreign economic program accomplished? Russia's efforts in Eastern Europe left those countries in an extremely poor condition. Even though the Russians tried to redeem themselves after 1956, it was too late to remedy the basic wounds and fractures that will pain those countries for years to come. In China and the neutralist world, Russian efforts have been much more constructive. Undoubtedly, their foreign aid program has won them numerous friends and increased their international prestige. While there is much to be criticized, on the whole the Russians have tried to promote economic growth in the non-Communist countries they have aided. No country in Africa, Asia, or Latin America is poorer today because of its experience with the U.S.S.R. (Some countries, such as China, Cuba, Guinea, Indonesia, and Ghana, may have been their own worst enemies, but the Russians cannot be blamed for this.) Most neutralist countries are considerably better off because of Russian economic help. This pertains especially to those countries where military purchases from the Soviet Union have been at a minimum and where political involvement with the U.S.S.R. has been circumspect.

With few exceptions, the Russians have stressed basic industrial projects. With Soviet assistance, new industries have been built at an astonishing rate. At times, excessive enthusiasm on all sides has led to the creation of over-ambitious projects, but this should not detract from the basic contributions which have been made. The Russians seem to have a knack for the spectacular. Much of the Soviet success has been due to concentrating on certain key projects, which are generally in-

Table XI-1

SOVIET AND CHINESE LOANS IMMEDIATELY PRIOR TO THE ALGERIAN CONFERENCE
(in Millions of Dollars)

Recipient	China Amount of loan	Date	Soviet Union Amount of loan	Date
Afghanistan	28	March, 1965	39	June, 1964
Algeria	50	October, 1963	100 128	September, 1963 May, 1964
Cambodia	5-10	November, 1964	12	November, 1964
Ceylon	4	February, 1964		
Congo-Brazzaville	25	1965	9	December, 1964
Ghana	22	February, 1964		
Indonesia	50	1965		
Iran			39	July, 1963
Iraq			140	March, 1965
Kenya	28	1964-65	3	1964
Pakistan	90	July, 1964- January, 1965	11-70	July, 1964
Senegal			7	November, 1964
Somalia	21 3	August, 1963 January, 1965		
Tanzania	29 14	June, 1963 June, 1965	42	August, 1964
Turkey			168	April, 1964
U.A.R.	80	January, 1965	277	May, 1964
Uganda	15	1965	15	December, 1964
Yemen	28	May, 1964	72	March, 1964
Zambia	.5	February, 1964		

dustrial in nature. These major impact projects not only excite the imagination, but result in productive and visible monuments. The workmanship and administrative efficiency that go into these showpieces are often more impressive than those in the U.S.S.R. itself. On occasion, the Russians have also been able to suggest improvements in already projected plans; in the case of the Aswan Dam, their suggestions saved Egypt considerable domestic and foreign currency. The Russians are also to be commended for training native technicians and turning over to them the operation of aid projects. In addition to on-the-job training, the Russians have invited large numbers of foreigners to the U.S.S.R. for training in Soviet schools. On occasion, such policies have backfired; native technicians have failed to perform properly; and the Russians have been criticized either for poor training or for poor quality of equipment. Nevertheless, their efforts deserve praise.

The successful Soviet projects are also distinguished by the efficiency and flexibility of Soviet administrative procedures. When a project is singled out for priority handling, the full resources of the Soviet Union are put behind it. The Bhilai steel mill was considered to be as important as any steel mill in the Soviet Union, and Soviet specialists in the field had authority to make decisions without referring to Moscow. When it is necessary to obtain a decision in the U.S.S.R. about a priority project, the answer is usually fast in coming.

It is in the field of public relations that the Russians appear to be at their best. Their preference for impact projects, together with their sense of timing, creates exciting drama and wins them applause from the recipients, their own people, and even their competitors. Because there was no need to seek the approval of any legislative body for its projects, the Soviet Union was able to announce its willingness to finance the Aswan Dam very soon after the Americans withdrew. They reacted the same way after the United States decided against financing the Bokaro steel mill in India. Similarly, as soon as the French proclaimed they would no longer help Guinea, Russian promises of aid were immediately sent off to Conakry, just as they were sent to Tunisia when the French bombed the naval base at Bizerte. Until recently, it was a rarity when an international crisis or realignment of power was not followed by a new Soviet aid agreement.

But perhaps the Russians' most notable accomplishment is that through the combined use of political expansion and foreign aid they have stimulated the use of economic aid by others. It was largely because of the fear of Russian expansionism in Europe that the United States introduced the Marshall Plan for European reconstruction. Until the Russian feelers in Afghanistan and India, American foreign aid to Africa and Asia was at a minimum. For example, annual American promises of aid to India, which were only $4.5 million in 1951, rose to $87 million in 1954 and to more than $100 million in 1959. In addition, the decision to counter Soviet aid helped bring about the creation of numerous international and financial institutions whose sole purpose was to aid economic development. The International Bank for Reconstruction and Development (World Bank) was joined by the International Finance Corporation, the International Development Association, the Development Assistance Committee, and the Inter-American Development Bank.

From the Soviet point of view, perhaps the most important contribution of the foreign aid program was that it made neutralism a practical alternative. The very existence of the alternative of Soviet aid provided needed leverage for the numerous countries that obtained their independence in the 1950's and 1960's. After the unexpected Russian decision to finance the Aswan Dam, the West and the developing countries learned that the Soviet Union was prepared to commit immense quantities of resources for countries that were willing to stand up to the NATO powers. Consequently the emergent countries did not have to worry as they once did that Western boycotts would ensure submission. It is entirely possible, for example, that Premier Mohammed Mossadegh's attempted nationalization of the Iranian oil companies in 1951 might have been successful if it had taken place only five years later. As Soviet support for Egypt indicates, by 1956 the Russians had decided to support actively just such provocative challenges.

What Soviet Aid Has Not Been Able To Do

If Soviet aid and trade has helped to produce neutralism and has increased the national prestige of the Soviet Union, it has not helped to bring a Communist regime to power. Even when the Communists did take over in a developing country, as in Cuba, it was done without Soviet aid. Although the Russians were probably delighted by their success in promoting and winning the support of the neutralist movement, eventually they began to wonder about the imminence of Communism in the rest of the Afro-Asian–Latin American bloc where Soviet aid had been applied. As we have seen, this provoked some conflict over the ultimate purpose of Soviet aims, especially when "neutralism" in favor of the U.S.S.R. became "neutralism" for the West.

Similarly, Russian aid and trade policies have not always been warmly received by fellow Communist states. The list of the openly disenchanted includes Yugoslavia, Albania, China, North Korea, and Rumania. At one time or another, protest has also come from Hungary, Poland, East Germany, and even Bulgaria and Czechoslovakia. As a result, even CMEA, which has some merit as an institution for stimulating foreign trade, is regarded with considerable hostility. Thus, although Russia's economic policies toward its satellites at one time brought short-run advantages, the long-run effects have brought dissension and economic inefficiency for the bloc as a whole.

As we have seen, the Russians, like other aid dispensers before them, have not yet discovered how to avoid mistakes in the implementation and administration of their foreign aid and trade programs. The frivolous nature of some projects such as the luxury hotels in Burma and Guinea, and the unproductive nature of others, such as the stadiums in Guinea, Mali, and Indonesia, have generated complaints about poor Soviet advice. Improper storage, erratic shipping procedures, and poor quality of materials are beginning to attract as much attention as Soviet successes. Like their Western competitors, the Russians have sometimes failed to make adequate feasibility studies. Many of these difficulties are due to the relative inexperience of the Russians, but they are also due to problems inherent in any underdeveloped country.

The Russians are also beginning to realize that while their system has the advantage of permitting swift action in priority situations, it also has shortcomings. After all, there can only be so many priority projects. Those projects that are not in the priority category move very slowly, and often run afoul of the Soviet bureaucracy. The emphasis being placed on the so-called Liberman reforms indicates how much remains to be done to bring about improved quality and efficiency within the U.S.S.R. itself. Until such reforms are implemented successfully, Soviet industrial aid and trade will not be completely satisfactory. The very debate over the reforms helps to focus world attention on Soviet economic difficulties. Similarly, Russia's inability to solve its own agricultural problems generates a skepticism with regard to Russia's agricultural aid programs. Russia's agricultural problems also embarrass those Soviet critics who complain that the United States stresses agricultural at the expense of industrial help. All of this detracts from attempts to make the Soviet Union a model of economic development for the poorer countries of the world.

One particular aspect of Soviet domestic economic policy deserves special mention because of its effect on Soviet foreign aid. The keystone of the Soviet aid program is its emphasis on industrial help. Yet there seem to be an increasing number of situations where lack of restraint in applying such a policy has come in for criticism. The Russians have a tendency to build factories on a scale more suited to Soviet conditions than to conditions in the developing countries. This disregard for scale and the tendency to concentrate on industrial projects have been partly due to the absence of the interest rate in Soviet calculations on plant size and feasibility. The loan fee of 2.5 per cent that the Russians charge is not the same as the capital charge used to determine the amount of capital (capital intensity) in a particular project. The capital or interest charge is used by project designers to decide on the optimum scale of the plant. The more limited the availability of capital, the higher the interest charge will be and the more likely it is that the planners will be persuaded to use less capital. In all likelihood, the plant will be smaller in size and less mechanized. In some cases, if the interest rate is high enough, a change in plans may be necessary and no factory will be built at all. The absence of a capital charge signifies that capital is free and that there need be no limit on the amount of capital that is used. This is what leads to excessive scale and unprofitable operations.

Because American project calculations take into account the capital charge, American factories in Africa and Asia tend to be smaller in size. Americans recognize that capital is a commodity in short supply. This helps to explain why they are more cautious than the Russians in building industrial projects in the less developed countries. Such enterprises must not only earn enough revenue to meet current expenses for inputs like labor and raw material, but they must also meet capital expenses. It is not true, as the Russians assert, that Americans are reluctant to build factories in the less developed countries because they fear subsequent competition with their own domestic industry. American investment and factory construction in Western Europe indicate that the possibility of future competition does not inhibit overseas investment by Americans. It is just that the risks are greater, the supply of capital is smaller, and the chances of profitability are more remote in the Afro-Asian bloc. Ironically, as the Liberman reforms take hold in the U.S.S.R. and as the Russians begin to use capital charges in their economic calculations at home, it is only to be expected that a similar calculation will enter into Soviet foreign aid projects. This in turn should induce a more conservative attitude as to the size and economic feasibility of industrial projects financed by the Soviet Union. The increase in interest charges to 4 per cent on a 1966 loan to Brazil indicates that this may be happening.

The Russians are likely to move in this direction not only because of domestic economic reforms but also because they are now harvesting the fruit of past unrestrained policies. Many of the less developed countries find themselves with serious balance-of-payments problems once their debt repayments to the Soviet Union fall due. As we have discovered, even the more conservative countries of Asia and Africa are having such difficulties. Where the national leaders are profligate spenders and/or dreamers, the chaos is likely to be monumental. The "go-go" generation of revolutionaries—Nkrumah, Sukarno, Ben Bella, Sékou Touré, Nasser, and Castro—have generally been unable to sublimate their frenetic energy and the political plotting of the soap box to the methodical plodding of the drawing board and accounting ledger. In addition to a common penchant for such useless endeavors as stadiums, statues, and oversized factories, these firebrands have also obligated their countries to pay for large quantities of economically unproductive military equipment; this further complicates their already serious balance of payments. In Egypt, Ghana, Cuba, Guinea, and Indonesia, this has led to default on the repayment of Soviet debt or at least requests for debt postponement. As Soviet aid projects are completed and more and more countries find themselves having to begin to repay their debts, this is bound to become more serious and generate considerable friction between the Russians and those they help.

The sale of munitions highlights another problem area in Soviet external affairs. The countries of Communist Europe, especially the Soviet Union and Czechoslovakia, have become major munitions manufacturers. Partly out of choice and partly out of necessity, they are now important suppliers of arms to the Afro-Asian bloc. In some cases, the Communists have been forced to sell weapons in order to retain the friendships and to protect the inroads already won. In other instances, they encourage the sale of arms in order to keep their munitions industry producing at full capacity. A curious aspect of the Communist arms business is that the Russians almost never publicize their sales of weapons to neutralist countries. Although they mention the military help and equipment they give other Communist countries—Cuba, Vietnam, Poland, and China—there is virtually no indication of the scope of the Russian and Czech arms traffic to non-Communist areas. As a result, most Russian citizens are ignorant of such activities. Presumably they would be as disturbed about the profits of the munitions industries in their own countries as they are about such profits when earned by Western firms.

But while the munitions industries in the Soviet Union may do their best to promote the sale of arms, the finance ministry undoubtedly opposes such transactions. The sale of military goods not only complicates the repayment problems of the recipient country, but almost always creates additional unrest in the region. Now that the Russians are owed over several billion dollars' worth of economic and military debts in various areas around the world, they are discovering for the first time that they have a vested interest in the status quo. They found that the governmental changes that took place in Algeria and Indonesia in 1965 and in Ghana in 1966 were distressing for economic as well as for political reasons. Similarly, military or political disturbances in India jeopardize the billion-dollar investment the Russians have in that country. As we saw, such considerations help explain Russia's moderating influence in the clashes between India and Pakistan. Thus the Russians are beset by the same dilemma as other donors of foreign aid. Although they like to sell military equipment, they realize that the political aftermath as well as the financial effect on their nonmilitary loans may be unfortunate.

The Russians have not been able to do away with yet another feature of foreign aid and trade which has been sharply criticized: tying strings to their economic help. The Russians were especially domineering in dictating policy to their satellites. Aid was offered and then withdrawn in Yugoslavia, Albania, and China because these countries refused to accede to Soviet political demands. It was subsequently resumed in Yugoslavia. As the Chinese put it in the *Peking Review* of September 18, 1964, "After receiving aid [Albania] was plundered, its internal affairs interfered in and it was even confronted with subversion." Other countries that have found themselves penalized or threatened economically or politically because of some indiscretions include Finland, Israel, Cuba, Algeria, Guinea, Indonesia, Ghana, and Iraq.

It would be a futile exercise to determine who pulls the most strings, the United States or the Soviet Union. The fact remains, however, that both countries have interfered when they deemed it to be in their short-run interest. No country likes to spend large sums of money for the benefit of another country only to see the recipient refuse to follow advice. Like parents with their adolescent children, the reaction is even stronger when the recipient begins to criticize or attack the donor. It is unrealistic to expect that economic support will be maintained under such circumstances even by the most altruistic of nations.

Lessons for the United States

With time, Soviet foreign economic policy has produced experiences and reactions similar to those of the United States. As their investment in foreign aid increases, it is likely that the Russians will become more cautious. Whether they pull strings, whether they worry about the repayment of the credits that they have extended, whether they are attacked for not providing enough industrial help, or whether they are criticized for the ineffectiveness of their aid, the Russians find themselves with problems that are all too familiar to Americans. What lessons are there in all of this for the United States and its aid program?

The most obvious conclusion is that foreign aid and trade with the developing nations is by its very nature a challenging and often thankless task. The returns are slow in coming, and failure and criticism are as much to be expected as success and praise. Patience, perhaps, is what is needed more than anything else. Consequently, it is encouraging to see that we have no monopoly on impatience.

Impatience, plus dissension among Communist allies and economic troubles at home, led to a moratorium on new aid promises by the Russians in late 1961. All of 1962 passed without a single major new commitment. This was a complete reversal of the pattern of the preceding years; it also meant the Russians had to watch the formation of an independent Algeria in July, 1962, in silence. It was not until fourteen months later, in September, 1963, that the Russians decided to offer any major promise of aid and finally announced a loan to Algeria. Then, as we have seen, the competitive battle with the Chinese generated a sharp increase in aid. A second reason for the extension of new loans was that the Russians found themselves trapped by what can be called the "quicksand effect." Once they have undertaken to support a country like Egypt or India in its program of economic development, it becomes extremely difficult to refuse requests for supplemental aid. Failure to promise new aid creates the risk that the political gains from past aid will be lost. Thus as we saw, against the advice of his economic counselors and the Soviet Presidium, Khrushchev announced a new loan to the United Arab Republic of $277 million in May, 1964. Carried away by the flush of enthusiasm over the completion of the first stage of the Aswan Dam, he was just a man who couldn't say no.

A third factor explaining the resumption of Soviet aid commitments is the traditional one of seizing new opportunities to penetrate new areas. In the early 1960's the nations of the CENTO pact became restless and disappointed with American support. Since most of these countries have common borders with the Soviet Union, the temptation to develop improved economic relations with these areas was too much for the Russians to resist. Thus, for all three reasons, the Russians resumed their aid program until early 1965, when it was cut back again because of growing economic problems at home and an increasing awareness that the means and ends of Soviet foreign aid were contradictory.

Nonetheless, whatever Soviet shortcomings or hesitations, in terms of per dollar expenditure on foreign aid, the Russians seem to have done better than the United States. In India, the United States has offered almost $6 billion and the Russians only $1–1.5 billion; in Egypt, the respective figures are $1 billion and $820 million. Yet Russian aid has had much more of an impact and is considered to have contributed more to the industrialization of both countries. It is true that this is partially because the Russians are newer at the game and not all of their promises have yet had to meet the test of reality. As their projects are completed, there is certain to be more criticism mixed in with the praise. Yet there are some techniques the United States would do well to copy from the Soviet Union.

A praiseworthy feature of Soviet aid is its flexibility. The U.S. foreign aid program tends to move from one extreme to another. First, we stress grants in aid. When that does not bring immediate results, we adopt a loan policy. We should be much more willing to use a little of both. When necessary, the Russians can move very rapidly to implement their aid program. American procedures are often time-consuming and cumbersome. Without restricting our flexibility, we might profit from preparing a prepackaged "shelf" of prototype aid projects that could be quickly utilized and put into operation. This might make it possible to reduce the months usually required to produce working plans for such basic projects as sugar mills, canneries, dairies, and lumbermills. Of course, it would still be necessary to make adjustments to local conditions, but the existence of standardized plans might reduce much of the frustration created by the excessive delays that often precede the actual construction of American aid projects.

Where we are already more flexible, we should do more to publicize the fact. For instance, American aid officials should make an effort to show that American aid is not limited to privately sponsored projects. Our aid is divided much more evenly between private and state enterprises than is Russian aid, which tends to be concentrated on government projects. Here we tend to be more flexible than the Russians, but few people know about it.

The Russians could also teach us something about public relations in foreign aid. Soviet officials and the Russian press go out of their way to draw attention to Soviet efforts. It would help if senior American officials, especially the President and the Vice President, would make a point of inspecting or inaugurating American-sponsored projects on their foreign tours, as Soviet officials do. Similarly, American firms should be encouraged to publicize their work on American-sponsored foreign aid projects. This would help inform the public about the existence of such projects and would also be a way of indicating how foreign aid appropriations benefit American businessmen. After all, this is no more than what American corporations presently do after each space shot. They vie with one another to show off their engineering and technical accomplishments. They should do the same about their foreign aid accomplishments.

To provide an image for its over-all efforts, the United States should adopt the Soviet practice of building "flagship projects." Projects such as the Aswan Dam and the Bhilai steel mill focus world-wide attention on Soviet foreign aid and lend an atmosphere of substance to all their efforts. One of the greatest shortcomings of the American aid effort is its diffusion. Few Americans can name one American project. Had the United States undertaken to build the Bokaro steel mill, it could have served as a symbol of tangible American support. The prestige from such a project would probably flow over to other important but less exciting American projects, such as agricultural help and educational and technical assistance, where the results are highly useful in the long run but less apparent in the short run. The United States should undertake one or two such flagship projects and commit itself to the necessary financial credits for more than one year. Although political hand-biting by the recipients may occur in the course of construction, this is something the United States must be prepared to tolerate. There have been sufficient swings in the political pendulum in the last twenty years to indicate that if one waits long enough, a hostile regime will eventually be replaced by a more favorable government. In the meantime, the aid project can make a basic contribution to economic development; this should redound more to our benefit than to the Soviet Union's.

Americans should also take a somewhat less skeptical and hostile attitude toward Soviet aid. Although we should not forget that behind Soviet aid there are political motives and ambitions just as there are in American aid, we should nevertheless recognize that in the long run, a successful aid project that strengthens and stabilizes an economy will help the United States more than the U.S.S.R. While the two may be connected, we should distinguish between subversion, which is destructive, and aid, which is constructive. History so far shows that Communism does not flourish or spread in countries that seem to be solving their economic problems. Logically, therefore, instead of discouraging Soviet aid, we should encourage it. Every project they undertake is one less we have to bear. There are short-run political risks in such a policy, but the long-run effects, both economic and political, seem to be in our favor. Experience shows that if the aided country prospers because of Soviet aid, it is less likely to become Communist. On the other hand, if

Soviet aid is unsuccessful, the Russians are often made to share the blame for the country's problems and the country is likely to turn to the West for support. This has been the case in Indonesia and Ghana. In countries where the Russians have been excluded, for example, Guatemala, Communism often seems to make the greatest inroads. Although the absence of Soviet aid in such countries is not the main reason why there is a strong Communist movement in the country, it is an interesting paradox.

Recognizing that Soviet aid may not always be detrimental to American interests, it is worth noting the emergence of a new and promising phase in the administration of American foreign aid. Largely at the initiative of sincere and committed aid and foreign service officials from both countries, there are a growing number of cases where the United States and the U.S.S.R. are attempting to coordinate their aid efforts in a particular country. There are immense advantages for all parties concerned in such a trend. Already it is possible to find some such joint efforts. In Afghanistan we saw how American roads end where Russian roads begin. In Ghana, water provided by American projects will irrigate sugar cane which is to be processed in a Polish sugar mill. Other cooperative efforts may only take the form of a discussion as to what each country plans to do. Even this can help to eliminate or reduce duplication and overcapitalization. On occasion it may even lead to a component-building process whereby one project supplements another. There seems little doubt that while both donors benefit from such an approach, the one who benefits the most is the recipient country.

Nonetheless it would be unrealistic to assume that American-Soviet cooperation in foreign aid will take place on a significant scale. This is not entirely to be regretted. Regardless of the advantages that coordination and cooperation may bring, history still shows that in the long run foreign aid, investment, and trade are most beneficial when rendered as a result of international competition. At best, coordination is most effective in a context of over-all competition. When a developed and powerful country or a group of large countries has a franchise to do as it pleases in a smaller country, the results are usually not entirely salutary from the poorer country's point of view. This has been true of American operations in Latin America and Soviet activities in Eastern Europe. Accordingly, Russian interest in Latin America has forced the United States to take a less selfish look at Latin America. Similarly, greater American and Western economic interest in Eastern Europe has caused the Soviet Union to re-examine its economic relations in that area. The West could probably bring about further improvement in conditions there if it took even more interest in Eastern Europe by offering better trade and credit privileges to the East European countries which seemed particularly deserving. In the past the most successful foreign aid projects have resulted where the United States, the Soviet Union, other Western countries, and, now, the Chinese have found themselves engaged in courting the favors of a particular country. For the country whose affections are being sought, this may be all to the good. To the extent that it can play off one faction against another, it is possible that it may be able to obtain more foreign aid and political concessions than it would if there were no competition from the other powers. The threat of Communist penetration has given birth to the Marshall Plan and to the Alliance for Progress, among other projects; the promise of neutralism has sparked a $4-billion aid program by the Soviet Union to the developing countries; and the likelihood of a Chinese takeover of the 1965 Afro-Asian Conference in Algeria caused the Russians to resume their foreign aid program and increase their loans by over half a billion dollars.

The role of international foreign aid is gradually changing from what it was in the late 1950's and early 1960's. Then acceptance of aid from a particular donor often implied strict adherence to the donor's particular point of view. With time this has changed. While there is still a danger of economic subversion under the guise of Soviet aid or trade, more and more, the developing nations seem to have learned how to balance off the various lures of the donor countries without losing their equilibrium. As long as the U.S.S.R. continues to invest in various projects overseas and as long as the recipient countries continue to reject Communism, there is a growing likelihood the U.S.S.R. will act as a moderating force in these areas. Conceivably some day the Chinese may react the same way. In the meantime, the United States should continue to compete and even cooperate with the Soviet Union in the developing countries, both Communist and non-Communist.

APPENDIXES

APPENDIX 1

ITEM 16: DELIVERY OF EQUIPMENT AND MATERIAL FOR COMPLETE PLANTS
BY SOVIET UNION
(In Thousands of Dollars)

	Afghanistan	Algeria	Burma	Cambodia	Ceylon	Ethiopia	Ghana	Guinea	India	Indonesia	Iran
1955	1,007								78		
1956	1,724								5,794		
1957	3,344								43,330		
1958	9,728				482				98,136		
1959	14,696				3				34,179		226
1960	17,409							102	18,141	5,017	
1961	18,570						78	9,100	39,569	9,022	
1962	19,288				927		2,625	7,395	64,671	7,403	
1963	23,894	591	947		2,867		4,585	7,344	81,285	9,694	
1964	27,842	1,985	2,065	577	6,834	2,182	4,507	3,912	132,537	18,508	
1965	29,922	5,905	458	222	4,269	6,095	8,096	1,859	84,239	13,169	
Total	167,424	8,481	3,470	799	15,382	8,277	19,891	29,712	601,959	62,813	226

Sources: See page 253.

Iraq	Mali	Pakistan	Somalia	Sudan	Syria	Tunisia	Turkey	U.A.R.	Yemen	Total
										1,085
								27		7,545
								485	44	47,203
					1,927		222	1,230	500	112,225
239					1,018		1,215	15,657	2,001	69,234
4,264		8			2,005		3,696	15,835	2,111	68,588
15,925	577	242			8,598		1,388	35,169	463	138,701
29,721	2,667	3,898	48	81	2,168		224	41,488	120	182,724
25,902	3,361	4,308	2,736	2,556	1,716	666	129	48,073	50	220,704
17,960	4,111	22,986	5,076	3,752	1,036	4	7	60,978	265	297,124
5,375	2,526	3,332	5,659	1,000	4,367	2,188	6	86,018	1,535	267,187
99,386	13,242	14,774	13,519	7,389	22,835	2,858	6,887	304,960	7,089	1,412,320

UNITED STATES, CHINA, AND SOVIET UNION:
ECONOMIC AID COMMITMENTS, 1946-66[a]
(in Millions of Dollars)

		United States		China, Loans	Soviet Union	
	Total	Food for Peace	Grants	and Grants	Loans	Grants
Afghanistan	295	84	154	28	377	150
Algeria	162	158	4	55-60	228	
Argentina	711	18	10		100	
Brazil	2,518	603	112		100	
Burma	111	46	26	84-88	10-15	
Cambodia	256	3	253	55-60	12	6
Ceylon	91	68	16	31-41	30	
Congo (Brazzaville)	4		2	25	9	
Ethiopia	150	15	68		100	2
Ghana	166	7	9	42	82	
Guinea	69	27	35	32	61-85	
India	5,882	2,753	385		806[b]	
Indonesia	1,345	289	222	100-108	367-75	
Iran	837	113	379		39	
Iraq	53	25	19		183	
Kenya	36	14	17	18-28	3	
Laos	419	4	415	(c)	4	
Mali	14	1	10	20	61	
Morocco	484	192	19		(c)	
Nepal	86	44	37	43-71	3	11
Pakistan	2,937	1,097	638	90	80-100	
Senegal	17	6	7		7	
Somalia	47	7	32	23	52	
Sudan	89	18	55		22	
Syria	83	63	2	16-20	237	
Tanzania	44	18	9	43	42	
Tunisia	449.	213	110		29	
Turkey	2,120	419	938		168-78	
U.A.R.	1,081	851	68	85	821	
Uganda	17	1	11	15	16	
Yemen	39	10	29	44-49	92	
Zambia	24		3	.5		
Total	20,636	7,167	4,094	859-938	4,141-4,208	169

Sources: See page 253.

(a) Figures for United States to mid 1965.

(b) Plus a reported $800 million to be given during the Fourth Five-Year Plan.

(c) Quantity unknown.

Convention for the Creation of the Soviet-Romanian Oil Co. Entered into Between the Government of the U.S.S.R. and the Government of the Romanian Kingdom *

Article I: The Government of the U.S.S.R. and the Royal Romanian Government establish by the present convention the organizations, companies, and groups which will constitute the Soviet-Romanian company for the exploration, exploitation, refining, and marketing of crude oil and its products:

For the U.S.S.R., Union Ucrneft and (Union) Soiusneftexport.

For Romania, the Companies Creditul Minier, Redeventa, and the other companies or groups possessing shares of Romanian companies.

The above-mentioned organizations, companies and groups shall be given the necessary rights by the respective Governments in accordance with previous agreements so that they may be able to conform in every respect with the conditions provided in the present convention.

Consequently, the two Governments mutually guarantee the carrying out by the above-mentioned organizations, companies, and groups of the conditions of the constitution and financing of the Soviet-Romanian company.

Article II: The Soviet-Romanian company for the exploration, exploitation, refining, and marketing of crude oil and its products shall have the status of a Romanian private juridical organ of the type of a limited company according to the Romanian laws.

In the course of its activity the Soviet-Romanian company shall have the same rights as any other company with Romanian capital.

The duration of the company is unlimited.

The main office of the company shall be in Bucharest.

Article III: The purpose of the company shall be to prospect, explore, exploit, refine, and market liquid oil on areas belonging to the Romanian state or on areas belonging to private persons, directly or together with the other

* Reprinted from Nicolas Spulber, *The Economics of Communist Eastern Europe* (Cambridge, Mass., and New York: The Technology Press of The Massachusetts Institute of Technology and John Wiley and Sons, 1957), by permission of The MIT Press, Cambridge, Mass. Copyright © 1957 by The Massachusetts Institute of Technology.

companies or persons, as well as to refine and market the products of liquid oil.

Article IV: The company shall have a social capital of five thousand million lei to be paid in equal parts by the two contracting parties, Soviet and Romanian, mentioned in Article I.

The contributions of the two parties shall be covered as shown below:

A. The contribution of the Soviet party:

1. Installations, casing, and materials necessary for the exploration and exploitation of oil up to the total value of 740 million lei, according to a list decided upon by the contracting parties and approved by the two Governments.

The evaluation of installations, casing, and materials shall be made on the basis of average prices of the first half of 1939 in Romania.

2. The shares of the companies mentioned in Annex I having a par value of 1,760 million lei.

B. The contribution of the Romanian party:

1. Shares or assets of Romanian companies at their nominal value.

2. Areas that become available to the Romanian state as a result of the extension of prospected areas in the proportion of 50 per cent, and areas which are ceded as of now, in accordance with Article 95 of the Oil Law, to the companies of the Romanian group of the Soviet-Romanian company.

The above-mentioned lands shall be brought as a contribution by the Romanian group to the Soviet-Romanian company on the basis of an agreement between this group and the Soviet group.

The evaluation of the lands brought by the Romanian group as its contribution shall be made on the basis of the Romanian prices of the first six months of 1939 by a commission of experts in which the members of the two groups shall be in equal number. In case of nonagreement the commission of experts shall submit the matter for arbitration to the Romanian Government, which shall make a decision in agreement with the Government of the U.S.S.R.

3. 50 per cent of the royalties due yearly to the Romanian state until such time as the contributions of the two contracting parties become equal.

The crude oil shall be evaluated at the average prices in Romania in the first six months of 1939.

The capital subscribed by the two founder members shall be completely paid within three years of the date of the constitution of the company.

Within two years of the expiration of the first term of three years granted for the total payment of the subscribed capital, the two founder members shall contribute the assets (installations, land, etc.) up to the amount established as their contribution.

The difference resulting between the evaluation of the contributions and their real value, namely:

    (a) between the par value of shares and the value of investments which constitute the assets by which these shares will be replaced within the aforementioned term, and

    (b) between the evaluation of investments (materials, royalties, lands) at the average prices of the first quarter of 1939 and their commercial value at the time of their transfer to the society, shall constitute a reserve of the company which shall be taxed as capital, according to Romanian laws, and not as profit, in view of the fact that it cannot be considered or used as profit.

As regards the transformation of shares, it is pointed out that the assets corresponding to the shares contributed or which will be contributed in exchange for the share (b) of the Romanian contribution shall be evaluated as contributions to the corresponding par value of the respective share.

The difference between their evaluation and the real value of the shares shall be estimated at the end of the five-year period mentioned in Article IV, points 2 and 3, and shall also be entered into the accounts as a reserve fund.

If, as a consequence of these operations, there is a difference in the total value of the assets paid in exchange for shares by one of the contracting parties and that paid by the other contracting party, the group whose asset is smaller shall either be free to contribute the difference in similar goods evaluated on the same basis or shall compel the other group to withdraw its surplus in order to equalize the contributions.

This equalization shall be made by means of preliminary agreements as the need arises between the Soviet and Romanian groups of the company.

Article V: 1. The Soviet-Romanian company may obtain from the Romanian state rights of prospecting, exploration, and concessions for the exploitation of liquid oil in accordance with the present laws.

2. In general, at auctions in which several offers on equal terms are made for the same rights, among which is an offer of the Soviet-Romanian company, the offer of this company shall be preferred.

3. Besides the mining rights of the state, the Soviet-Romanian company may benefit also from the rights of private owners in accordance with conventions which it may conclude with them in conformity with present laws.

4. The Soviet-Romanian company may build the necessary pipelines to carry crude oil within the oil field and to carry it from the oil field to the refineries.

5. After the contribution of royalties for the completion of the capital is effected, the Soviet-Romanian company may purchase and refine the royalties which it owes to the state from the oil produced on the company's own

lands, as well as on the lands of the companies whose shares or assets enter into the composition of the capital of the Soviet-Romanian company.

6. The company shall be given the most favorable terms granted to oil companies for buying and selling of foreign exchange at the National Bank of Romania.

7. The company shall also be given the most favorable terms as regards the premiums granted by the Romanian state on imports and exports to oil companies.

8. The Soviet-Romanian company shall be granted by the Romanian authorities, without any difficulty, the foreign currency it requires for purchasing from abroad the materials and equipment necessary for its operations from the foreign currency that results from the company's own exports payable in such currency.

Article VI: Each of the founder members shall receive an equal number of shares of the capital subscribed.

The shares of the company shall be of nominal value.

The shares of the Soviet or Romanian group may be transferred only with the authorization of the respective government.

Article VII: 1. The administration of the company shall be carried out in accordance with the Romanian commercial code and with present Romanian laws, with the clarification contained in the following paragraph:

Special mention is made that the Board of Directors shall be composed of an equal number of members representing the Soviet and Romanian groups. The Chairman of the Board of Directors shall be Romanian, the Vice-Chairman Russian, the General Manager Russian, and the Assistant General Manager Romanian.

2. The liquidation of the company may be effected only after a preliminary agreement between the two Governments.

In that event the liquidation shall be made according to the Romanian commercial code.

3. All provisions concerning the organization and the functioning of the company shall be mentioned in a charter drawn up on the above-mentioned principles; the charter shall have a legal status in accordance with the Romanian commercial code.

Article VIII: The present convention shall be effective as of the date of signature. It shall be ratified by the two Governments within thirty days of the date.

Annex 1

LIST OF THE ROMANIAN OIL COMPANIES whose shares and assets represent the Romanian contributions to the Sovrompetrol Company: Creditul Minier;

Redeventa; Subsolul Romanesc; Astramina; Geosina; Neopetrol; Petrolul; Auxiliara Minera; Sarver; Montana; Satelit; Luceafarul; Corana Romana; Consortiul Petrolifer; Compania Romana de Petrol; Doicesti; Socop; Integrupul (Petrolul Romanesc, Petrol Govora, Forajul and Int. Grigorescu); Soc. Generala de Mine si Petrol; Titan; Int. Fr. Ciufu; Noris; Rasnov; Revoil; Petrol Obor.

APPENDIX 4

Agreement with the U.S.S.R. Concerning the Project for the Implementation of the High Dam, Approved by Decree No. 8 of January 9, 1959 (Official Gazette No. 2n.)

December 27, 1958

The governments of the U.A.R. and the U.S.S.R., impelled by the friendly relations which exist between them, and in their desire to strengthen economic and technical cooperation between them on a basis of equality and non-intervention in internal affairs and full respect for the dignity and national sovereignty of each of the two countries, and in view of the great importance of the High Dam project at Aswan to the national economy of the U.A.R., have agreed upon the following:

1. In answer to the desire of the Government of the U.A.R. to develop its national economy, the Government of the U.S.S.R. expresses its readiness to cooperate with the Government of the U.A.R. in constructing the first stage of the High Dam at Aswan.

The first stage comprises the construction of the front part of the main dam, with a height of 50 meters and a length of 600 meters, and the downstream coffer dam with a height of 27 meters and a length of 600 meters; together with work on the diversion of the waters and the sluices, as well as the supply of equipment, and instruments necessary for this work. The two parties will agree on measures in the course of study of the details, or whenever the need arises in the course of implementation.

The first stage also includes projects for converting the basins and the projects of irrigation and land reclamation for the purpose of utilizing the surplus waters resulting from this stage. The volume of assistance offered by the Soviet side will be determined by the agreement of the two parties as regards the implementation of these projects, after the U.A.R. has completed the studies necessary for the execution of these projects.

It is agreed that all the expenses which will be assumed by the Soviet side, whether for the construction of the Dam itself or for implementation of the works of irrigation and the conversion of the basins, imputed to the loan, will be covered within the limit of the loan offered, according to Article 5 of this agreement.

2. In implementation of the cooperation stipulated in Article 1:

a) The Government of the U.S.S.R. undertakes, through the medium of Soviet organisms, to prepare for the execution of the work as well as the necessary research which will be agreed upon by the two parties, with the aim of introducing amendment or modification to the details of the drawings whenever it is deemed necessary, conforming to the agreement with the competent U.A.R. authorities, on condition that this should take place in the shortest time possible and according to the conditions and hydraulic specifications and the basic information drawn up by the U.A.R., on condition that these modifications agree with the final plans for the Dam.

b) The Government of the U.S.S.R. will supply the sluices, machinery and equipment—with a supply of necessary spare parts—as well as the material required for the construction and functioning of the first stage, and the projects related to it, in a perfect manner; material which is not available in the U.A.R.

c) The Government of the U.S.S.R. will offer the technical aid necessary for construction. To accomplish this it will send the required number of Soviet experts to the U.A.R., according to the agreement concluded between the two parties.

3. The Government of the U.A.R. will create a special organism for the management of the project. It will be entrusted with questions of an administrative, technical and financial nature. The implementation of the work which the Government of the U.A.R. will demand within the framework of the first stage will be entrusted to contractors agreed upon by the two parties, and this on the basis of the employment of Soviet equipment and the cooperation of Soviet specialists and experts.

The contract to be concluded between the Government of the U.A.R. and the contractors will include, apart from the plans and specifications of the work, all the obligations of the contractors and the services and facilities which the Government of the U.A.R. will extend.

The above-mentioned organism will supervise the contractors to make sure of the implementation of the obligations required of them according to the contract, and this organism will be charged with the services and facilities stipulated in the article.

4. The Soviet organisms will be responsible for the technical management relating to the construction work of the first stage of the High Dam at Aswan and the execution of all work in a perfect manner, and will also be responsible for the fitting of the machines and their operation within the time limit agreed upon by both parties, and on condition that the special organ-

ism and the contractors mentioned in Article 3 fulfill their obligations as to the operations of research, fitting and construction, according to the implementation programme with regard to similar operations following the agreement between the two countries.

To this effect the Soviet organisms have delegated to the U.A.R. a highly efficient Soviet expert as well as the necessary number of engineers, technicians and skilled Soviet workers, according to the agreement concluded between the two parties.

The Soviet expert, with the collaboration of the organism mentioned in Article 3, will attend to the organisation of work between the Soviet and U.A.R. specialists for the technical supervision of the said work.

5. The Government of the U.S.S.R. offers the U.A.R. Government a loan of 400 million roubles (the rouble is equal to 0.222168 grammes of pure gold) to cover cost of the operations to be carried out by the Soviet organisms for all matters relating to the execution of the projects as well as the studies and researches, the delivery of machinery, equipment and material on the basis of Soviet port prices free of charge (FOB), and the travel fares of Soviet experts from the U.S.S.R. to the U.A.R. and back, in accordance with Article 2.

In the event the total value of the above-mentioned machinery, sluices, equipment and material estimated on the basis of Soviet port prices free of charges, plus the transportation expenses of Soviet specialists and the expenses of Soviet organisms which comprise the technical assistance included in the framework of this agreement, exceeds the amount of the loan, that is, 400 million roubles, the Government of the U.A.R. will pay the excess amount to the U.S.S.R. by supplying it with U.A.R. merchandise, according to the trade and payments agreement in force between the U.A.R. (Egyptian Region) and the U.S.S.R.

6. The Government of the U.A.R. will reimburse the utilized sums of the loan, granted to it in accordance with Article 5 of this agreement, in twelve equal annuities commencing one year after the complete execution of the work on the first stage of the High Dam at Aswan and the filling up of the basin, on condition this is not later than January 1, 1964. The date of the utilization of the loan with regard to machinery, equipment and material will be that of the acknowledgment of the receipt of consignment. For expenses relating to the plans, studies and research, and the expenses of the delegation of Soviet experts and specialists sent to the U.A.R., the date of the utilization of the loan will be that of the vouchers.

The rate of interest on the loan is 2.5 per cent per annum, starting from the date of the utilization of each part of the loan, and will be settled in the course of the first three months of the year following that of their falling due.

7. The Government of the U.A.R. will reimburse the loan and its interest

by depositing in Egyptian pounds (the rate of the Egyptian pound being 2.55187 grammes of pure gold) the sums due in a special account opened at the U.A.R. Central Bank (Egyptian Region) on behalf of the U.S.S.R. State Bank.

The price of the rouble with regard to the Egyptian pound is estimated on the basis of the gold balance between the two foreign currencies on the day of payment.

The Soviet organisms will use all the sums deposited to their account to buy articles from the U.A.R. (Egyptian Region) in accordance with the trade and payments agreement in force between the U.A.R. (Egyptian Region) and the U.S.S.R.

It is also possible to transfer all sums deposited in this account to sterling pounds or to whatever other transferable foreign exchange following agreement between both parties. If the rate of the Egyptian pound is changed, the evaluation of the balance opened on behalf of the U.S.S.R. State Bank will be referred to the date of this change of the Central Bank of the Egyptian Region of the U.A.R. in accordance with the modifications with the gold contained in the Egyptian pound.[1]

8. The Central Bank of the Egyptian Region of the U.A.R. and the U.S.S.R. State Bank will open special accounts to register the operations relating to the loan offered in accordance with this agreement and its execution, as well as the interest due by virtue of this agreement; and the two banks will agree upon the financial and technical measures necessary for its implementation.

9. The Government of the U.A.R. will pay for the Soviet party all the expenses incurred by the Soviet organisms relative to the expenses of food and accommodation, as well as the travel expenses of Soviet experts—inside the

---

[1] It is agreed that the U.S.S.R. will not use the sums deposited in the said account except for the purchase of merchandise from the U.A.R. It is also agreed that at the time of the utilization of the said amounts the U.S.S.R. will enjoy the same rights, advantages and discounts accorded by the U.A.R. for exports in free foreign exchange in conformity with the system in force at the time.

The U.S.S.R. will be entitled to demand payment in sterling pounds or in a freely convertible foreign currency which will be subject to the agreement of the two parties concerned only in exceptional cases which will not permit the U.A.R. to employ the same payment concerning exports in free currency or when the U.A.R. will be unable to offer the merchandise required by the U.S.S.R. within a period of six months.

With regard to Article 5 which stipulates that the rate of the rouble in gold is 0.222168 grammes of pure gold, it is agreed that if the price of the rouble changes in relation to the gold standard before reimbursement of the loan, the balance will be modified in conformity with the change, so that the value of the balance in question remains as is.

U.A.R.—delegated to offer their technical services according to this agreement and by virtue of the conditions stipulated in the special contracts. The settlement of these expenses will be made by adding these sums in Egyptian pounds to the "collect" account opened at the Central Bank of the U.A.R. (Egyptian Region) in favor of the U.S.S.R. State Bank, by virtue of the payments agreement in force between the U.A.R. (Egyptian Region) and the U.S.S.R.

10. The supply of machinery, equipment and material, as well as the preparations for the project, the studies and research and the dispatch of Soviet specialists to the U.A.R., will take place in accordance with the agreements to be concluded between the U.A.R. and the competent Soviet organisms, in conformity with Article 2.

The contracts will determine in particular the sums, date, prices and guarantees concerning each kind of material and machinery, and the responsibility of each party with regard to the circumstances independent of the will of each of them, as well as the violation of the provisions of invention patents, and the provisions and conditions relating to the implementation of obligations of the Soviet party according to this agreement.

The cost of equipment, machinery and material delivered to the U.A.R. by the U.S.S.R. by virtue of this agreement will be determined on the basis of prices in effect on world markets.

11. Without prejudice to the provisions of Article 5 concerning the utilization of the loan for covering the cost of material, machinery and equipment, Soviet ports delivery free of charge on the basis of FOB prices, the furnishing of equipment, material and machinery presented by the U.S.S.R. will be covered by an insurance policy (CIF) in the ports of the U.A.R. (Egyptian Region).

The expenses for shipment and insurance will be paid separately on the basis of the actual value, in accordance with the trade and payments agreement in force between the U.A.R. (Egyptian Region) and the U.S.S.R.

The maritime transportation of the above-mentioned equipment, machinery and material will be effected in accordance with the agreement of maritime transportation concluded between the two countries on September 18, 1958.

12. In case of litigation or contention between the competent authorities in the U.A.R. and the Soviet organisms concerning any question relating to this agreement or its execution, representatives of the governments of the U.A.R. and the U.S.S.R. will consult together so as to come to an understanding on the subject of the above-mentioned contention or litigation.

This agreement will be in force after its ratification, on condition that this is done at the soonest possible time. It will become effective with the exchange of documents of ratification in Moscow.

Agreement Concerning the Economic and Technical Assistance Accorded by the U.S.S.R. to the U.A.R., to Complete the High Dam at Aswan in its Final Form

August 27, 1960

The Government of the United Arab Republic and the Government of the Union of Soviet Socialist Republics in their desire to extend the friendly relations between the two countries.

And the creation of economic and technical cooperation between them on a basis of equality, non-interference in internal affairs and complete respect for the national dignity and sovereignty of each of the two countries.

And owing to the great economic, national importance of the creation of the Aswan High Dam with regard to the Government of the United Arab Republic.

And in execution of the agreements concluded in the letters exchanged on January 15 and 17, 1960, between the President of the United Arab Republic and the Premier of the Union of Soviet Socialist Republics concerning the participation of the Soviet Union in the completion of the High Dam project at Aswan.

Have decided on the following:

Article 1. The Government of the Union of Soviet Socialist Republics, inspired by the desire to assist in the economic development of the United Arab Republic and in answer to the will of the Government of the United Arab Republic, has agreed to collaborate with the Government of the United Arab Republic in completing the final stage of the High Dam project at Aswan.

This stage includes the following work:

a) Completing the construction of the Dam in its final form with an overall height of 111 meters from the river bed.

b) Installing a hydro-electric power station in the course of the diversion canal on the eastern bank of the river, with a capacity of 2.1 million kw.

c) Constructing an overflow channel allowing a discharge of 200 million cubic meters daily, so that the maximum level of storage waters does not exceed 182 meters.

d) Establishing two transmission lines transmitting electric power from the High Dam in Aswan to Cairo, each with a tension of 400–500 kilovolts and a length of 900 kilometers, including three or four transformer stations.

Other transmission lines will also be established with a tension of 132–220 kilovolts and approximately 1,000 kilometers long, including from 10 to 20 transformer stations.

e) Projects of irrigation and reclamation in the lands depending on the High Dam waters, whose area is approximately two million feddans, including the lands depending on the waters resulting from the first stage of the High Dam.

It should be noted that this information is preliminary and will be agreed upon by the two parties in the course of the discussions concerning the details of the design or when the need arises during the process of execution.

Article 2. In realization of the collaboration mentioned in Article 1 of this agreement, the Government of the U.S.S.R. undertakes the following:

a) It undertakes, by means of the Soviet organisations, to draw up the complete designs, blueprints, specifications and the list of quantities, in conformity with the hydraulic circumstances and information supplied by the U.A.R.; and when the need arises it undertakes to carry out the necessary researches and studies. Furthermore it undertakes to draw up the plans for implementing the work necessary for the completion of the High Dam in its final form, in accordance with the agreement reached.

All these aforementioned jobs must be completed in the shortest possible time, thereby making it possible to complete the construction of the Dam at a level of 155 meters by 1967 and completing it in its final form in 1968.

b) Designing, manufacturing, supplying and installing all the sluice gates with the mechanical and electrical annexes necessary for their operation; and also supplying all the necessary spare parts.

c) Designing, manufacturing, supplying, installing, testing and operating all the equipment necessary for the hydro-electric power station and the sluice-gates necessary for it, so that the station units and sluice-gates will be completed, installed and ready for operation according to the following schedule.

First—the first three units	1967
Second—the second three units	1968
Third—the third three units	1969
Fourth—the fourth three units	1970

Also designing, manufacturing, supplying, installing and testing all the equipment necessary for the two transmission lines each with a tension of 400/500 kilovolts and 900 kilometers long, going from Aswan to Cairo (with the exception of the construction and installation of pylons for supporting the electric lines), including three or four transformer stations equipped with commuters for regulating the tension. Furthermore it will install transmission lines with a tension of 132/220 kilovolts and approximately 1,000 kilometers long, including from 10 to 12 transformer stations comprising communications and precautionary instruments and centres for distributing pressure which operate according to the system of sonic waves. All this will be undertaken according to the agreement reached by the two parties in a manner that will insure the operation of a line with a tension of 400/500 kilovolts which are approximately 1,000 kilometers long in the course of 1967. As for the second line with a tension of 400/500 kilovolts it will begin operating in 1968.

Furthermore it undertakes to provide sufficient quantities of spare parts for all the above-mentioned equipment.

d) Supplying and installing the additional construction instruments necessary to complete the final stage of the High Dam project, in addition to the materials necessary for the completion of the High Dam project and which are unavailable in the United Arab Republic, according to the dates agreed upon.

e) Extending the technical assistance necessary for construction. For this purpose the required number of Soviet experts will be sent, according to the agreement reached by the two parties.

f) Extending the technical assistance necessary for training Arab technicians, in the Soviet Union or the United Arab Republic, with regard to the work connected with the High Dam project, if the Government of the United Arab Republic so desires.

g) The Soviet organisations will undertake the work requiring special experience, and whose nature and the basis on which they will be carried out will be determined in the letters exchanged between the two parties at the signing of this agreement.

h) Carrying out the necessary tests to insure the soundness of the Dam and also carrying out final tests on the sluice gates and the hydroelectric power station when the storage waters reach their maximum level, which is 182 meters. It is understood that this will be realized not later than 1975.

i) Supplying, installing and operating the mechanical and electrical equipment necessary for the irrigation and land reclamation projects mentioned in Article 1 of this agreement.

It is understood that the dates mentioned above are founded on the basis that the U.A.R. side will furnish the required information and will undertake the obligations stipulated in this agreement and all that will be agreed upon by the two parties.

Article 3. The U.S.S.R. Government will grant the Government of the U.A.R. a loan of approximately 900 million roubles (the rouble contains

0.222168 grammes of pure gold) to cover the expenses of the Soviet organisations with regard to the designs of the project, research work, studies, and supplying and installing the sluice-gates and hydro-electric power generating units, equipment and materials according to Article 2 of this agreement on the basis of Soviet ports delivery prices (FOB), and the transportation expenses of Soviet experts supplied to offer technical assistance according to this agreement, to and from the United Arab Republic.

If the total expenditure mentioned above exceeds the loan, fixed in this Article at 900 million roubles, the Government of the U.A.R. will reimburse the balance to the Government of the U.S.S.R. in the form of merchandise from the United Arab Republic, in conformity with the trade and payments agreements in force between the United Arab Republic (Egyptian Region) and the Government of the U.S.S.R.

Article 4. The U.A.R. Government will reimburse the sums used from the loan granted to it in accordance with Article 3 of this agreement in twelve equal annuities, starting one year after the completion of the High Dam in its final form, and the implementation of the hydro-electric power station which will be ready to generate not less than 10 million kilowatts of electricity, provided that this is not done later than January 1st, 1970. As for the part of the loan which will be utilized from January 1st, 1969, to execute the remaining parts of the project, it will be reimbursed according to the same conditions of payment, one year after the execution of all these jobs, provided this is not done later than January 1st, 1972.

The rate of interest on the loan is 2.5 per cent annually. Interest is payable from the date of the utilization of every part of the loan, and is to be paid in the course of the first three months of the year following upon the year in which they fall due. The date of the utilization of the loan with regard to equipment, instruments and materials is considered as the date of the shipping voucher. As regards the expenditures connected with the work involved in designing, research and studies, and also the expenses incurred by sending Soviet experts to the United Arab Republic, the date of the utilization of the loan is considered as the date of the bills concerning these matters.

Article 5. Apart from the stipulations present in this agreement, the stipulations of Articles (3), (4), (7), (8), (9), (10), (11), (12) of the agreement concluded between the Union of Soviet Socialist Republics and the U.A.R. in which the U.S.S.R. undertakes to extend technical and economic assistance with regard to the construction of the first stage of the High Dam at Aswan and which was signed on December 27, 1958, are in force. Also in force are the stipulations and conditions mentioned in the letters exchanged between the two parties on the same date as the signing of the said agreement, and will be effective as of the date of this agreement.

Article 6. This agreement shall be ratified within the shortest time possible and are considered as an integral part of the exchange of the ratification documents in Cairo.

This agreement was written in Moscow on August 27, 1960, in two copies, one in Arabic and one in Russian, each of which has the same legal power.

Moussa Arafa,

(*representing the Government of the United Arab Republic*)

Y. F. Arkhiboff,

(*representing the Government of the Union of Soviet Socialist Republics*)

Agreement on Economic and Technical Cooperation Between the Union of Soviet Socialist Republics and the Republic of Egypt

The Government of the Union of Soviet Socialist Republics and the Government of the Republic of Egypt mutually desiring to further consolidate friendly relations and develop economic and technical cooperation between the two countries have agreed to the following:

Article 1. The Government of the Union of Soviet Socialist Republics, meeting the wishes of the Government of the Republic of Egypt, expresses its consent to cooperate with the Government of Egypt in carrying out plans for national economic development of Egypt in geological work, mining, oil exploration and production of oil products, metallurgical, engineering, electric, chemical, textile, food, pharmaceutical and light industries.

This cooperation shall be carried out in establishing new industrial enterprises as well as in extending the productive capacities or by adapting them to manufacture new products.

Annex 1 to this Agreement enumerates the Industrial Enterprises which will be established or extended by the Egyptian Party with the cooperation of the Soviet Party and indicates the manner in which this cooperation will be carried out in each Industrial Enterprise.

Annex 2 to this Agreement enumerates the Industrial Enterprises which all or some of them will be established or extended by the Egyptian Party with the cooperation of the Soviet Party. The two Parties will agree upon the industrial enterprises of this list which will be established or extended with the cooperation of the Soviet Party and upon the scope of this cooperation.

Industrial enterprises and other projects which are to be established by the Egyptian Party in cooperation with the Soviet Party under this Agreement shall be hereinafter referred to as "Industrial Enterprises."

Article 2. In order to carry out the cooperation in establishing and extending the Industrial Enterprises, as stipulated in Annex 1 of this Agreement, the Soviet Organizations shall:

1. Fulfill projecting works to the extent which will be agreed upon by the two Parties.

2. Deliver machinery and equipment with standard set of spare parts for Industrial Enterprises as well as some materials which are not available in Egypt and are needed for establishing the said enterprises.

3. Render technical assistance in:

   a) Selecting the construction sites.

   b) Collecting the initial data necessary for projecting work in connection with Industrial Enterprises.

   c) Establishing the Industrial Enterprises by author's inspection and advice.

   d) Mounting of machinery and equipment (supervision of mounting).

   e) Adjustment of equipment and putting these enterprises into operation.

   f) Reaching projected capacities of the Industrial Enterprises;

   g) Carrying out geological and exploration work.

   h) The proper training (practical and theoretical), of the Egyptian specialists for the said Industrial Enterprises whether in Egypt or in the U.S.S.R. This includes training on processes and operations of machinery and equipment of said Industrial Enterprises.

4. Render technical assistance in organizing the training of skilled personnel for Egyptian industry and for these purposes, work out and hand over to the Egyptian authorities schemes and plants for vocational training of Egyptian nationals, as well as depute to Egypt Soviet specialists and instructors for the purpose of rendering assistance to Egyptian authorities in training.

Number of Soviet specialists, to be sent to Egypt in accordance with this article, their specialties, periods and conditions of their deputing as well as numbers of Egyptian personnel to be received in the U.S.S.R. for training, periods of training and other terms and conditions shall be mutually agreed upon, in each case, by corresponding Soviet Organizations and Egyptian authorities.

Article 3. The Government of the U.S.S.R. shall hand over through Soviet Organizations to the Government of the Republic of Egypt drawings and documents of technological processes required for the production of the Industrial Enterprises as stipulated in the project reports prepared by the Soviet Organizations.

The said documentation shall be handed over free of charge but for actual expenses involved in their reproduction and handing over. It is understood that this documentation shall be used only for the said production within the territory of the Republic of Egypt and shall not be transferred to any foreign judicial or private persons.

Deviations from this provision may only be allowed with the approval of the corresponding Soviet Organization in each case.

Article 4. The Government of the U.S.S.R. and the Government of the Republic of Egypt agree that for the execution of this Agreement the Soviet Party may cooperate with the corresponding Organizations of People's Democratic countries in projecting work, deliveries of equipment, machinery and materials as well as in rendering other kinds of technical assistance stipulated under this Agreement.

Article 5. In pursuance of cooperation provided for in Article 1 of this Agreement the Egyptian authorities shall, on dates to be mutually agreed upon, hand over to Soviet Organizations all initial data necessary for designing the Industrial Enterprises, design and execute all building work and auxiliary services on the basis of the project reports agreed upon, install the machines and equipment of the Industrial Enterprises and provide all the necessary public utilities inside and outside the premises of the Industrial Enterprises.

Article 6. The Government of the Union of Soviet Socialist Republics shall extend credit to the Government of the Republic of Egypt to the amount of seven hundred million roubles (0.222168 grammes of fine gold in one rouble), interest accruing at the rate of $2\frac{1}{2}$ per cent per annum. This credit shall be utilized during the period of four years from the date of entry into force of this Agreement to pay for:

a) Cost of equipment, and machinery, as well as some materials necessary for establishment of Industrial Enterprises which are not available in Egypt on the basis of FOB prices Soviet ports.

b) Cost of projecting and geological and exploration work, as well as cost of preparation of plans and schemes for training of skilled personnel, carried out by Soviet Organizations.

c) Actual expenses involved in the reproduction and handing over of technical documentation in accordance with Article 3 of this agreement.

Should the gold parity of the rouble change before the full utilization of the credit mentioned above, the balance of the credit will be adjusted accordingly so as to assure that the gold value of the balance will remain the same.

In case the cost of above services provided by the Soviet Party exceeds the sum of the credit of 700,000,000 roubles, the excess shall be paid by the Egyptian Party by deliveries to the U.S.S.R. of Egyptian goods in accordance with Trade and Payments Agreement in force between the U.S.S.R. and Egypt.

Article 7. The Government of the Republic of Egypt shall repay parts of credit used under Article 6 of this agreement for each Industrial Enterprise in 12 equal annual installments one year from the date of completion of delivery from U.S.S.R. of complete equipment stipulated in corresponding contracts, for each Industrial Enterprise.

The date of use of credit for delivery of machines, equipment and materials shall be considered the date of the Bill of Lading; for designing and geological and exploration work as well as for other kinds of technical assistance the date of the Invoice.

Interest shall accrue from the date on which each particular part of credit is used, and shall be paid within the first three months of the year, following the year for which it is accrued.

Article 8. Repayment of credit and payment of interest accrued thereof shall be made by the Government of the Republic of Egypt by means of transferring of corresponding sums in Egyptian pounds to a separate account opened by the National Bank of Egypt in favour of the State Bank of the U.S.S.R.

Roubles shall be recalculated into Egyptian pounds based on the gold parity of the rouble and the Egyptian pound on the day of such repayment.

Amounts transferred to this account will all be utilized by Soviet Organizations for purchase of goods in Egypt in accordance with Trade and Payments Agreements in force between U.S.S.R. and Egypt; and/or may be freely converted into pounds sterling or any freely convertible currency which will be agreed upon between the two governments.

In case of any change in the parity of the Egyptian pound, the balance of the account of the State Bank of the U.S.S.R. with the National Bank of Egypt on the date of this change shall be revalued proportionally to the change of the gold value of Egyptian pound.

Article 9. In order to keep record of the utilization and repayment of the credit provided by this Agreement and payment of interest thereof the State Bank of the U.S.S.R. and the National Bank of Egypt shall mutually open special credit accounts and shall work out financial technical arrangements necessary for the implementation of this Agreement.

Article 10. The Government of the Republic of Egypt shall pay to Soviet Party all expenses of the Soviet Organizations in connection with deputing Soviet specialists to Egypt for rendering technical assistance provided for under this Agreement, as well as all expenses of Soviet Organizations connected with training of the Egyptian specialists in the U.S.S.R.

The payment in question shall be made by transferring corresponding sums in Egyptian pounds to the credit of "the collector account" opened with the National Bank of Egypt in favour of the State Bank of the U.S.S.R. in accordance with payments agreements in force between the

Government of the U.S.S.R. and the Government of the Republic of Egypt.

Article 11. Fulfillment of projecting work, delivery of machinery, equipment and materials from the U.S.S.R. geological and exploration work, training of Egyptian nationals, deputing of Soviet specialists to Egypt and rendering other kinds of technical assistance provided under this Agreement shall be effected according to contracts to be concluded between appropriate Soviet Organizations and Egyptian authorities.

Volume of deliveries, dates, prices and guarantees for quality of equipment and machinery and their conformity with respective projected capacities, liabilities of the parties in circumstances beyond control of either party, infringement of patents as well as any other details concerning fulfillment by the parties of obligations under this Agreement are to be determined in the contracts mentioned above. Prices of equipment, machinery and materials delivered to Egypt under this Agreement shall be based on world market prices.

Article 12. Without prejudice to Article 6 stipulating the utilization of the credit to cover cost of machinery, equipment and materials at the price FOB Soviet ports, delivery of machinery, equipments and materials to be supplied by the U.S.S.R. shall be CIF Egyptian ports. Insurance and freight shall be paid by the Egyptian authorities separately as actual rate in accordance with the Soviet-Egyptian Trade and Payments Agreements in force.

Article 13. The Government of the U.S.S.R. expresses its willingness to fulfill the requirements of the Government of the Republic of Egypt concerning the purchase in the U.S.S.R. of spare parts (in addition to standard sets delivered with the equipments) and some kinds of raw materials necessary for normal operation of Industrial Enterprises to be established with the help of the U.S.S.R. Deliveries of spare parts and raw materials shall be effected in accordance with Soviet-Egyptian Trade and Payments Agreement in force.

Article 14. The Government of the U.S.S.R. and the Government of the Republic of Egypt, in the shortest possible time after entry into force of this Agreement, shall mutually inform each other as to the Soviet Organizations and respectively the Egyptian authorities which will be authorized for signing contracts pursuant to this Agreement.

Article 15. In case any dispute or difference may arise between the Soviet Organization and the Egyptian authorities relating to any matter connected with this Agreement or its execution the representatives of the Government of the U.S.S.R. and the Government of the Republic of Egypt shall consult each other and take possible steps to arrive at a solution of the said dispute or difference.

Article 16. The present Agreement is subject to ratification in the shortest possible time and shall come into force on the date of exchange or ratifications that will take place in Cairo.

Done on the 29th day of January, 1958, at Moscow in two original copies in Russian and Arabic, both texts being equally authentic.

APPENDIX 6

Agreement Between His Majesty's Government of Nepal and the Government of the Union of Soviet Socialist Republics on Rendering Economic and Technical Assistance by the Union of Soviet Socialist Republics to the Sovereign Kingdom of Nepal

His Majesty's Government of Nepal (hereinafter referred to as HMG) and the Government of the Union of Soviet Socialist Republics (hereinafter referred to as the Government of the U.S.S.R.),

Being desirous of further strengthening the friendly relations and of developing the economic intercourse between the two countries, and in conformity with the Joint Nepalese-Soviet Communiqué of June 23, 1958,

Have agreed as follows:

Article 1. The Government of the U.S.S.R. in response to the desire of HMG concerning rendering by the Soviet Union assistance in development of the economy of Nepal declares its readiness to render to HMG a free of charge economic and technical assistance to the amount of 30 million roubles [$7.5 million].

Article 2. On the account of the free of charge assistance, granted in accordance with Article 1 of this Agreement, the Government of the U.S.S.R. shall provide technical assistance to be rendered by Soviet organizations to Nepalese State organizations, existing or to be sponsored, authorized by HMG:

a) in construction of

a Hydro-Electric Power Plant of the capacity up to 1,200 KW at Panauti in East Number One district of Nepal with 25 Kilometers transmission line;

a Sugar Factory of crushing capacity up to 1,000 tons of sugar cane per day, with a repair shop and a laboratory;

a Cigarette Factory of the capacity up to 2 milliard cigarettes per year with two shifts work, with a Diesel Power plant forming a part of the Factory to ensure its technological process;

b) in carrying out survey work on laying motorable roads, extending from East to West along the Terai Region of Nepal of the distance up to 1,050 Kilometers, by deputing to Nepal Soviet specialists for rendering advice to HMG's Departments concerned and by delivery of necessary survey equipment.

Article 3. The technical assistance in construction of the projects stipulated in Article 2 of this Agreement shall be performed by the Soviet organizations by means of:

carrying out designing work;

delivery of equipment and such materials as are necessary for construction and not available in Nepal;

deputing to Nepal Soviet specialists (engineers, technicians and skilled workers) for rendering technical assistance in selecting construction sites, in carrying out survey work, in collecting initial data for designing, in construction (advice and supervision), in mounting, in adjusting of the equipment and in putting it into operation;

industrial-technical (shop-floor) training both in Nepal and in the U.S.S.R. of the Nepalese national personnel to work at the projects and construction of which is to be effected with the assistance of the U.S.S.R. in accordance with this Agreement;

handing over technical documentation and information as are necessary for organization and productions of the articles of manufacture, stipulated by project reports of the enterprises constructed in accordance with this Agreement. The aforesaid documentation and information shall be used only for the production of the articles of manufacture mentioned above within the territory of Nepal and are not to be handed over to foreign individuals or legal entities.

Article 4. HMG shall perform through authorized Nepalese organizations the execution of all construction and mounting works both in regard to the projects provided under this Agreement and ancillary services in conformity with the worked-out projects, and shall provide the projects under construction with manpower, electricity, water, transport facilities, approach roads, building materials and necessary municipal services as well as secure financing and costs involved in construction of these projects and execution of works provided under this Agreement.

The respective HMG's Departments shall hand over to the Soviet organizations all initial data required for the designing of the projects provided under this Agreement, project assignments previously agreed upon by the parties.

Article 5. Expenses of the Soviet organizations involved in the delivery of equipment and materials and in rendering other kinds of technical assistance and service provided under this Agreement shall be paid for from the amount of 30 million roubles (one rouble contains 0.222168 grammes of fine gold), stipulated in Article 1 of this Agreement.

Should the cost of the above deliveries and services of the Soviet Party exceed the amount of the free of charge assistance of the 30 million roubles, the excess amount is to be paid by HMG on dates to be agreed upon by the parties through deliveries of Nepalese goods to the U.S.S.R. and/or in Indian rupees, or in freely convertible currency to be specified upon the agreement between the Rastra Bank of Nepal and the State Bank of the U.S.S.R.

Article 6. Delivery of the equipment and materials from the U.S.S.R., as provided in this Agreement, shall be effected by the corresponding Soviet organizations to the respective HMG's Departments on CIF Calcutta Port terms.

It shall be the responsibility of the respective HMG's Departments to procure licenses, attend to the necessary customs formalities, bear the expenses connected with insurance and transit of the aforesaid equipment and materials from Calcutta to the place of delivery in Nepal, arrange at their cost unloading from ships and transportation of the aforesaid equipment and materials from the Port of Calcutta to the place of delivery as well as to pay any customs duties, taxes or any other charges which may be levied in India and Nepal on the aforesaid equipment and materials.

Article 7. To secure local currency for financing local expenses of the Soviet Organizations in Nepal incurred in connection with the stay of Soviet specialists deputed in Nepal and in rendering other kinds of technical assistance and services, provided in this Agreement, the Government of the U.S.S.R. shall secure delivery of goods to HMG or to Nepalese organizations authorized by it which will arrange for the sale of goods at the internal market of Nepal.

Nomenclature, quantity and prices of these goods as well as dates and conditions for their delivery and sale will be the subject for a special Agreement between the two parties. Hereby it is understood that the payment for goods to be delivered by the Soviet organizations shall be effected by HMG immediately after their sale, however, not later than 180 days from the date of delivery of the aforesaid goods at the disposal of HMG in the Port of Calcutta, by remitting corresponding amounts in Nepalese rupees to a special account of the State Bank of the U.S.S.R. to be opened with the Rastra Bank of Nepal on behalf of HMG.

In case of a modification of the official rate of exchange of the Nepalese rupee with respect to the Indian rupee, the balance appearing on the above account of the State Bank of the U.S.S.R. with the Rastra Bank of Nepal on the date of such modification shall be revalued according to the modified official rate of exchange of the Nepalese rupee.

Article 8. For the purpose of keeping records of utilization of the free of charge assistance in the sum of 30 million roubles made available under this Agreement, the Rastra Bank of Nepal and the State Bank of the U.S.S.R. shall open in favor of each other special record accounts in roubles and mutually establish technical procedure for effecting the aforesaid accounts and records connected with them.

Article 9. HMG and the Government of the U.S.S.R. have agreed that in pursuance of this Agreement the Soviet party may cooperate with respective organizations of the countries of the People's Democracies in the deliveries of equipment as well as in rendering other kinds of technical assistance provided under this Agreement.

Article 10. Execution of designing work, delivery of equipment and materials from the U.S.S.R., delegation of Soviet specialists to Nepal and rendering by the Soviet party of other kinds of technical assistance provided under this Agreement shall be effected on the basis of contracts to be entered into between competent Nepalese State organizations and the respective Soviet organizations authorized for this purpose by the governments of the two countries.

The contracts will specify the scope, dates, prices and other terms and conditions for the execution of designing work, delivery of equipment and materials, delegation of Soviet specialists to Nepal and rendering other kinds of technical assistance resulting from this Agreement.

The prices of equipment and materials subject of delivery from the U.S.S.R. to Nepal as well as goods to be purchased by the Soviet organization in Nepal shall be fixed on the basis of the world market price.

The respective HMG's departments shall expeditiously grant permits for the export of goods to be purchased by the Soviet organizations from the Nepalese organizations.

Article 11. HMG and the Government of the U.S.S.R. shall mutually inform each other in the shortest time possible after entry into force of this Agreement as to what HMG's Departments and Soviet organizations respectively will be authorized by them to enter into contracts for the purpose of implementing this Agreement.

Article 12. In case any dispute or difference occurs between HMG's Departments concerned and the Soviet organizations with regard to any matter arising out of this agreement or in connection with its implementation, representatives of HMG and the Government of the U.S.S.R. shall consult with each other and endeavor to arrive at a mutual settlement of the aforesaid dispute or difference.

The present Agreement shall enter into force on the day of its signing.

Done in the City of Kathmandu, this 24th Day of April, 1959, in Duplicate, in the Nepalese, Russian and English languages, all texts being equally authentic.

Protocol to the Agreement Between the Government of the Union of Soviet Socialist Republics and His Majesty's Government of Nepal on Rendering Economic and Technical Assistance by the Union of Soviet Socialist Republics to the Sovereign Kingdom of Nepal, Dated April 24, 1959

The Government of the Union of Soviet Socialist Republics and His Majesty's Government of Nepal proceeding from the friendly relations that exist between the two countries and in connection with the appeal of His Majesty's Government of Nepal to render assistance by the Union of Soviet Socialist Republics in financing the local costs of the Nepalese Party on the construction of the enterprises stipulated in the Soviet-Nepalese Agreement, dated April 24, 1959, have agreed as follows:

Article 1. The Government of the Union of Soviet Socialist Republics meeting half-way the wishes of His Majesty's Government of Nepal expresses its consent to render assistance in financing the local costs of the Nepalese Party during 1962–1965 for the sum up to 3,200 thousand roubles on the construction of the enterprises stipulated in the Soviet-Nepalese Agreement, dated April 24, 1959.

Article 2. In the course of rendering the assistance stipulated in Article 1 of the present Protocol the Government of the Soviet Union loans to His Majesty's Government of Nepal a credit in the amount of 2,500 thousand roubles bearing an annual interest charge of 2.5 per cent of the total loan, out of which 239 thousand roubles in cash, will be transferred from the Account of the State Bank of the U.S.S.R opened in Nepal Rastra Bank in conformity with the Soviet-Nepalese Protocol, dated January 27, 1960, and by the supply of commodities for the remaining total 2,261 thousand roubles.

Besides, the Government of the Soviet Union will ensure the supply of commodities valued at the rest sum of 700 thousand roubles on account of the free-of-charge grant aid to Nepal according to the Soviet-Nepalese Agreement, dated April 24, 1959.

The gain from the realization of Soviet commodities in the local market of Nepal will be utilized by His Majesty's Government to finance the above local costs.

Commodities, quantity, date of delivery and other conditions of the supply of goods will be the subject of a separate Agreement between the Contracting Parties.

Article 3. The payment of the credit stipulated in Article 2 of the present Protocol will be carried out by annual equal payments during the five years starting from January 1, of the year following the year when each enterprise stipulated in the above Soviet-Nepalese Agreement, dated April 24, 1959 is set working but not later than January 1, 1966.

The credit of the sum of 1,400 thousand roubles will be paid off after the Sugar Mill is set working; the credit of the sum of 200 thousand roubles will be paid off after the Cigarette Manufacturing Factory is set working and the credit of the sum of 900 thousand roubles will be paid off after the Hydro-Power Station is set working.

The credit interest will be charged from the date of utilizing the corresponding part of the credit and will be paid off during the first three months of the year following the one for which it has been charged; it being known that the date of utilizing the credit, in case of the supply of the commodities, will be the date of the Bill of Lading; in case of the cash loan the date will be that of the transfer authorization of the State Bank of the U.S.S.R.

The last payment of the interest charge will be completed simultaneously with the last payment in the repayment of the main credit. In case of any alteration of the present gold content of the rouble (one rouble contains .98712 grammes of pure gold) all sums involved (used and unused parts of the credit, the debt balance of the main debt, and the balance of the interest which has been charged but not as yet been paid) will be recalculated so as to preserve the present gold equivalent of the rouble and the credits concerned.

Article 4. Payment to clear off the credit and to pay the interest charged on it will be carried out by means of the supply of Nepalese commodities to the U.S.S.R. and/or with the Indian rupees and/or with freely converted currency determined on agreement between the State Bank of the U.S.S.R. or on behalf of the State Bank of the U.S.S.R. by the Foreign Trade Bank of the U.S.S.R. and Nepal Rastra Bank.

The Parties will coordinate for each calendar year the commodities, quantity and date of the supply of Nepalese goods to the U.S.S.R. three months before the coming of the next year of the repayment of the credit and payment of the interest charge.

While repaying the credit and paying the interest charged on it in freely converted currency and/or in Indian rupees, the conversion of the payment currency into roubles will be carried out according to the gold parity of the currencies on the day of payment.

Article 5. With the object of the registration and calculation of the utilization and repayment of the interest on it the State Bank of the U.S.S.R. or on behalf of the State Bank of the U.S.S.R. the Foreign Trade Bank of the U.S.S.R. and Nepal Rastra Bank will determine, in conference, a technical order of maintaining accounts on the credit.

Article 6. The present Protocol comes into force on the day when it is signed.

Done in Kathmandu in duplicate in the Russian and English languages both texts being equally authentic on this sixth day of February, one thousand nine hundred and sixty-two.

Notes

Introduction

1. See Nicolas Spulber, *The Economics of Communist Eastern Europe* (Cambridge, Mass: The MIT Press, 1957); and Joseph Berliner, *Soviet Economic Aid* (New York: Frederick A. Praeger, 1958).

2. *Ekonomicheskaia Gazeta,* July 14, 1965, p. 34; V. I. Zolotarev, *Vneshniaia Torgovlia Sotsialisticheskikh Stran* (Moscow: Vneshtorgizdat, 1964), p. 80; A. Petrushev, "Bratskoe Sotrudnichestvo—Zalog Uspekha," *Vneshniaia Torgovlia,* March, 1965, pp. 6–7.

CHAPTER 1. *Satellite Aid to the Soviet Union*

1. This is the case despite the existence of several excellent studies that are well documented and unemotional in tone. See especially Spulber, *op. cit.,* and Margaret Dewar, *Soviet Trade with Eastern Europe, 1945–1949* (London: Royal Institute of International Affairs, 1951).

2. The information that follows was taken mainly from S. D. Sergeev, *Ekonomicheskoe Sotrudnichestvo i Vzaimopomoshch' Stran Sotsialisticheskogo Lageria* (Moscow: Vneshtorgizdat, 1959), pp. 114ff (hereafter cited as Sergeev, 1959); Jan Wszelaki, *Communist Economic Strategy: The Role of East-Central Europe* (Washington, D.C.: National Planning Association, 1959), pp. 68ff; A. K. Kozik (ed.), *Ekonomicheskoe Sotrudnichestvo i Vzaimopomoshch' Mezhdu Sovetskim Soiuzom i Evropeiskimi Stranami Narodnoi Demokratii* (Moscow: Izdatel'stvo Akademiia Nauk SSSR, 1958), pp. 52–55; Victor Winston, "The Soviet Satellites—Economic Liability?," *Problems of Communism,* January, 1958, p. 15. Especially helpful was Spulber, *op. cit.,* pp. 36ff.

3. D. F. Fokin (ed.), *Vneshniaia Torgovlia SSSR 1946–1963* (Moscow: I.M.O., 1964), p. 73.

4. The West Germans are still saddled with similar expenses for the United States, England, and France, although the payments were reduced in 1952 and 1957.

5. Wszelaki, *op. cit.,* p. 68; Winston, *op. cit.,* p. 15; Penelope Hartland Thumberg, "The Soviet Union in the World Economy," *Dimensions of Soviet Economic Power,* Hearings of the Joint Economic Committee, Congress of the United States (Washington, D.C.: Government Printing Office, 1962), pp. 415–25. Wolfgang Stolper says it amounted to as much as one-quarter of the East German GNP in some years; see *The Structure of the East German Economy*

(Cambridge, Mass.: Harvard University Press, 1960), p. 5. Abram Bergson uses a lower figure, although his estimate covers the years 1948–53, after much of the looting had taken place. He estimates the Russians received total reparations from all countries worth $2 billion (1938 prices) in this period; see *The Real National Income of Soviet Russia Since 1928* (Cambridge, Mass.: Harvard University Press, 1961), p. 100.

6. For further information on what follows, see Spulber, *op. cit.*, p. 39.

7. *Ibid.*, pp. 172, 181.

8. See I. G. Pisaretz, *Vneshne-Ekonomicheskie Sviazi Pol'skoi Narodnoi Respubliki* (Moscow: Vneshtorgizdat, 1962), p. 77; also Spulber, *op. cit.*, p. 176.

9. See John Michael Montias, "Unbinding the Polish Economy," *Foreign Affairs*, April, 1957, p. 80.

10. See N. I. Ivanov, *Ekonomicheskoe Sotrudnichestvo i Vzaimopomoshch' Stran Sotsializma* (Moscow: Sotsekgiz, 1962), p. 176; Spulber, *op. cit.*, p. 434.

11. See Spulber, *op. cit.*, pp. 173–75.

12. See Ministry of Foreign Affairs of the Federal People's Republic of Yugoslavia, *White Book on the Aggressive Activities by the Governments of the USSR, Poland, Czechoslovakia, Hungary, Rumania, Bulgaria, and Albania Toward Yugoslavia* (Belgrade, 1951), p. 331 (hereafter cited as *White Book*); *Peking Review*, No. 9 (May 8, 1964), p. 7, and No. 38 (September 18, 1964), p. 22; *The New York Times*, September 11, 1964, p. 11.

13. See Frederic L. Pryor, *The Communist Foreign Trade System* (Cambridge, Mass.: The M.I.T. Press, 1963), pp. 136–37.

14. "Terms of Trade Between the Soviet Union and Smaller Communist Countries, 1955–57," *Review of Economics and Statistics*, May, 1959; "The Terms of Soviet-Satellite Trade: A Broadened Analysis," *ibid.*, May, 1960; "Mutual Price Discrimination in Soviet Bloc Trade," *ibid.*, November, 1962. A study of relative oil prices in Cuba and Eastern Europe shows that the Russian charge the Cubans only half as much as they do the other satellites.

15. "Soviet Foreign Trade Pricing and the Question of Discrimination," *Review of Economics and Statistics*, May, 1962; "Soviet Bloc Mutual Discrimination: Comment," *ibid.*, November, 1962; "More on Soviet Bloc Trade Discrimination," *Soviet Studies*, July, 1965, p. 44.

16. "Psevdonauchnye Issledovaniia Burzhuaznykh Ekonomistov," October, 1963, p. 13.

17. Pryor, *op. cit.*, p. 144; Dewar, *op. cit.*, p. 50.

18. Heinz Kohler, "East Germany's Terms of Trade 1950–61," *Kyklos*, February, 1963, p. 286.

19. Much of what follows is taken from Max Beloff, *Soviet Policy in the Far East 1944–1951* (London: Oxford University Press, 1953), pp. 25–41.

20. Merle Goldman, *The Chinese Communist Party and Its Literary Critics* (Cambridge, Mass.: Harvard University Press, in press), Chapter 4.

21. Beloff, *op. cit.*, p. 40.

22. Vsevolod Holubnychy, "Soviet Economic Aid to China," *Bulletin of the Institute for the Study of the USSR*, January, 1956, p. 4. He quotes from *Voprosy Ekonomiki*, February, 1952, p. 53.

23. Most of what follows is taken from M. V. Meshcheriakov, *Ocherk Ekonomicheskogo Sotrudnichestva Sovetskogo Soiuza i Mongol'skoi Narodnoi Respubliki* (Moscow: Vneshtorgizdat, 1959); also from Akademiia Nauk SSSR Institut Narodnov Azii, *Mongol'skaia Narodnaia Respublika 1921–1961* (Moscow: Izdatel'stvo Vostochnoi Literatury, 1961).

24. Dennis J. Doolin, *Territorial Claims in the Sino-Soviet Conflict* (Stanford, Calif.: The Hoover Institution, 1965), pp. 15, 43.

25. Akademiia Nauk SSSR Institut Narodnov Azii, *op. cit.*, p. 116; M. F. Kovrizhnyi (ed.), *Vneshniaia Torgovlia Stran Narodnoi Demokratii* (Moscow: Vneshtorgizdat, 1960), p. 199; A. D. Stupov (ed.), *Ekonomicheskoe Sotrudnichestvo i Vzaimopomoshch' Sotsialisticheskikh Stran* (Moscow: Akademiia Nauk SSSR, 1962), p. 214; S. D. Sergeev, *Ekonomicheskoe Sotrudnichetvo i Vzaimopomoshch' Sotsialisticheskikh Stran* (Moscow: Vneshtorgizdat, 1964), p. 177 (hereafter cited as Sergeev, 1964).

26. Konrad Il'chen, *Druzhba v Deistvii* (Moscow: Izdatel'stvo Inostrannoi Literatury, 1962), p. 160 (translated from the German); Meshcheriakov, *op. cit.*, p. 98; Sergeev, 1959, p. 116.

27. The most detailed analysis of the JSC available in English is contained in Spulber, *op. cit.*, Chapter 6.

28. Most of the figures in the following discussion are drawn from the *White Book;* also from Spulber, *op. cit.*

29. *White Book,* p. 37.

30. *Ibid.*, p. 306.

31. See Milovan Djilas, *Conversations with Stalin* (New York: Harcourt, Brace and World, 1962), pp. 131–35. Djilas describes the Albanian and Soviet resentment over the Yugoslav JSC in Albania. He also quotes Stalin as saying that the JSC were not conducive to good relations between friendly and allied countries.

32. Figures for Bulgaria are drawn from S. D. Sergeev and A. F. Dobrokhotov, *Narodnaia Respublika Bolgariia* (Moscow: Vneshtorgizdat, 1962), p. 189 (hereafter cited as Sergeev, 1962); Spulber, *op. cit.;* Wszelaki, *op. cit.*

33. Figures for Hungary are drawn from M. A. Usievich, *Razvitie Sotsialisticheskoi Ekonomiki Vengrii* (Moscow: Akademiia Nauk SSSR, 1962); Spulber, *op. cit.;* Wszelaki, *op. cit.;* Dewar, *op. cit.*

34. V. P. Komissarov and A. N. Popov, *Den'gi Kredit i Finany Evropeiskikh Stran Narodnoi Demokratii* (Moscow: Sotsekgiz, 1960), p. 235.

35. Figures for Rumania are drawn from Spulber, *op. cit.;* Wszelaki, *op. cit.;* Sergeev, 1959.

36. John Michael Montias, "Background and Origins of the Rumanian Dispute with Comecon," *Soviet Studies,* October, 1964, p. 126; *The New York Times,* May 14, 1966, p. 4.

37. M. F. Kovrizhnykh, A. B. Frumkin, and V. S. Pozdniakov, *Vneshniaia Torgovlia Stran Narodnoi Demokratii* (Moscow: Vneshtorgizdat, 1955), pp. 52–53.

38. Sergeev, 1959, p. 115; Beloff, *op. cit.*, pp. 14, 73–77.

39. *People's China,* February 16, 1955, pp. 3–4.

40. Letter of the Central Committee of the Chinese Communist Party in reply to the letter of the Communist Party of the Soviet Union, dated November 29 1963; in *Peking Review,* No. 9 (May 8, 1964), p. 7.

41. Letter of the Central Committee of the Communist Party of the Soviet Union to the Central Committee of the Chinese Communist Party, March 7, 1964; in *Peking Review,* No. 9 (May 8, 1964), p. 7.

42. *Vneshniaia Torgovlia,* April, 1958, p. 48.

CHAPTER 2. *Soviet Aid to the Satellites*

1. For example, compare N. N. Liubimov, *Sovremennye Mezhdunarodnye Ekonomicheskie Otnosheniia* (Moscow: Mezhdunarodnoe Otnoshenie, 1964), p. 128; Ivanov, *op. cit.,* p. 177; Komissarov and Popov, *op. cit.,* p. 234; and Sergeev, 1964, pp. 393, 396–97.

2. See Khrushchev's speech in *Pravda,* December 10, 1963, p. 1; Pryor, *op. cit.,* p. 170.

3. I. P. Oleinik, *Pobeda Sotsializma v Rumynii* (Moscow: IZL, 1962), p. 76.

4. Liubimov, *op. cit.,* p. 128; N. Mitrofanova, "Mezhdunarodnoe Sotsialisticheskii Kredit," *Den'gi i Kredit,* October, 1964, p. 84.

5. V. N. Polezhaev, *Vneshniaia Torgovlia Vazhnyi Faktor Mirnogo Sosushchestvovaniia* (Moscow; Vneshtorgizdat, 1952), p. 44.

6. Sergeev, 1964, p. 181. Fokin (ed.), *op. cit.,* says 200,000 tons of grain were provided.

7. Sergeev, 1964, p. 182; Spulber, *op. cit.,* p. 434. Fokin, *op. cit.,* p. 69, says it was $23 million.

8. Pryor, *op. cit.,* p. 201.

9. Kozik, *op. cit.,* p. 168; Liubimov, *op. cit.,* p. 128; Zolotarev, *op. cit.,* p. 330.

10. Sergeev, 1964, p. 180.

11. One source indicates that in 1955 the Soviet Union transferred about $6.7 million in convertible currency to Czechoslovakia for the purchase of needed food and raw materials outside the bloc. The same source reports that this type of aid was repeated in 1956, when $28 million was transferred. Neither transaction, however, seems to have been considered as a loan, and no other sources carry this information. Kovrizhnyi, *op. cit.,* p. 263n.

12. A. G. Zverev, *Finansy i Sotsialisticheskoe Stroitel'stvo* (Moscow: Gosfinizdat, 1957), pp. 329–31.

13. It should be noted, however, that the volume of Equipment and Material for Complete Plants (Item 16) shipped to Poland did not increase until 1961. See Table II-2.

14. Zverev, *op. cit.,* p. 331; Komissarov and Popov, *op. cit.,* p. 58. Kozik, *op. cit.,* p. 178, says that only $10 million in convertible currency was provided.

15. Kozik, *op. cit.,* p. 178. Sergeev, 1964, p. 174, says a total of $262 million was provided, much of it supplied in 1958. However, shipments of Equipment and Material for Complete Plants did not increase significantly until 1959.

16. A. F. Kudriashov, *Mir Sotsializma v Tsifrakh i Faktakh* (Moscow: Politizdat, 1963), p. 58.

17. Sergeev, 1964, pp. 182–88. Kudriashov, *op. cit.*, p. 58, Sergeev, 1959, p. 118. V. P. Komissarov and A. N. Popov, *Mezhdunarodnye Ekonomicheskie Otnosheniia GDR* (Moscow: I.M.O., 1963), p. 91 (hereafter cited as Komissarov and Popov, 1963). Sergeev, 1964, p. 184, says East Germany loaned only $15 million.

18. Albania's exclusion was so complete that the editors of the annual statistical handbook for foreign trade did not mention Albania in the 1962 handbook. Albania has reappeared in the summary handbook which covers the years 1959 to 1963 (*VT SSSR 1959–63*).

19. Mitrofanova, *op. cit.*, p. 84. By 1960, deliveries of Equipment and Material for Complete Plants was higher to Bulgaria than to any other East European country; this situation continued through 1965.

20. Liubimov, *op. cit.*, p. 129; J. F. Brown, "Eastern Europe," *Survey*, January, 1965, p. 71.

21. It is necessary to repeat that these figures refer to economic loans for which explicit and official sources can be found. The actual totals may be higher or lower.

22. L. S. Bagrianskaia, "Ekonomicheskoe Sotrudnichestvo Sovetskogo Soiuza s Koreiskoe Narodno-demokraticheskoi Respublikoi," *Narody Azii i Afriki*, January, 1965, pp. 20–21.

23. E. Karavaev, "Torgovo-Ekonomicheskoe Sotrudnichestvo SSSR i DRV," *Vneshniaia Torgovlia*, October, 1965, p. 6.

24. Kovrizhnyi, *op. cit.*, p. 172. Liubimov, *op. cit.*, p. 135, says that *socialist* aid as of 1961 amounted to $500 million. This apparently excludes Chinese aid.

25. *The New York Times*, April 7, 1965, p. 14.

26. For details of the agreements, see *Vneshniaia Torgovlia*, September, 1961, p. 5; and October, 1959, p. 6.

27. Doolin, *op. cit.*, p. 43.

28. Liubimov, *op. cit.*, p. 95; *Ekonomicheskaia Gazeta*, October 5, 1963, p. 15.

29. Emphasis added. *Pravda*, April 3, 1964, p. 1; Kudriashov, *op. cit.*, p. 69; *Soviet News*, August 17, 1964, p. 79.

30. U.S. Department of State, *Current Backgrounds*, No. 464, p. 14.

31. Iu. V. Gankovskii (ed.), *SSSR i Strany Vostoka, Ekonomicheskoe i Kulturnoe Sotrudnichestvo* (Moscow: Vostochnoi Literatury, 1961), p. 18.

32. *Soviet News*, August 14, 1964, p. 74; *Ekonomicheskaia Gazeta*, August 22, 1964, p. 19; Zolotarev, *op. cit.*, p. 194. One source claims that $4 billion in new plant construction was undertaken by the Russians (*Ekonomicheskaia Gazeta*, October 5, 1963, p. 15).

33. *Soviet News*, August 14, 1964, p. 74.

34. Kudriashov, *op. cit.*, p. 69; *Soviet News*, August 17, 1964, p. 79.

35. Colin Garrat, "China as a Foreign Aid Donor," *Far Eastern Economic Review*, January 9, 1961, p. 81.

36. *Peking Review*, No. 9 (May 8, 1964), p. 7.

37. *Soviet News*, August 14, 1965, p. 75.

38. *Pravda*, April 3, 1964, p. 5.

39. *Ibid.*; *Soviet News*, August 14, 1964, p. 75.

40. *Red Flag*, November 19, 1963.

41. *Peking Review*, No. 9 (May 8, 1964), p. 7.

42. Quoted by Raymond L. Garthoff, "Sino-Soviet Military Relations," *The Annals*, September, 1963, p. 81; *The New York Times*, June 24, 1957.

43. N. Ptichkin, "Mogushii Uskoritel' Ekonomicheskogo Progressa," *Vneshniaia Torgovlia*, October, 1963, p. 4; N. Ptichkin, "Organizatsiia Bratskogo Sotrudnichestva," *Vneshniaia Torgovlia*, April, 1964, p. 17.

44. This estimate has been provided by Egon Neuberger.

45. For the text of agreement establishing IBEC, see *Vneshniaia Torgovlia*, August, 1964, p. 47. The capital quota is given on p. 48.

46. *The New York Times*, March 30, 1964, p. 43; April 28, 1965, p. 67; June 21, 1965, p. 43; August 3, 1965, p. 43.

47. For an analysis of the debate, see John Michael Montias, "Background and Origins of the Rumanian Dispute with Comecon," *op. cit.*, p. 147.

48. Francis Osvald, "Cross Currents in Prague," *Survey*, October, 1963, p. 48.

49. *Peking Review*, July 3, 1964, p. 20; September 18, 1964, p. 22.

50. *Peking Review*, No. 9 (May 8, 1964), p. 7.

CHAPTER 3. *The United Arab Republic*

1. Supplement to *Vneshniaia Torgovlia*, November, 1965, p. 1.

2. Herman Finer, *Dulles Over Suez* (Chicago: Quadrangle, 1964), p. 27.

3. *Arab Scribe*, April, 1964, p. 83.

4. *Ibid.*, p. 84.

5. Finer, *op. cit.*, p. 48.

6. See I. Komzin, *The High Aswan Dam* (Moscow: Foreign Languages Publishing House, n.d.), p. 24.

7. Vasilii Galaktionov, "Plotina Asuana," *Novy Mir*, February, 1961, p. 184.

8. This information obtained in personal interviews in Egypt.

9. Dr. Said El Naggar, *Foreign Aid to the UAR* (Cairo: Institute of National Planning, 1963), p. 54.

10. *Izvestiia*, September 14, 1961, p. 2.

11. Sadd-El-A'ali Authority, *Aswan High Dam: Diversion of Nile* (Aswan High Dam Authority, Aswan, May, 1964).

12. *The High Dam: Bulwark of Our Future* (Cairo: Information Department, Government of Egypt, 1963), p. 24.

13. *Ibid.*, p. 26; *Aswan High Dam: Diversion of Nile*, sixth page from end of pamphlet (no page numbers).

14. *Ethiopian Herald*, May 7, 1964, p. 3. At the Volta Dam in Ghana, an American aid project about one-quarter to one-half the size of the Aswan Dam, there were ten deaths.

15. Egypt's foreign debt was estimated to total $2.5 billion as of 1965; reserves were down to $30 million (*The Wall Street Journal*, April 28, 1965, p. 1). A further complication was the war in Yemen, to which Nasser decided to commit large quantities of Egyptian troops and funds. Reportedly, the U.S.S.R. agreed to cancel $460 million of the military debt in September, 1965 (*The New York Times*, December 30, 1965, p. 5).

16. These figures were obtained from officials in Cairo. The $8.3 million amounts to one-twelfth of the $100 million for the first stage of construction. This loan was made for a twelve-year period.

17. *The New York Times,* June 15, 1965, p. 4; November 5, 1965, p. 9. *U.S. Economic Assistance to the UAR* (Cairo: U.S. AID Mission, April 1, 1964), p. 2.

18. *Vedomosti Verkhovnogo Soveta SSSR,* April 7, 1965, p. 316; Central Bank of Egypt, *Economic Review,* V, No. 2 (1965), p. 161.

19. Central Bank of Egypt, *Report of the Board of Directors for the Year 1962/63* (Cairo, September, 1963), p. 26; *Pravda,* May 25, 1964, p. 2; D. Fokin, "Vneshniaia Torgovlia SSSR v 1963 Godu," *Vneshniaia Torgovlia,* November, 1964, p. 16 (Fokin does not include the $44-million loan in his totals); B. Sobolev, "Sovetskaia Pomoshch' Stranam Azii i Afriki," *Finansy SSSR,* January, 1964, p. 40; *Vedomosti Verkhovnogo Soveta SSSR,* April 7, 1965, p. 316.

20. A. Nekrasov, "Cooperation and Disinterested Aid," *International Affairs,* March, 1963, p. 81; P. Beliaev, "Nashe Sotrudnichestvo s OAR," *Vneshniaia Torgovlia,* February, 1963, p. 17.

21. Government of India, Ministry of Finance, Department of Economic Affairs, *Report of the Committee on Utilisation of External Assistance* (New Delhi, 1964), p. 8.

22. In *The Ugly Russian* (New York: Trident Press, 1965), p. 30, Victor Lasky mistakenly transposed my report about the bulldozers and burnt-out boilers from Helwan in Egypt to the Bhilai steel mill in India.

23. *Soviet News,* February 12, 1965, p. 79.

24. *Ibid.,* December 20, 1965, p. 136.

CHAPTER 4. *India*

1. V. K. R. V. Rao and Dharm Narain, *Foreign Aid and India's Economic Development* (New York: Asia Publishing House, 1963), p. 45.

2. Government of India, Ministry of Finance, Department of Economic Affairs, *External Assistance 1962* (New Delhi, 1963), pp. 25, 32, 41 (hereafter referred to as *External Assistance 1962,* and so on for the issues of succeeding years).

3. Fokin, *op. cit.,* p. 119; Rao and Narain, *op. cit.,* p. 29.

4. Government of India, Ministry of Finance, Department of Expenditure (Projects Coordination Division), *Annual Report on the Workings of Industrial and Commercial Undertakings of the Central Govt. for the Year 1962–63* (March, 1964), pp. 31–33; *External Assistance 1963,* pp. 108–10; Hindustan Steel Limited, *Eighth Annual Report 1961–62* (Calcutta, 1962), p. 12; *Ninth Annual Report 1962–63* (Calcutta, 1963), p. 8; *Tenth Annual Report 1963–64* (Calcutta, 1964), p. 8; Press Bureau of German Industry, *Newsletter* (New Delhi), March 24, 1965, p. 2.

5. *The Hindustan Survey of Indian Industry 1961,* p. 43.

6. Press Bureau of German Industry, *Newsletter,* March 10, 1965, p. 2.

7. Public Relations Department, Bhilai Steel Mill, *Expansion of the Bhilai Steel Mill* (Bhilai, n.d.).

8. *Statesman,* May 31, 1965.

9. *Economic Times* (Bombay), December 23, 1964. There have been similar complaints about a surplus of useless equipment at Bhilai (*Indian Express,* June 1, 1965).

10. Similar pressures had the same effect in Pakistan (*Far Eastern Economic Review,* September 22, 1960, p. 679).

11. Obstinacy may also pay off. Ceylon, after a change in government, has agreed to compensate various Western firms for property nationalized in 1962. However, this compromise was extracted by withholding American foreign aid for three years. There is some question whether this is the proper way to exercise the power of the American government and what the over-all benefit to the United States has been. It seems unwise, to say the least, to tie American policy to the whims of private oil firms over which the U.S. Government has little control.

12. *The New York Times,* September 2, 1962, p. 6; M. Neresov, "Pakistan Dolzhen Imet 'Sviou Nefet,' " *Sovremennyi Vostok,* December, 1960, p. 58; V. Bol'shakov, "Sovetskii Soiuz Pomogaet Industrializatsii Druzhestvennykh Stran," *Vneshaniaia Torgovlia,* January, 1962, p. 14.

13. *Christian Science Monitor,* January 4, 1963, p. 13. *Lok Sabha Debates,* March 16, 1964, 7th sess., Third Series, XXVII, p. 5650.

14. *Lok Sabha Debates,* March 16, 1964, pp. 5650–55; *Times of India,* March 13, 1964.

15. See *The Economist,* July 31, 1965, p. 467.

16. Officials of the Chemical Construction Corporation have denied that they quoted a price three times that of the Florida firm. But although repeatedly requested to, they have not made public the price of the Florida project. They also deny that they subsequently lowered the bid on the Indian plant to $9 million.

17. *The Hindu Survey of Indian Industry 1961,* p. 107.

18. Rao and Narain, *op. cit.,* p. 31.

19. See Government of India, *Report of the Committee on Utilisation of External Assistance 1964,* p. 29.

20. *Red Flag,* October 21, 1963.

21. *The New York Times,* January 4, 1964, p. 15; January 9, 1964, p. 10.

22. *The New York Times,* August 4, 1965, p. 8. In November, 1965, a Pakistan newspaper reported that India had received two new squadrons of MIG-21 jets and ground-to-air and air-to-air missiles (*The New York Times,* November 4, 1965, p. 11).

23. *Red Flag,* October 21, 1963.

24. *External Assistance 1962,* p. 59; *External Assistance 1963,* p. 45.

25. Sergeev, 1959, p. 164.

26. "Is the USSR Superior to the West as a Market for Primary Products?," *Review of Economics and Statistics,* August, 1964, p. 287.

27. Only Finland had a volume of trade equal to India's in 1964 (*VT SSSR,* p. 12). *Vneshniaia Torgovlia,* March, 1965, *Supplement,* p. 5.

28. Government of India, Ministry of Commerce and Industry, Department of Commercial Intelligence and Statistics, *A Guide to Official Statistics of Trade, Shipping and Custom Revenue of India* (Calcutta, December 31, 1962).

29. *Economic Times* (Bombay), May 16, 1964, p. 5; *The Hindu* (Madras), June 12, 1965.

30. *Economic Times* (Bombay), June 11, 1964.

31. At least one American importer has expressed the view that as of January, 1965, the Czechs and the Yugoslavs, but not the Russians, have been involved in the reselling of cashew nuts to the United States. (Personal communication from Hollander Trading Corporation and Mitchel Beck Company.)

32. Government of India, Ministry of Finance, *Explanatory Memorandum on the Budget of the Central Government for 1964–65* (New Delhi, February 27, 1964).

33. *Statesman*, May 31, 1965; Rao and Narain, *op. cit.*, p. 60.

34. *Explanatory Memorandum on the Budget of the Central Government for 1964–65*, p. 113.

CHAPTER 5. *Afghanistan*

1. N. M. Gurevich, "Razvitie Fabrichno-Zavodskoi Promyshlennosti v Afganistane," *Narody Azii i Afriki*, March, 1962, p. 48.

2. Iu. M. Golovin, *Afganistan Ekonomika i Vneshniaia Torgovlia* (Moscow: Vneshtorgizdat, 1962), p. 149.

3. L. B. Teplinskii, *Sovetsko-Afganskoe Otnosheniia 1919–1960* (Moscow: Sotsekgiz, 1961), pp. 115–18.

4. Afghanistan official figures indicate that $24 million of Russian aid was utilized in 1963. This virtually coincides with Item 16 in the Soviet Trade Handbook (*VT SSSR 1963*, p. 184). See the discussion of Item 16 in Chapter 4.

5. United States Government, Agency for International Development and Department of Defense, *Proposed Mutual Defense and Development Program, FY 1966* (Washington, D.C.: Government Printing Office, 1965).

6. Iu. M. Golovin, *Sovetskii Soiuz i Afganistan* (Moscow: Izdatel'stvo Vostochnoi Literatury, 1962), p. 90.

7. *Ibid.*, p. 80.

8. Golovin, *Afganistan Ekonomika i Vneshniaia Torgovlia*, p. 157.

CHAPTER 6. *Indonesia*

1. Most of the material that follows was obtained in interviews with Indonesian, American, and Russian officials in Indonesia. In addition, I have relied heavily on the excellent study of Dr. Alexander Shakov entitled "Foreign Economic Assistance to Indonesia 1950–61," an unpublished dissertation at the London School of Economics, University of London, August, 1962. Dr. Shakov was also most helpful in providing me with more current information.

2. Shakov, *op. cit.*, p. 419; K. Krishna Moorty, "Russians Harsh to Sukarno," *Far Eastern Economic Review*, April 25, 1963, p. 229.

3. V. Arkhipov, "Ekonomika i Gosudarstvennye Finansy Indonezii," *Finansy SSSR*, February, 1965, p. 86.

4. Sobolev, *op cit.*, p. 38. Additional information about the faulty equipment in Indonesia and other Afro-Asian countries may be found in the statement on "Sino-Soviet Bloc Aid: Myths and Facts," by the Honorable Frank M. Coffin,

Deputy Administrator for Program, Agency for International Development, Before the Senate Foreign Relations Committee on May 12, 1962.

5. As of mid-1963, the total was $610 million. S. M. Nesterov (ed.), *Mezhdunarodnyi Ezhegodnik Politika i Ekonomika* (Moscow: Gospolitzdat, 1964), p. 34.

CHAPTER 7. *Asia*

1. These data were obtained from official sources in Nepal.
2. *Red Flag,* October 21, 1963.
3. Chinese Embassy in Afghanistan, *News Bulletin,* June 24, 1964, p. 3.
4. *Izvestiia,* July 12, 1964, p. 4.
5. *Vedomosti Verkhovnogo Soveta SSSR,* August 6, 1957, p. 477.
6. I. Mozheiko, "Litsom k Litsu s Sovetskim Chelovekom," *Vneshniaia Torgovlia,* November, 1963, p. 29.
7. *Soviet News,* June 16, 1965, p. 142; *Pravda Ukrainy,* March 9, 1963, p. 4.
8. *Pravda,* July 5, 1962, p. 4. I am indebted to Holland Hunter for drawing this response to my attention.
9. *Izvestiia,* July 12, 1964, p. 4.
10. Nesterov, *op. cit.,* p. 31; Thomas L. Hughes, "The Communist Economic Offensive Through 1963." Research Memorandum, RSB-43, Department of State, Bureau of Intelligence and Research (Washington, D.C., June 18, 1964), p. 23.
11. *Soviet News,* August 6, 1954, p. 58; Hughes, *op. cit.,* p. 24; "Krepnet Sotrudnichestvo Mezhdu SSSR i Kambodzhei," *Vneshniaia Torgovlia,* June, 1963, p. 8.
12. Almost all the information about Chinese activity in Cambodia is taken from *Far Eastern Economic Review,* May 9, 1963, pp. 320–21.
13. *Vedomosti Verkhovnogo Soveta SSSR,* June 18, 1958, pp. 563–67; *The New York Times,* June 7, 1963, p. 43; and January 18, 1965, p. 40.
14. Liubimov, *op. cit.,* p. 241.
15. L. Kliuchkovskii, "Problemy Vneshnei Torgovli Pakistana," *Vneshniaia Torgovlia,* October, 1964, pp. 24, 29; *The New York Times,* March 27, 1964, p. 6.
16. *Vedomosti Verkhovnogo Soveta SSSR,* April 10, 1963, p. 316.

CHAPTER 8. *The Middle East*

1. V. Zaitsev, "Soglasenie s Alzhirom v Deistvii," *Vneshniaia Torgovlia,* June, 1964, p. 19.
2. "Vo Imia Bratskoi Druzhby," *Vneshniaia Torgovlia,* July, 1964, p. 17; *Soviet News,* September 4, 1964, p. 108.
3. V. Naborov, "Zhiznenno Vazhnye Problemy," *Vneshniaia Torgovlia,* September, 1963, p. 24; Hughes, *op. cit.,* p. 32.
4. "The Socialist World System and the National-Liberation Movement," *World Marxist Review,* No. 3 (1963), p. 70.
5. *Vedomosti Verkhovnogo Soveta SSSR,* April 23, 1959, pp. 278–85.
6. *Soviet News,* March 19, 1965, p. 144; May 5, 1965, p. 67. M. Beloshevich, "Dorogi Druzhby," *Vneshniaia Torgovlia,* March, 1966, p. 11.

7. Hughes, *op. cit.*, p. 26; *Time*, January 15, 1965, p. 31.

8. *Vedomosti Verkhovnogo Soveta SSSR*, May 27, 1965, p. 491.

9. Nesterov, *op. cit.*, p. 31.

10. Nekrasov, *op. cit.*, p. 81; *Soviet News*, August 6, 1965, p. 59; Ministerstvo Inostrannykh Del SSSR, *SSSR i Arabskie Strany 1917–1960 gg.* (Moscow: Gospolitizdat, 1961), p. 415.

11. Sobolev, *op. cit.*, p. 39; *The New York Times*, July 30, 1963, p. 1.

12. *China Quarterly*, October, 1964, p. 182; *The New York Times*, October 23, 1964, p. 19.

13. *Ta Kung Pao*, January 18, 1961, p. 4.

14. V. Kudryavstev, "Problems of Afro-Asian Solidarity," *International Affairs*, May, 1963, p. 53.

15. *Red Flag*, October 21, 1963.

16. S. Skachkov, V. Sergeev, and G. Sheviakov, *Pomoshch' i Sotrudnichestvo vo Imia Mira* (Moscow: Gospolitizdat, 1962), p. 5. The Russians reportedly provided Turkey with a $10-million loan in 1957 and an offer of up to $500 million in 1960, but the Russians have not acknowledged either. However, their foreign trade statistics do indicate about $6-million worth of help under Item 16. *VT SSSR 1955–59*, p. 561; *VT SSSR 1961*, p. 206; *VT SSSR 1963*, p. 232; Hughes, *op. cit.*, p. 28; *The New York Times*, June 17, 1962, p. 2. See also Appendix Table 2.

17. Sobolev, *op. cit.*, p. 39; *Sovetskaia Torgovlia*, December 24, 1963, p. 1.

18. *Soviet News*, November 11, 1964, p. 78.

19. *Sovetskaia Rossia*, December 24, 1964, p. 4.

CHAPTER 9. *Latin America*

1. *The New York Times*, April 8, 1965, p. 63; and August 12, 1965, p. 1. The only other Communist countries that seem to have gained any foothold in Argentina are Czechoslovakia and Poland. Poland is reported to have provided a loan, although of unspecified amount. For a general discussion of Soviet and satellite efforts in Latin America, see Evgeny Glovinsky, "The Economic Relations of the USSR with Latin America," *Studies on the Soviet Union*, New Series, II, No. 3 (1962), p. 64; Akademiia Nauk SSSR, *Ekonomicheskie Problemy Stran Latinskoi Ameriki* (Moscow: Akademiia Nauk SSSR, 1963), pp. 359–69; Sergeev, 1964, p. 397.

2. *Vedomosti Verkhovnogo Soveta SSSR*, September 2, 1965, p. 807.

3. Theodore Draper, *Castroism: Theory and Practice* (New York: Frederick A. Praeger, 1965).

4. Liubimov, *op. cit.*, p. 132; Sergeev, 1964, p. 183; I. Arkhipov, "Soviet-Cuban Economic Cooperation," *International Affairs*, December, 1963, p. 50.

5. N. Kukharev, "Svobodnaia Kuba Idet Vpered," *Vneshniaia Torgovlia*, November, 1963, p. 21.

6. *Vedomosti Verkhovnogo Soveta SSSR*, April 15, 1964, p. 303.

7. *The London Sunday Telegraph*, June 25, 1961, p. 17.

CHAPTER 10. *Africa*

1. S. Tanin, *Gosudarstvennyi Stroi Gvineiskoi Respubliki* (Moscow: Gosiurizdat, 1960), p. 10.

2. *Pravda*, March 3, 1960; Sobolev, *op. cit.,* p. 40.

3. *The New York Times*, July 4, 1965, p. 38. However, it should be noted that an earlier venture in 1963 by Alaskan Airlines met with complete failure in Guinea.

4. *Vneshniaia Torgovlia*, September, 1961, p. 17. This and other information was obtained from official sources in Conakry.

5. New China News Agency, July 7, 1964.

6. G. Fadin, "Na Prochnoi Osnove," *Vneshniaia Torgovlia*, August, 1965, p. 28; *Vedmosti Verkhovnogo Soveta SSSR*, July 27, 1961, p. 716.

7. I. Chernyshev and L. Beneson, "SSSR Sodeistvuet Industrializatsii Zhilishchnogo Stroitel'stva," *Vneshniaia Torgovlia*, November, 1964, p. 29.

8. *The Wall Street Journal*, August 26, 1965, p. 20.

9. Sergeev, 1964, p. 397.

10. *Vedomosti Verkhovnogo Soveta SSSR*, September 16, 1961, p. 847; Sobolev, *op. cit.,* p. 40.

11. *Soviet News*, March 26, 1965, p. 160; Sobolev, *op. cit.,* p. 4.

12. *Soviet News*, June 16, 1965, p. 142; *Ekonomicheskaia Gazeta*, June 9, 1965, p. 35.

13. P. A. Petrov, *Sudan: Ekonomika i Vneshniaia Torgovlia* (Moscow: Vneshtorgizdat, 1961), pp. 69–75.

14. *Soviet Daily News* (Soviet Embassy, Addis Ababa), No. 79 (May 5, 1964), pp. 2–3.

15. *Vedomosti Verkhovnogo Soveta SSSR*, March 30, 1962, pp. 391–92.

16. *Soviet News*, February 12, 1965, p. 79; *The New York Times*, June 18, 1961, p. 32; and July 28, 1964, p. 4; *The New York Times Magazine*, August 8, 1965, p. 46.

17. *The New York Times Magazine*, August 8, 1965, p. 46.

18. *Soviet News*, December 18, 1964, p. 151; and August 6, 1965, p. 58.

19. *Soviet News*, May 19, 1964, p. 107.

20. *China Quarterly*, October, 1964, p. 182; *The New York Times*, June 5, 1965, p. 7.

21. *Soviet News*, August 26, 1964, p. 89; *The New York Times*, June 10, 1965, p. 7.

22. *Soviet News*, December 2, 1964, p. 118; April 20, 1965, p. 36; *The New York Times*, February 16, 1966, p. 5.

23. *Sovetskaia Torgovlia*, July 6, 1963, p. 1; November 30, 1963, p. 4; *Vneshniaia Torgovlia*, March, 1963, p. 27; *Soviet News*, April 27, 1965, p. 51; *The New York Times*, February 21, 1964.

CHAPTER 11. *Conclusion*

1. *The New York Times*, May 30, 1966, p. 4.

Sources for Tables *

TABLE II-1

Albania: S. D. Sergeev, *Ekonomicheskoe Sotrudnichestvo i Vzaimopomoshch' Stran Sotsialisticheskogo Lageria* (Sergeev, 1959), pp. 13, 114; A. K. Kozik (ed.), *Ekonomicheskoe Sotrudnichestvo i Vzaimopomoshch' Mezhdu Sovetskim Soiuzom i Evropeiskimi Stranami Narodnoi Demokratii*, p. 194; V. P. Komissarov and A. N. Popov, *Den'gi Kredit i Finansy Evropeiskikh Stran Narodnoi Demokratii* (Komissarov and Popov, 1960), p. 236; Konrad Il'chen, *Druzhba v Deistvii*, pp. 64–70; M. F. Kovrizhnyi (ed.), *Vneshniaia Torgovlia Stran Narodnoi Demokratii*, p. 80.

Bulgaria: Margaret Dewar, *Soviet Trade with Eastern Europe 1945-1949;* S. D. Sergeev and A. F. Dobrokhotov, *Narodnaia Respublika Bolgariia* (Sergeev, 1962), pp. 4, 41, 199; V. I. Zolotarev, *Vneshniaia Torgovlia Sotsialisticheskikh Stran*, p. 234; A. G. Zverev, *Finansy i Sotsialisticheskoi Stroitel'stvo*, p. 330; Kozik, *op. cit.*, p. 188; N. N. Liubimov (ed.), *Sovremennye Mezhdunarodnye Ekonomicheskie Otnosheniia*, p. 129; *Vneshniaia Torgovlia*, May, 1963, p. 17; *Survey*, January, 1965, p. 71; *The New York Times*, May 7, 1965, p. 8; Kovrizhnyi, *op. cit.*, p. 97; V. P. Sergeev, *Ekonomicheskie Sviazi Stran Sotsializma*, p. 35; N. Mitrofanova, "Mezhdunarodnoe Sotsialisticheskii Kredit," *Den'gi i Kredit*, October, 1964, pp. 83–84.

China: Zolotarev, *op. cit.*, pp. 194–95; *Vneshniaia Torgovlia*, September, 1961, p. 5, and October, 1959, p. 6; *Soviet News*, August 14, 1964, p. 75.

Cuba: *Vedomosti Verkhovnogo Soveta SSSR*, April 15, 1964, p. 303; Liubimov, *op. cit.*, p. 105; *Boston Globe*, February 15, 1966, p. 10; *Soviet News*, February 15, 1966, p. 88.

Czechoslovakia: D. F. Fokin (ed.), *Vneshniaia Torgovlia SSSR 1946-1963*, p. 69; Dewar, *op. cit.*, pp. 20–28; Kovrizhnyi, *op. cit.*, p. 263n; S. D. Sergeev, *Ekonomicheskoe Sotrudnichestvo i Vzaimopomoshch' Sotsialisticheskikh Stran* (Sergeev, 1964), p. 181.

Germany: Il'chen, *op. cit.*, pp. 98–103; Kozik, *op. cit.*, p. 168; Liubimov, *op. cit.*, p. 128; Zverev, *op. cit.*, p. 330; Komissarov and Popov, 1960, p. 236; Kovrizhnyi, *op. cit.*, p. 145; L. I. Frei, *Mezhdunarodnye Raschety i Finansirovanie Vneshnei Torgovli Sotsialisticheskikh Stran*, p. 232.

Hungary: Dewar, *op. cit.*, pp. 69–70; M. A. Usievich, *Razvitie Sotsialistichekoi Ekonomiki Vengrii*, pp. 76, 147, 211; Zverev, *op. cit.*, p. 331; A. F. Kudriashov, *Mir Sotsializma v Tsifrakh i Faktakh*, p. 58; Kozik, *op. cit.*, p. 178; Liubimov,

* Complete publication information is given in the Bibliography, pp. 254–58.

op. cit., p. 129; V. P. Komissarov and A. N. Popov, *Mezhdunarodnye Ekonom-icheskie Otnosheniia GDR* (Komissarov and Popov, 1963), p. 91; Sergeev, 1959, p. 118.

Korea: Liubimov, *op. cit.*, pp. 130–31; Zolotarev, *op. cit.*, pp. 204–5; Sergeev, 1959, p. 119; Sergeev, 1964, p. 187; Kovrizhnyi, *op. cit.*, pp. 181–84; A. D. Stupov, *Sotsialisticheskaia Industrializatsiia Stran Narodnoi Demokratii*, p. 167; *Vneshniaia Torgovlia*, February, 1963, pp. 9–10; V. P. Kadyshev, *SSSR na Vneshikh Rynkakh*, p. 40; Frei, *op. cit.*, p. 233.

Mongolia: Kovrizhnyi, *op. cit.*, pp. 195–200; Liubimov, *op. cit.*, p. 131; *Vneshniaia Torgovlia*, June, 1961, p. 5; and February, 1963, p. 8; Stupov, *op. cit.*, p. 214; Sergeev, 1964, pp. 176–79; Il'chen, *op. cit.*, p. 160; Akademiia Nauk SSSR, Institut Narodov Azii, *Mongol'skaia Narodnaia Respublika 1921–1961*, p. 116; *Sovetskaia Torgovlia*, July 11, 1963, p. 4; Zolotarev, *op. cit.*, p. 208; *The New York Times*, January 1, 1962, p. 6; and September 1, 1964, p. 11.

Poland: Liubimov, *op. cit.*, p. 128; N. I. Ivanov, *Ekonomicheskoe Sotrudnichestvo i Vzaimopomoshch' Stran Sotsializma*, pp. 176–79; D. F. Fokin (ed.), *Vneshniaia Torgovlia SSSR 1946–1963*, pp. 16, 68, 73; Komissarov and Popov, 1960, p. 234; Dewar, *op. cit.*, p. 43; *Pravda*, July 2, 1950, p. 2; Il'chen, *op. cit.*, p. 115; Kozik, *op. cit.*, p. 55; Zverev, *op. cit.*, p. 331; Sergeev, 1959, p. 110; *Ekonomicheskaia Gazeta*, December 7, 1963, p. 35; Zolotarev, *op. cit.*, pp. 221–26; Kovrizhnyi, *op. cit.*, p. 218; Frei, *op. cit.*, p. 231.

Rumania: Fokin, *op. cit.*, pp. 68, 101; I. P. Oleinik, *Pobeda Sotsializma v Rumynii*, pp. 76, 206; Stupov, *op. cit.*, p. 247; Kozik, *op. cit.*, p. 56; Sergeev, 1959, p. 111; Liubimov, *op. cit.*, p. 129; Komissarov and Popov, 1960, p. 235; Il'chen, *op. cit.*, pp. 121–25; Kovrizhnyi, *op. cit.*, p. 235; Frei, *op. cit.*, p. 232.

Vietnam: Zolotarev, *op. cit.*, p. 209; Sergeev, 1964, p. 175; Liubimov, *op. cit.*, pp. 92–93, 134; Stupov, *op. cit.*, p. 123; Ivanov, *op. cit.*, p. 200; Sergeev, 1962, p. 202; *Vneshniaia Torgovlia*, June, 1961, p. 5; and February, 1963, p. 10; *Ekonomicheskaia Gazeta*, April 14, 1965, p. 41; Frei, *op. cit.*, p. 233.

Yugoslavia: Liubimov, *op. cit.*, p. 130; Nicolas Spulber, *The Economics of Communist Eastern Europe*, p. 434; Jan Wszelaki, *Communist Economic Strategy: The Role of East-Central Europe*, p. 72; Zverev, *op. cit.*, pp. 329–30; *Vneshniaia Torgovlia*, April, 1958, p. 49.

U.S. Government Sources: George S. Carnett and Morris H. Crawford, "The Scope and Distribution of Soviet Economic Aid," *Dimensions of Soviet Economic Power*, Hearings of Joint Economic Committee (Washington, D.C.: Government Printing Office, 1962), p. 474; see also p. 427. These figures make no distinction between industrial loans and loans for purchase of the joint stock companies and cancellation of reparation debt.

TABLE II-2

Ministerstvo Vneshnei Torgovli SSSR, *Vneshniaia Torgovlia Soiuza SSR za 1955–1959 gody* (*VT SSSR 1955–1959*); *VT SSSR, 1959–1963*; *VT SSSR, 1965*.

Table II-3

1949: Stupov, *op. cit.*, p. 187.
1949–58: M. Sladkovskii, "Razvitie Torgovli Sovetskogo Soiuza s Kitaiskoi Narodnoi Respublikoi," *Vneshniaia Torgovlia*, October, 1959, pp. 3, 6, 9.
1959–60: *VT SSSR, 1960*, p. 9.
1961–63: *VT SSSR, 1959–63*, p. 17.
1964–65: *VT SSSR, 1965*, p. 13.

Table II-4

Afghanistan: *The New York Times*, March 23, 1965, p. 4; and April 1, 1965, p. 9.
Albania: Kovrizhnyi, *op. cit.*, p. 60; *Christian Science Monitor*, February 15, 1963, p. 6.
Algeria: New China News Agency, October 11, 1963; *China Quarterly*, October, 1964, p. 182; Colin Garratt, "China as a Foreign Aid Donor," *Far Eastern Economic Review*, January 19, 1961, p. 81.
Burma: *International Affairs*, October, 1961, p. 116; *The New York Times*, March 1, 1964, p. 3.
Cambodia: Chinese specialists in Hong Kong; *The New York Times*, November 12, 1964, p. 14; *International Affairs*, October, 1961, p. 116.
Ceylon: Chinese specialists in Hong Kong; *Asian World*, December, 1964, p. 32; *International Affairs*, October, 1961, p. 117; *The New York Times*, March 1, 1964, p. 24.
Congo-Brazzaville: *The New York Times*, September 9, 1964, p. 11; and March 8, 1965, p. 1.
Cuba: *International Affairs*, October, 1961, p. 117.
Ghana: *Ekonomicheskaia Gazeta*, December 25, 1961, p. 36; *China Quarterly*, October, 1964, p. 182; *The New York Times*, February 5, 1964, p. 18; and July 16, 1964, p. 9.
Guinea: Official sources in Guinea; *International Affairs*, October, 1961, p. 117; *The New York Times*, September 20, 1961, p. 20.
Hungary: Kovrizhnyi, *op. cit.*, p. 60.
Indonesia: Chinese specialists in Hong Kong; *The New York Times*, December 8, 1963, p. 7; January 29, 1965, p. 1; and January 8, 1965, p. 2; *International Affairs*, October, 1961, p. 117; Iu. Kapelinskii *et al.*, *Razvitie Ekonomiki i Vneshneekonomicheskikh Sviazei Kitaiskoi Narodnoi Respubliki* (Moscow: Vneshtorgizdat, 1959), p. 490; *Mirovaia Ekonomika i Mezhdunarodnye Otnosheniia*, March, 1960, p. 85. See also Table VI-1.
Kenya: *The New York Times*, June 13, 1965, p. 21; *China Quarterly*, October, 1964, p. 182.
Laos: *The New York Times*, December 6, 1962, p. 33.
Mali: Official sources in Mali; *International Affairs*, May, 1961, p. 86; *Far Eastern Economic Review*, February 13, 1964, p. 350.

Mongolia: Garratt, *op. cit.*, p. 84; Kovrizhnyi, *op. cit.*, pp. 61–62, 200.

Nepal: *International Affairs*, October, 1961, p. 117; official sources in Nepal; *The New York Times*, August 30, 1965, p. 10.

North Korea: Garratt, *op. cit.*, p. 84; Kapelinskii, *op. cit.*, p. 469; Daniel Wolfstone, "China's Foreign Aid," *Far Eastern Economic Review*, January 19, 1961, p. 81; Kovrizhnyi, *op. cit.*, p. 184.

North Vietnam: Garratt, *op. cit.*, p. 84; Kovrizhnyi, *op. cit.*, p. 172.

Pakistan: *The New York Times*, January 24, 1965, p. 1; *China Quarterly*, October, 1964, p. 182.

Somali: *The New York Times*, January 20, 1963, p. 58; September 8, 1963, p. 30; October 3, 1963, p. 6; and January 25, 1965, p. 76; Chinese specialists in Hong Kong.

Syria: Afro-Asian News Service, March 10, 1964; *Khartoum Morning News*, May 8, 1964, p. 1; *The New York Times*, April 19, 1963, p. 60.

Tanzania: *The New York Times*, June 5, 1965, p. 7; *China Quarterly*, October, 1964, p. 182.

U.A.R.: *International Affairs*, October, 1961, p. 117; *The New York Times*, January 4, 1965, p. 3; official sources in Egypt; *The Wall Street Journal*, July 22, 1965, p. 28.

Uganda: *The New York Times*, February 16, 1966, p. 5.

Yemen: *China Quarterly*, October, 1964, p. 182; *International Affairs*, October, 1961, p. 117; Kapelinskii, *op. cit.*, p. 490.

Zambia: *The New York Times*, February 21, 1964.

TABLE II-5

Donors:

Albania: A. F. Kudriashov, *Mir Sotsializma v Tsifrakh i Faktakh*, p. 58.

Bulgaria: Sergeev, 1964, pp. 185–87; Kudriashov, *op. cit.*, p. 58.

China: Kovrizhnyi, *op. cit.*, pp. 60–61, 172, 184; *International Affairs*, October, 1961, p. 117; Sergeev, 1959, p. 118; Kapelinskii, *op. cit.*, p. 469; *Christian Science Monitor*, February 15, 1963, p. 6.

Czechoslovakia: Sergeev, 1964, pp. 182–85; Fokin, *op. cit.*, p. 16; Oleinik, *op. cit.*, p. 206; Liubimov, *op. cit.*, p. 129; Mitrofanova, *op. cit.*, p. 85.

East Germany: Sergeev, 1964, p. 190; Kudriashov, *op. cit.*, p. 58; Komissarov and Popov, 1963, p. 58; Stupov, *op. cit.*, p. 167; Mitrofanova, *op. cit.*, p. 85.

Hungary: Komissarov and Popov, 1960, p. 237; Sergeev, 1964, p. 185; Sergeev, 1959, p. 119.

Poland: Sergeev, 1964, p. 188; Kudriashov, *op. cit.*, p. 58; Liubimov, *op. cit.*, p. 119; *Vneshniaia Torgovlia*, November, 1963, p. 21; Mitrofanova, *op. cit.*, p. 85.

Rumania: Sergeev, 1964, pp. 185–88.

TABLE III-1

Bulgaria: Central Bank of Egypt, *Economic Review*, V, No. 2 (1965), p. 162.

China: *International Affairs*, October, 1961, p. 117; *The New York Times*, January 4, 1965, p. 3; and July 3, 1965, p. 7; *The Wall Street Journal*, July 22, 1965, p. 28.

Czechoslovakia: *International Affairs*, October, 1961, p. 117; *International Affairs*, January, 1960, p. 36; Dr. Said El Naggar, *Foreign Aid to the UAR* (Cairo: Institute of National Planning, 1963), pp. 60–62; Central Bank of Egypt, *Report of the Board of Directors for the Year 1962/63* (Cairo, September, 1963), p. 25; Central Bank of Egypt, *Economic Review*, V, No. 2 (1965), p. 162. The estimate of $277 million (as of May, 1964) was supplied by American Embassy officials.

East Germany: Komissarov and Popov, 1963, pp. 167–69; Il'chen, *op. cit.*, p. 243; *International Affairs*, November, 1961, p. 118; and January, 1960, pp. 38–39; *The New York Times*, January 4, 1965, p. 3; January 29, 1965, p. 7; February 1, 1965, p. 8; and March 2, 1965, p. 8.

Hungary: *International Affairs*, January, 1960, p. 38; and November, 1961, p. 118; Central Bank of Egypt, *Report of the Board of Directors for the Year 1962/63*, p. 26. The figure was confirmed by American officials in Cairo. Thomas L. Hughes, in "The Communist Economic Offensive Through 1963" (Department of State, Bureau of Intelligence and Research, June 18, 1964, mimeo.), p. 26, lists an additional $20 million. This is because he considers the loan of October, 1962, as a new loan rather than a refinancing of the earlier loan.

Poland: Central Bank of Egypt, *Report of the Board of Directors for the Year 1962/63*, p. 25; *International Affairs*, January, 1960, p. 38; and November, 1961 pp. 115–17. The $20-million figure was confirmed by American authorities in Cairo. The extra $25 million, for which there is no official confirmation, is from *The New York Times*, January 4, 1965, p. 3.

Rumania: There is no official confirmation. The figure is from *The New York Times*, January 4, 1965, p. 3.

Table IV-1

Government of India, Ministry of Finance, Department of Economic Affairs, *External Assistance 1963*, pp. 50–57; *Statesman*, May 31, 1965; *The New York Times*, May 18, 1965, p. 5; Frei, *op. cit.*, p. 239.

Table IV-2

Columns 1, 3, 5: *VT SSSR 1955–59*, pp. 12, 44; *VT SSSR 1959–63*, pp. 12, 352; *VT SSSR 1965*, pp. 12, 239; *Dengi i Kredit*, October, 1960, p. 21.

Columns 2, 6: *Direction of Trade Annual 1958–62* (Washington, D.C.: International Monetary Fund, 1964), p. 341; Series T, Vol. XI, No. 9, p. 333. *Direction of Trade Annual 1960–64*, p. 231.

Column 4: Official sources in India.

Table IV-3

Eastern Economist, June 12, 1964, p. 1360; and June 26, 1964, p. 1454.

TABLE IV-4

Government of India, Ministry of Finance, *Explanatory Memorandum on the Budget of the Central Government for 1964* (New Delhi, 1964), pp. 112, 182, 184, 185, 188, 190.

TABLE V-1

Lines 1–7: Official data of the Government of Afghanistan.
Line 8: *Vedomosti Verkhovnogo Soveta SSSR*, April 22, 1964, p. 316.
Line 9: *Vedomosti Verkhovnogo Soveta SSSR*, July 24, 1964, p. 566.

TABLE VI-1

Bulgaria, V. P. Sergeev, *op. cit.*, p. 398.
China: K. Krishna Moorty, "Russians Harsh to Sukarno," *Far Eastern Economic Review*, April 25, 1963, p. 229; Alexander Shakov, "Foreign Economic Assistance to Indonesia: 1950–1961," p. 601; *The New York Times*, January 8, 1965, p. 2.
Czechoslovakia: Moorty, *op. cit.*; Shakov, *op. cit.*, p. 464; official sources in Indonesia.
East Germany: Sergeev, 1964, p. 395; Komissarov and Popov, 1963, p. 162.
Hungary: Official sources in Indonesia.
Rumania: V. P. Sergeev, *op. cit.*, p. 396.
Poland: Shakov, *op. cit.*, p. 600, Sergeev, 1964, p. 395, Moorty, *op. cit.*, p. 229.
U.S.S.R.: B. Sobolev, "Sovetskaia Pomoshch' Stranam Azii i Afriki," *Finansy SSSR*, January, 1964, p. 38; Shakov, *op. cit.*, p. 600.

TABLE IX-1

VT SSSR 1959–1963, pp. 20–21; *VT SSSR, 1965*, p. 15.

TABLE IX-2

Col. 1: *The New York Times*, August 15, 1962, p. 3; June 21, 1963, p. 19; July 6, 1965, p. 3; and April 10, 1966, p. 31.
Col. 2: *VT SSSR 1961*, p. 228; *VT SSSR 1963*, p. 259; *The New York Times*, February 18, 1965, p. 7; *VT SSSR 1965*, p. 320.
Col. 3: *Vedomosti Verkhovnogo Soveta SSSR*, May 26, 1960, p. 243.
Col. 4: *Pravda*, December 20, 1960, p. 1.
Col. 5: *The New York Times*, October 6, 1961, p. 2; January 10, 1962, p. 69; and May 16, 1963, p. 12; *Ekonomicheskaia Gazeta*, May 11, 1963, p. 31.
Col. 6: *The New York Times*, June 2, 1963, p. 1.
Col. 7: *Pravda*, January 23, 1964, p. 1.

Col. 8: *Vedomosti Verkhovnogo Soveta SSSR,* May 26, 1960, p. 243; *Pravda,* December 20, 1961, p. 1; June 7, 1963, p. 4; and January 23, 1964, p. 1.

Col. 9: *The New York Times,* March 12, 1963, p. 1; January 24, 1963, p. 3; and October 26, 1964, p. 12.

APPENDIX 1

VT SSSR 1955–1958; VT SSSR 1959–1963; VT SSSR 1965.

APPENDIX 2

United States Government, Agency for International Development and Department of Defense, *Proposed Mutual Defense and Development Program, FY 1967* (Washington, D.C: Government Printing Office, 1966), pp. 223–25, 229–31. For Chinese and Russian aid, see text.

Bibliography

AGENCY FOR INTERNATIONAL DEVELOPMENT and DEPARTMENT OF DEFENSE. *Proposed Mutual Defense and Development Program, FY 1967.* Washington, D.C.: Government Printing Office, 1966.

AKADEMIIA NAUK SSSR. *Ekonomicheskie Problemy Stran Latinskoi Amerika.* Moscow. Akademiia SSSR, 1963.

————. Institut Narodov Azii. *Mongol'skaia Narodnaia Respublika 1921–1961.* Moscow: Vostochnoi Literatury, 1961.

AVARIN, V. IA. *Problemy Industrializatsii Suverennykh Slaborazvitykh Stran Azii.* Moscow: Akademiia Nauk, 1960.

BELOFF, MAX. *Soviet Policy in the Far East, 1944–1951.* London: Oxford University Press, 1953.

BERLINER, JOSEPH S. *Soviet Economic Aid.* New York: Frederick A. Praeger, 1958.

COFFIN, FRANK M. "Sino-Soviet Bloc Aid: Myths and Facts." Mimeographed. April 12, 1962.

COMMITTEE ON FOREIGN RELATIONS, U.S. SENATE. *A Background Study on East West Trade.* Washington, D.C.: Government Printing Office, May, 1965.

DANTSIG, B. M. *Ekonomicheskoe Polozhenie Stran Azii Afriki i Latinskoi Ameriki.* Moscow: Vneshtorgizdat, 1959.

DEWAR, MARGARET. *Soviet Trade with Eastern Europe 1945–1949.* London: Royal Institute of International Affairs, 1951.

DOOLIN, DENNIS J. *Territorial Claims in the Sino-Soviet Conflict.* Stanford, Calif.: The Hoover Institution, 1965.

EL-NAGGAR, SAID. *Foreign Aid to United Arab Republic.* Cairo: Institute of National Planning, December 15, 1963.

FITUNI, L. A., and V. D. SHCHETININ. *Problemy Pomoshchi Ekonomicheski Slaborazvitym Stranam.* Moscow: IMO, 1961.

FOKIN, D. F. (ed.). *Vneshniaia Torgovlia SSSR 1946–1963.* Moscow; IMO, 1964.

FREI, L. I. *Mezhdunarodnye Raschety i Finansirovanie Vneshnei Torgovli Sotsialisticheskikh Stran.* Moscow: IMO, 1965.

GANKOVSKII, IU. V. (ed). *SSSR i Strany Vostoka.* Moscow: Vostochnoi Literatury, 1961.

GANSHIN, G. A. *Ekonomika Kitaiskoi Narodnoi Respubliki.* Moscow: IMO, 1959.

GARTHOFF, RAYMOND L. "Sino-Soviet Military Relations," *The Annals,* September, 1963.

GOLOVIN, IU. M. *Afganistan: Ekonomika i Vneshniaia Torgovlia.* Moscow: Vnesh torgizdat, 1962.

———. *Sovetskii Soiuz i Afganistan.* Moscow: Vostochnoi Literatury, 1962.

HINDUSTAN STEEL LIMITED. *Annual Report 1961–62, 1962–63,* and *1963–64.* Ranchi, India, 1962, 1963, 1964. (HSL)

HUGHES, THOMAS L. "The Communist Economic Offensive Through 1963." Research Memorandum, RSB-43, Department of State, Bureau of Intelligence and Research. Washington, D.C., June 18, 1964. Mimeo.

IL'CHEN, KONRAD. *Druzhba v Deistvii.* Moscow: Inostrannoi Literatury, 1962. Translated from the German.

INSTITUT MEZHDUNARODNYKH OTNOSHENII. *Voprosy Vneshnei Torgovli.* Moscow: IMO, 1960.

INTERNATIONAL MONETARY FUND, INTERNATIONAL BANK FOR RECONSTRUCTION AND DEVELOPMENT. *Directions of Trade—Annual 1958–62.* Washington (*DOT Annual 1958–62* or the relevant period).

ISKANDAROV, R. G. *K Vorposy o Pomoshchi Slaborazvitym Stranam.* Moscow: VPSH i AON pri TsK KPSS, 1960.

———. *Sovetskii Soiuz—Slaborazvitym Stranam.* Moscow: Znanie Series III, No. 8, 1961.

IVANOV, N. I. *Ekonomicheskoe Sotrudnichestvo i Vzaimopomoshch' Stran Sotsializma.* Moscow: Sotsekgiz, 1962.

JOINT ECONOMIC COMMITTEE, U.S. CONGRESS. *Dimensions of Soviet Economic Power.* Washington, D.C.: Government Printing Office, 1962.

KADYSHEV, V. P. *SSSR na Vneshnikh Rynkakh.* Moscow: Vneshtorgizdat, 1964.

KAKHAROV, A. K., and G. M. PROKHOROV. *Druzheskaia Pomoshch i Vzaimovygodnoe Sotrudnichestvo.* Moscow: Vostochnoi Literatury, 1959.

KAPELINSKII, IU. N., I. A. KISVIANTSEV, M. S. PANKIN, IU. A. PEKSHEV, V. P. SENIN, and V. G. SYCHEV. *Razvitie Ekonomiki i Vneshneekonomicheskikh Sviazei Kitaiskoi Narodnoi Respublikii.* Moscow: Vneshtorgizdat, 1959.

KOMISSAROV, V. P. and A. N. POPOV. *Den'gi Kredit i Finansy Evropeiskikh Stran Narodnoi Demokratii.* Moscow: Sotsekgiz, 1960.

———. *Mezhdunarodnye Ekonomicheskie Otnosheniia GDR.* Moscow: IMO, 1963.

KOMZIN, IVAN. *The High Aswan Dam.* Moscow: The Foreign Languages Publishing House, n.d.

KOVNER, MILTON. "Soviet Aid Strategy in Developing Countries," *Orbis,* Fall, 1964.

KOVRIZHNYI, M. F. (ed.). *Vneshniaia Torgovlia Stran Narodnoi Demokratii.* Moscow: Vneshtorgizdat, 1961.

KOZIK, A. K. (ed.). *Ekonomicheskoe Sotrudnichestvo i Vzaimpomoshch' Mezhdu Sovetskim Soiuzom i Evropeiskimi Stranami Narodnoi Demokratii.* Moscow: Akademii Nauk SSSR, 1958.

KUDRIASHOV, A. F. *Mir Sotsializma v Tsifrakh i Faktakh.* Moscow: Politizdat, 1963.

LARICHENKO, M. V. *Ekonomicheskoe Sotrudnichestvo SSSR so Stranami Azii Afriki i Latinskoi Ameriki.* Moscow: Gospolitizdat, 1961.

LIUBIMOV, N. N. (ed.). *Sovremennye Mezhdunarodnye Ekonomicheskie Otnosheniia.* Moscow: IMO, 1964.

MESHCHERIAKOV, M. V. *Ocherk Ekomicheskogo Sotrudnichestva Sovetskogo Soiuza i Mongol'skoi Narodnoi Respubliki.* Moscow: Vneshtorgizdat, 1959.

MINISTERSTVO INOSTRANNYKH DEL SSSR. *SSSR i Arabskie Strany 1917–1960 gg.* Moscow: Gospolitizdat, 1961.

MINISTERSTVO VNESHNEI TORGOVLI SSSR. *Vneshniaia Torgovlia Soiuza SSR za 1955–1959 gody.* Moscow: Vneshtorgizdat, 1961 (*VT SSSR 1955–1959* and other relevant years).

MINISTRY OF FINANCE, GOVERNMENT OF INDIA. *Annual Report on the Workings of Industrial and Commercial Undertakings of the Central Government for the Year 1962–63.* New Delhi, March, 1964.

——. *Explanatory Memorandum on the Budget of the Central Government for 1964–65.* New Delhi, February 27, 1964.

MINISTRY OF FINANCE, DEPARTMENT OF ECONOMIC AFFAIRS, GOVERNMENT OF INDIA. *External Assistance, 1962.* New Delhi, 1963.

——. *External Assistance, 1963.* New Delhi, 1964.

——. *Report of the Committee on Utilisation of External Assistance.* New Delhi, 1964.

MINISTRY OF FOREIGN AFFAIRS OF THE FEDERAL PEOPLE'S REPUBLIC OF YUGOSLAVIA. *White Book on Aggressive Activities by the Governments of the USSR, Poland, Czechoslovakia, Hungary, Rumania, Bulgaria and Albania Toward Yugoslavia.* Belgrade, 1951.

MOROZOV, V. U. *Sovet Ekonomicheskoi Vzaimopomoshchi: Soiuz Ravnykh.* Moscow: IMO, 1964.

MULLER, KURT. *The Soviet Bloc and the Developing Countries.* Frankfurt, Germany: Forschungstelle der Friedrich-Ebert Stiftung, 1962.

NEKRASOV, A. "Soviet Aid: Past and Present," *International Affairs,* March, 1963.

NESTEROV, S. M. (ed.). *Mezhdunarodnyi Ezhegodnik Politika i Ekonomika.* Moscow: Politizdat, 1964.

NUKHOVICH, E. *Vneshniaia Politika Afganistana.* Moscow: IMO, 1962.

OLEINIK, I. P. *Pobeda Sotsializma v Rumynii.* Moscow: IZL, 1962.

PETROV, P. A. *Sudan: Ekonomika i Vneshniaia Torgovlia.* Moscow: Vneshtorgizdat, 1961.

PISARETZ, I. G. *Vneshne-Ekonomicheskie Sviazi Pol'skoi Narodnoi Respubliki.* Moscow: Vneshtorgizdat, 1962.

POLEZHAEV, V. N. *Vneshniaia Torgovlia Vazhnyii Faktor Mirnogo Sosushchestvovaniia.* Moscow, Vneshtorgizdat, 1952.

POTEKHIN, I. I. (ed.). *Afrika 1956–1961.* Moscow: Vostochnoi Literatury, 1961.

PRYOR, FREDERIC L. *The Communist Foreign Trade System.* Cambridge, Mass.: The MIT Press, 1963.

RAO, V. K. R. V., and DHARM NARAIN. *Foreign Aid and India's Economic Development.* New York: Asia Publishing House, 1963.

RIMALOV, V. *Economic Cooperation Between the USSR and Underdeveloped Countries.* Moscow: Foreign Language Publishing House, n.d.

——, and V. TIAGUNENKO. *Slaborazvitye Strany v Mirovom Kapitalisticheskom Khoziaistve.* Moscow: Sotsekgiz, 1961.

SERGEEV, S. D. *Ekonomicheskoe Sotrudnichestvo i Vzaimopomoshch' Sotsialisticheskikh Stran.* Moscow: Vneshtorgizdat, 1964.

——. *Ekonomicheskoe Sotrudnichestvo i Vzaimopomoshch' Stran Sotsialisticheskogo Lageria.* Moscow: Vneshtorgizdat, 1959.

———, and A. F. DOBROKHOTOV. *Narodnaia Respublika Bolgariia.* Moscow: Vneshtorgizdat, 1962.

SERGEEV, V. P. *Ekonomicheskie Sviazi Stran Sotsializma.* Moscow: Ekonomika, 1965.

SHAKOV, ALEXANDER. "Foreign Economic Assistance to Indonesia: 1950–1961." Unpublished dissertation at London School of Economics, London, August, 1962.

SKACHKOV, S., V. SERGEEV, and G. SHEVIAKOV. *Pomoshch' i Sotrudnichestvo vo Imia Mira.* Moscow: Gospolitizdat, 1962.

SOBOLEV, B. "Sovetskaia Pomoshch' Stranam Azii i Afrika," *Finansy SSSR,* January, 1964.

SPULBER, NICOLAS. *The Economics of Communist Eastern Europe.* Cambridge, Mass.: The MIT Press, 1957.

STUPOV, A. D. (ed.). *Ekonomicheskoe Sotrudnichestvo i Vzaimopomoshch' Sotsialisticheskikh Stran.* Moscow: Akademiia Nauk SSSR, 1962.

———. *Sotsialisticheskaia Industrializatsiia Stran Narodnoi Demokratii.* Moscow: Gosplanizdat, 1960.

SVESHNIKOV, M. N. *Sistema Raschetov Mezhdu Stranami Sotsialisticheskogo Sodruzhestva.* Moscow: Finansy, 1964.

TANIN, S. *Gosudarstvennyi Stroi Gvineiskoi Respubliki.* Moscow: Gosiurizdat, 1960.

TEPLINSKII, L. B. *Sovetsko-Afganskie Otnosheniia 1919–1960.* Moscow: Sotsekgiz, 1961.

USIEVICH, M. A. *Razvitie Sotsialisticheskoi Ekonomiki Vengrii.* Moscow: Akademiia Nauk SSSR, 1962.

VAGANOV, B. S. *Organizatsiia i Tekhnika Vneshnei Torgovli SSSR i Drugikh Sotsialisticheskikh Stran.* Moscow: IMO, 1963.

WSZELAKI, JAN. *Communist Economic Strategy: The Role of East-Central Europe.* Washington, D.C.: National Planning Association, 1959.

ZEVIN, L. "Vzaimnaia Vygoda Ekonomicheskogo Sotrudnichestva Sotsialisticheskikh i Razvivaiushchikhsia Stran," *Voprosy Ekonomiki,* February, 1965.

ZOLOTAREV, V. I. *Vneshniaia Torgovlia Sotsialisticheskikh Stran.* Moscow: Vneshtorgizdat, 1964.

ZVEREV, A. G. *Finansy i Sotsialisticheskoi Stroitel'stvo.* Moscow: Gosfinizdat, 1957.

Periodicals

Bulletin of the Institute for the Study of the USSR
Christian Science Monitor
Current Digest of the Soviet Press
Eastern Economist
Ekonomicheskaia Gazeta
Far Eastern Economic Review
Finansy SSSR
International Affairs
Izvestiia
Mirovaia Ekonomika i Mezhdunarodnye Otnosheniia
The New York Times

Peking Review
Planovoe Khoziaistvo
Pravda
Press Bureau of German Industry (New Delhi)
Problems of Communism
Review of Economics and Statistics
Scribe—Arab Review
Sovetskaia Torgovlia (newspaper)
Sovetskaia Torgovlia (journal)
Soviet Studies
Survey
Vedomosti Verkhovnogo Soveta
Vneshniaia Torgovlia
Voprosy Ekonomiki
The Wall Street Journal

Miscellaneous

Aswan High Dam Authority. *Aswan High Dam, May 1964.* Aswan, 1964.
——. *Aswan High Dam: Miracle of the 20th Century.* Aswan, 1964.
Union of Burma. *Inya Lake Hotel.* Rangoon.
United Arab Republic, Information Department. *The High Dam.* Cairo, 1964.
USSR-Nepal: 5 Years of Co-operation.

Index

Abramov, F., 8–9

Aeroflot, 170

Afghanistan, 45–47, 61, 85, 115–23, 133, 135, 174, 190–91, 200, 205–6

Africa, 51, 58, 60, 83, 152, 168–84, 186–87, 189, 192, 194–95

Afro-Asian Conference; see Algerian Conference

Agricultural aid: Russian, 49, 74, 100, 118, 127, 129, 145, 148–50, 154, 169, 174–76, 178, 180, 182–83, 193; Chinese, 173, 176–77, 180–81

Aid dispensing, 75–79, 126

Aid in kind, 117, 125–27, 129–30, 132, 136–37, 173–74, 180, 182; see also Barter

Airplanes; see Aviation aid

Alaskan Airlines, 246 (n. 3)

Albania, 7, 13, 16, 19, 24–26, 35, 42, 46–47, 51–52, 54, 192, 196, 237 (n. 31), 239 (n. 18)

Alexandrov, Alexei, 69

Algeria, 46–47, 71, 105, 147–49, 152, 154, 189, 190, 196–97, 205–6

Algerian Conference, 73, 79, 122, 130, 135, 149, 152, 176, 181, 188–89, 201

Alliance for Progress, 201

Amer, Abdel, 65

Apel, Erich, 9

Arab countries, 147–55

Arafa, Mussa, 69

Argentina, 51, 156–58, 161, 245 (n. 1)

Asia, 58, 60, 135–46, 152, 186–87, 189, 192, 194–95

Aswan Dam, xiii, 49, 61–76, 79, 82–85, 92–93, 116, 119, 138, 169, 188, 191–92, 197, 199, 212–21

Atomic aid, 48, 64, 118, 128, 150, 174

Australia, 51

Austria, 13, 15, 19

Aviation aid, 13, 14–20, 50, 71, 104–5, 116, 119, 148, 152, 169–70, 172, 174, 177, 246 (n. 3)

Balance of payments, 27, 71–73, 83, 95–96, 111–14, 120–21, 132–33, 157–59, 164–66, 175–76, 194–96

Banda, Hastings, 182

Bandung, 106, 125, 181; see also Algerian Conference

Banking, 6, 12, 16–17, 79, 210, 215–16, 225, 230–33

Barauni, 98–99, 102–3

Barter, 23, 26, 63–64, 67, 71–73, 83, 96, 104, 106, 109–11, 117–18, 130, 132–33, 142, 145, 156–63, 172, 175, 178, 180–82, 186; see also Aid in kind

Ba'th Party, 149–50

Batista, F., 156, 161

Belgium, 125

Ben Bella, Ahmad, 148–49, 195

Bergson, Abram, 236

Berlin Uprising; see East Germany

Berliner, Joseph, xii

Bethlehem Steel, 86

Bhilai, xiii, 61, 85–93, 99, 111, 116, 191, 199, 241 (n. 22), 242 (n. 9)

Bokaro, 91–94, 99–100, 114, 138, 191

Brazil, 156–61, 188, 194

British Guiana, 97

Bulganin, Nikolai, 116

Bulgaria, 5–7, 13, 17, 24–25, 28, 30, 32, 35–36, 53–56, 80, 131, 193, 239 (n. 19); aid to Communist countries, 35, 38, 161; aid to developing countries, 75, 130, 145, 149–50, 160, 173, 176–77

Burma, 46–47, 90, 110, 135, 141–43, 146, 170, 190, 193, 205–6

Burmah Shell, 95

Byroade, Henry, 64